MW01251191

MENNONITE MARTYRS

People Who Suffered for Their Faith
1920 - 1940

PERSPECTIVES on MENNONITE LIFE and THOUGHT

"Perspectives on Mennonite Life and Thought" is a series jointly published between Kindred Press, the Historical Commission of the General Conference of Mennonite Brethren Churches and the Center for Mennonite Brethren Studies of Winnipeg, Manitoba, Fresno, California and Hillsboro, Kansas.*

*Volumes 1-4 were published by the Center for Mennonite Brethren Studies (Fresno)

MENNONITE MARTYRS

People Who Suffered for Their Faith
1920 - 1940

Aaron A. Toews

Translated by John B. Toews

Winnipeg, MB Canada   **Kindred Press**   Hillsboro, KS USA

MENNONITE MARTYRS
People Who Suffered for Their Faith 1920 - 1940

Copyright © 1990 by the Centers for Mennonite Brethren Studies, Fresno, CA; Winnipeg, MB; and Hillsboro, KS.

All rights reserved. With the exception of brief excerpts for reviews, no part of this book may be reproduced without written permission of the publisher.

Canadian Cataloguing in Publication Data
> Toews, Aron A.
> Mennonite martyrs
> (Perspectives on Mennonite life and thought; no. 6)
> Translation of: Mennonitische Maertyrer der juengsten vergangenheit und der
Gegenwart. 1949.
> ISBN 0-919797098-9

> 1. Mennonites - Biography. 2. Christian martyrs - Biography. I. Title. II.
Series.

> BX8141.T64 1990   289.7'09'22   C90-097036-7

Published simultaneously by Kindred Press, Winnipeg, MB R2L 2E5 and Kindred Press, Hillsboro, KS 67063

Cover design by Sleeping Tiger Artworks, Winnipeg, Manitoba

Book design by Publishing Services, Winnipeg, Manitoba

Printed in Canada by Fraser Valley Custom Printers Inc., Chilliwack, b.C.

International Standard Book Number: 0-919797-98-9

Translator's Preface

Mennonitische Märtyrer began as an attempt to collect information on the fate of Mennonite ministers during the 1920s and 1930s. As the author indicates, public awareness and interest soon expanded the scope of the project. The compilation suffered a serious setback when fire destroyed the author's farm home in Namaka, Alberta. Its rapid spread not only destroyed the entire contents of the house, but also the precious manuscript and the materials associated with it. The task of reconstruction proved long and arduous. There was nevertheless a silver lining in the tragedy. The ensuing delay allowed the collection of new information and materials from the Russian Mennonite refugees who had found sanctuary in western Europe. These eyewitness accounts enriched both the scope and depth of the compilation.

Mennonitische Märtyrer was never intended to be anything more than a compilation. If significant information or a name listed by the author or suggested by the Mennonite constituency could be found, it was usually included in the collection. The primary objective was to preserve the stories at all costs. Much of the biographical information would have been irretrievably lost if it had not been gathered at that time. Sometimes the biographies written by relatives or friends were printed verbatim or they were reconstructed by the author from a series of different reports. While such an approach ensured veracity and authenticity, it also meant considerable variation in the literary quality of the accounts. Some are thoughtfully and skillfully arranged, others are little more than biographical listings. The translator tried to take this unevenness into account by appropriately reflecting the style and syntax of each contribution as well as its simplicity or sophistication.

The open-ended collection of material created a special problem for *Mennonitische Märtyrer*. Biographical sketches of every type and description were sent to the author. New names were constantly added to the list and interested parties suggested the inclusion of other types of material. In the end major and minor biographical sketches, poems, and a variety of narrative accounts were all included in the compilation. The lengthy biographies generally found their way into the first

1

volume, the shorter sketches into the second. For translation purposes, only biographies of significant length and ,hopefully, also of significant depth were selected. Not surprisingly the vast majority of translated martyrologies come from volume one. Excluding the many brief sketches containing only biographic essentials did not constitute a value judgment on the merit of these stalwart individuals. There was no intention of dismissing any of them as minor figures or of somehow minimizing their suffering and martyrdom. The longer biographies usually presented a more cohesive story of faith and suffering and so provided a better sampling of the Russian Mennonite experience during the 1920s and the 1930s.

The translator exercised editorial discretion in at least one other area. The author and his generation knew very little of the Russian Mennonite experience during the 1930s due to the lack of letter contact with their coreligionists in Russia. After WWII eyewitness reports from Mennonite refugees in Europe began to fill in the information gaps. As he continued to gather material for his compilation, the full scope of the tragedy became increasingly apparent to the author. The contents of the stories filled him with a sense of righteous indignation. In some of the accounts he expressed his outrage by way of editorial comment on the evils of Bolshevism in Russia. These rather frequent comments have not been translated. It seemed the individual stories spoke eloquently enough both to the prevailing unrighteousness and the suffering and death of the Christian believers.

The original German spelling was retained for all place and family names. Many of the reports exercised considerable liberty in the spelling of such names. Then, too, there were isolated references to remote camps, railway stations, mines or industrial complexes. When he originally compiled the biographies, Aron A. Toews found it impossible to verify the correctness of such spellings. Place and family names were therefore printed as they appeared in the original manuscripts. The translation retained the same practice even in the case of the better known geographic names of cities and provinces.

The biographical sketches contained in *Mennonitische Märtyrer* appear to have been inserted into the manuscript as they were completed. Occasionally, martyrs from a given settlement were listed separately, but this was certainly not the rule. A geographic classification by settlement was doomed by the frequent flight of the victim prior to his arrest or his forcible relocations afterwards. Similarly classification by denominational affiliation meant little in an era when all churches were closed and congregations scattered. Then too believers, themselves, frequently reported that the old lines of demarcation meant very little in the 1930s and so a sharp denominational awareness, as such, really did not exist. In the end it was decided simply to list the translated martyr biographies alphabetically.

Hopefully, this "modern martyrology" will enable future generations of English- speaking Mennonites to derive inspiration and benefit from these stories of faithfulness, suffering, and death.

Author's Preface

Nothing happens by chance in the lives of people who belong to the Lord. Everything occurs according to the unfathomable but wise decree of our God. In the earthly life of our Lord Jesus the Bible again and again says, "and it came to pass." That is also the story of this book.

Some years ago when I was asked to deliver a paper on the theme "Mennonite Martyrs in the Recent Past and at Present" for a ministerial conference in Alberta, I had no idea that this small beginning would become a large project. At that time the minister, H.H. Kornelsen, from Coaldale, Alberta presented a similar paper. It can be found at the beginning of this book. I was instructed to gather further material on the subject and publish it in the form of a brochure, but the project continued to expand. The author's experience was similar to that of the Mennonite writer, P.M. Friesen, who also received the assignment to prepare a pamphlet as a Jubilee commemoration for the Mennonite Brethren Conference. It took twenty-five years to complete the job and in the end produced a massive historical work. Personally, I only spent three years on this very specific area of Anabaptism.

The story of the Anabaptists, especially in its early stages, was mainly written with tears and blood. It has repeated itself during the last decades, especially in the case of the Mennonites in Russia who number about 100,000. To some degree even the Mennonites from Prussia, Holland, Alsace and Poland were affected.

Since all direct or letter contact with the coreligionists in the old homeland—Russia—has been interrupted for some years and still remains so, it was rather difficult for the author to obtain the necessary data. The mass flight of refugees from Russia to Western Europe during the past years has made it possible to obtain information about the terrible happenings behind the iron curtain. Even this source is limited because many thousands of the exiles, the condemned, and the prisoners were forcibly separated from their loved ones for decades. Since no correspondence was allowed between them one cannot, despite all inquiries, even determine their place of exile. Consequently, many of the biographies of the martyrs end with a sad comment: "There is no further information about the subsequent fate of the exile and prisoner." In the majority of such cases, we can be almost certain that they perished somewhere in the virgin forests of Siberia or the swamps of northern Russia.

People have repeatedly asked me, "Who belongs to the martyrs?" Many of our people did not exactly perish on account of their faith. We readily admit that among the many victims of the bloody revolution, the civil war, and the two World Wars, there were those who were not disciples of Jesus. Many of these, however, turned to God and called upon Him in their last hour amid torment and death throes. And the Word of the eternal God says, "Whoever shall call upon the name of the Lord shall be saved."

One thing is certain. Not all who have been designated a martyr's crown by humankind will receive it and some, whom we did not expect, will attain the crown of victory of the redeemed. We want to leave the matter to the Judge of this world who will judge each according to the work he has done (1 Corinthians 3:5-15).

It is for this reason that, in addition to the many who for reasons of faith were exiled and killed as martyrs, we have found a place in this book for those who were tortured and murdered in some terrible way. This was done in response to the request of the many relatives and friends who, for the sake of coming generations, wanted to erect a small memorial of love to their dear departed ones.

In his Bible Wordbook, H. Zeller writes, "The word 'martyr' does not come from torture (martern) but rather the opposite: [it comes] from the tortures applied to the 'martyr,' that is to the witness of Christ. The German word martern emerged from this. Martyrs are those children of God who, filled with a holy courage to witness, proclaimed Jesus as their Lord through the giving of their lives. It may be that they suddenly and violently had to offer their lives or that they had to endure countless miseries and difficulties for the sake of Christ, which is often more difficult."

Rightly or wrongly we have expanded Zeller's concept and will let it stand at that. One can also become a martyr due to national hatred, language, racial derivation, or one can become

5

a victim of mob violence, of the unfettered passions of the crowd, etc.

One particular difficulty in the writing of this book related to the fact that the author wished to accept only trustworthy facts which could be verified by witnesses. When numerous reports arrived from various persons which did not agree in all the details, it became difficult to determine the unbiased truth. If inaccuracies occur, please let me know so they can be corrected. In most cases the reports are based on the statements of eye and earwitnesses. In most of the accounts, I therefore identified the author by name. For many the exact mention of place, name and time may well serve the needs of a private family chronicle, though some may regard this information as superfluous. It is also intended to be a bit of history in miniature, a data base for a later historian.

Most of the accounts are original, written by various brothers and sisters from all walks and ranks. The heartrending portrayals of suffering, torture and death throes of our suffering coreligionists came from everywhere: Russia (mostly indirect); Germany, The Netherlands, Austria, Paraguay, Brazil, the USA and Canada.

I want to give a heartfelt thanks to all my co-workers for their contributions to this volume. Some of them, including a considerable number of insightful women among our people, provided me with a great deal of particularly valuable material. My work would have been impossible without all this manifold assistance.

For several years the many encouraging notes and good wishes for my work, again and again, encouraged me to continue with this difficult collection. I am thinking particularly of my recent departed friend and former colleague, Dr. Abram Warkentin, (Chicago) who, with kind words, persistently pled that I continually press forward until I completed the work. He knew what such a task meant from personal experience. The publication of his history book, Who is Who Among the Mennonites, was no small accomplishment.

Another difficulty related to the various spellings of personal and place names, especially those translated from other languages like Russian and Tatar. I would like to mention only a few like Tockmack, Tokmak, Tockmak, Soviet, Sowjet,

6

Ssowett and others as well as personal names like Klassen, KlaBen, Classen, ClaBen, Claassen; or Dueck, Dyck, Dick. Generally, I kept the original spelling which the contributor utilized.

The book lacks a chronological sequence of the various events and of the "Martyr Stories." We, nevertheless, have this in the books <u>Die Mennoniten-Gemeinden in RuBland waehrend der Kriegs = und Revolutionsjahre 1914-1920</u> published by Mennonitische Fluechtlingsfuersorge in Germany. There is also <u>Hildebrand's Zeittafel.</u>

I did not want to write a martyr history but only wished to portray individual martyrs among our people—how they patiently struggled, suffered, and died. In order to provide understanding for the novice, I have also included some general accounts.

The author should not be blamed if more martyrs are mentioned from one denomination than another. Again and again, I requested, in all Mennonite papers, that material be sent to me. To the best of my knowledge I have not left out any report which was sent. I had to shorten some reports because of limited space. Furthermore, I could not get information on all the people whom I knew of or who were mentioned to me. If it becomes necessary, perhaps this could be remedied in a new edition.

I would like to have given this task to the academically trained writers among our people but since no one was prepared to deal with the material I took it on with trepidation.

The Canadian Conference of the Mennonite Brethren generously placed funds for this task at my disposal, and I want to express my deepest thanks and fullest recognition to them.

May the Lord's richest blessing accompany this work. He also has regard for the small things. May these martyr figures speak to us mightily and strengthen our faith. May they cause us and our children to follow the footsteps of Jesus more faithfully, especially when we are confronted by a time of tribulation, which is not out of the question amid the threatening world events.

"But if you bear patiently with suffering when you are doing right, this is pleasing to God. To such experience you

7

have been called; for Christ also suffered for you and left behind an example, that you might follow in His footsteps" (1 Peter 2:20-21).

Aron A. Toews
Abbotsford, British Columbia
Canada
May 1948

CONTENTS

Johann J. Andres, Junior
Friedensruh, Molotschna, South Russia

This story, like many others, is told in 1946 by the daughter, Justine Schmidt (nee Andres), in the refugee camp near Novierenstein, Holland. Her husband was Heinrich Schmidt of Gnadenfeld who was exiled by the Russians to an unknown destination in 1941.

My father, Johann J. Andres, was born on January 15, 1891 in the village of Fuerstenau, Molotschna. He was the oldest of thirteen children and so had to help his mother a great deal with the household, especially since his father was working outside. As he grew up, he had to help his father on the farm. At the age of ten, he already worked for neighbors whenever he could and earned some money in this fashion. From childhood my father knew something about the seriousness of life.

At the age of eighteen, father was a full-time worker in the service of others. He came to the estate owner, Gerhard Nickel, in Barwenkowo, Charkow province. This G. Nickel, his father's cousin, had only daughters and so he hired Johann to help with all the work on the estate.

There Johann also learned to know my mother, Justina Hildebrandt, who lived in nearby Marjewka. After two years they celebrated their wedding in 1911 and soon moved to Friedensruh, where they purchased a farm. The Lord blessed them abundantly and gave them many healthy children, of which I was the oldest.

Following nineteen years of wedded bliss, my father was ruthlessly torn from his family and taken away. What was the reason? They did not possess many earthly goods. They had remained poor because they had lived through the war, revolution, civil war, and the famine which followed. No, the reason was that he had been elected as co-worker of the Word in the nearby Evangelical Mennonite Brethren Church. He was, as the government designated him, a cult servant, and these were to be eliminated because they blocked the course of the revolution— of course, according to their interpretation.

My mother remained alone with eight children. I was eighteen at the time and the youngest children, the twins, were four years of age. With a heavy heart and a deep concern about our future welfare, father left his family and the farm where he had worked for nineteen years. My mother was in complete despair. With a tearstained face, surrounded by her children, she watched father go and could only sigh, "God protect you." I can still see it in my mind's eye even though it was sixteen years ago.

Every night mother gathered us about her and we prayed to our heavenly Father to give us back our father. These were difficult years for us. We were visited by hunger and cold, destitution and misery. We thought God had abandoned us. Everything was taken from us; we were driven from house and home. We fled from one place to another, everywhere misunderstood and scorned— homeless! Since father was exiled we were disenfranchised and therefore had no right to work anywhere. For a time we lived in a small hut at the end of the village.

Our father was first taken to the prison in Halbstadt. He was there for one week, then taken to the city of Melitopol where he spent several weeks. From here it was steadily northward: first Charkow, then Tscheljabinsk, further to Kotlas and, finally, he came to his destination— Murmansk on the Polar Sea. He was able to write us several letters about his journey. He suffered indescribable hardship during this time: hunger, thirst, cold and vermin which literally consumed him.

Once they reached their destination, he and many of his fellow sufferers had to cut wood in the immense virgin forest. Tired and exhausted from the long journey, they were unable to fulfill their quotas and therefore did not get their allotment of bread. Instead they received less and less so that many, exhausted and overworked, became ill. He, himself, contracted rheumatism so he could no longer walk without a cane. He was taken into the hospital, where he wrote us that his food was somewhat better. As soon as he was better, he had to go to work again. They had to fell trees the entire day, from early in the morning until late in the evening. At lunch the piece of bread was thawed over the fire, eaten, and then it was back to work. In the evening, exhausted from their work, they returned to the barracks where each received a bowl of soup and a piece of bread. Things went on in this way day in and day out, year in and year out— it was always the same.

Father was gone for three years, returning in 1934. But he could not remain in his native village and so moved to the Caucasus with his family. Only we three eldest children remained in Mariawohl with our grandmother, J. Andres and Aunt Tina.

Our parents lived in the Caucasus for two years under wretched conditions. Mother could not endure the climate. She was always ill with fever. So they returned to the colony. When they returned, I was already married to Heinrich Schmidt from Gnadenfeld. For a time my parents lived in Mariawohl. Father went to the neighboring village of Paulsheim everyday to work in the collective. When he found accommodation, they moved to Paulsheim where they had a reasonable livelihood.

The year 1937 was a terrible time in our villages. Men were taken from their beds at night and led away, never to be seen again. Our father's turn came once again. He was among the first to be taken away. The lamentations and tears of the poor wives and mothers were of no avail.

Father left his family, steadfastly trusting in his God and Father. If God had been able to protect him for three years and return him to his family, He could do it again. Yet we never learned where he and all the exiles who walked that difficult path of suffering ended up. It seemed the earth had swallowed them.

When the unhappy war with Germany began in 1941, my four brothers, one of whom was only sixteen, were taken by the Russians. This was also the fate of my husband and my brother-in-law, Kaethe's husband, Jakob Quiring, from Paulsheim. My Uncle Jakob Andres and Aunt Tina's husband, Abram Mathies of Friedensruh were already exiled in 1937 and 1938.

In the fall of 1943 all of us fled to Warthegau in Poland, then Germany and Holland. We travelled throughout the entire winter on wagons, on foot, in rain, snow and cold. That is a chapter in and of itself. We were only women and children and my youngest brother, Willi. Even the dear old grandma from Mariawohl (the old Mrs. Johann Andres) was with us on the long difficult journey. We buried her enroute near the Polish border. In spite of her seventy-five years, she was quite healthy until our brother and husbands were taken. This affected her so severely that she had a stroke and for a time was very ill. She gradually recovered but her memory had suffered and she could not remember anything. Poor grandmother, who had done so much good in her life, perished so piteously during the flight. She was buried without a coffin! She only wanted to see her children once more before she died. How poor mother longed to see her loved ones in Canada. She had four sons in Ontario.

Here in Germany we had another great loss. Our youngest brother, Willi, who was with us and had not been taken by the Russians, was drafted into the German army. We never heard from him again.

My married sister Kaethe, Mrs. Jakob Quiring, also had two boys. The oldest died after her husband had left, the youngest became ill enroute and, as we had to flee, we left him in a hospital. All the later enquiries through the Red Cross have been ineffectual. Kaethe had a difficult cross but she bears it courageously. Our mother appears very careworn; she has seen some very difficult years.

We three sisters and mother, my sister-in-law, and my two children, Walter and Eugene, are all that are left of a large, happy family. We are homeless, wandering in this world and it often seems that in this whole wide world there is no place for us. Eight people are missing from the family of Johann Andres: the father, five sons and two sons-in-law—all men, the providers.

There are five orphaned women: mother, three daughters and one sister-in-law, together with two boys, the youngest of which has poliomyelitis and suffers severely from its consequences. These people are all on the way to Paraguay to find a new home. Does this not seem hopeless?

But what does the mother of these two boys write? "When during the journey we sometimes thought it was impossible to go on, we experienced [these words]: 'When the need is greatest God is nearest.'" In reality this means faith and trust in all circumstances. God will not allow them to be disgraced.

14

Bernhard Bargen
Minister and Evangelist

He was born in the village of Friedensdorf, south Russia in 1884. His parents lived on a small farm (Kleinwirtschaft). In 1889 or 1890, his family moved to the newly established Mennonite settlement of Neu-Samara on the Volga. The son Bernhard experienced all the difficulties associated with a new settlement. They lived in the village of Pleschanowo.

As an unconverted youth, his life was in danger on several occasions. Once during harvest time, he was working on the field with family members cutting grain. Over lunchtime, they left their forks in the wheat stack. At that time the grain was not bound by a binder but cut loose with a *hobogrejka*, a type of mower. The loose ears were then put into piles by workers using forks. With these forks they had made a shady nook using the loose grain. After lunch Bernhard wanted to test his strength against the other boys as such youngsters are wont to do. A hired hand was stronger than him and threw him onto the straw pile where the forks were. The tine of one of the forks entered his body below the shoulder blade. We could feel the tine in his throat. His older brother pulled out the fork by force. It was far from home, yet he began to walk in that direction. Enroute he met his father who was just driving to the field to change the horses as was customary during harvest. He placed Bernhard on the wagon and took him to the doctor. Thanks to the Lord's grace he was soon healed.

On another occasion he was hauling some water; the horses bolted and ran away. He got caught between the wagon and the brick fence. Though badly crushed, he remained alive. An elderly believer came to us from the village, tapped my brother on the shoulder and said, "Ben, Ben, the Lord does not desire the death of the sinner but that he be converted and live." My parents and my brothers and sisters were not converted at the time. In fact, no one ever spoke of conversion.

I understood very little about the matter at that time. Bernhard looked earnestly at the old gentleman but remained silent. Next came his years of state service at the Razin Forestry. In his second or third year of service, he was converted to the Lord. When he wrote to his parents of his

15

conversion, they were very happy even though they did not profess to belong to the Lord at the time.

We believe that he brought the entire family before the Lord during that period, for not long after he came home, the other family members were converted. During the next winter the Lord also drew me unto Himself. In 1908 Bernhard and his three sisters were baptized in the river and accepted into the Mennonite Brethren Church. Our parents were not opposed. They only said, "If you think it's the right thing to do we will not stop you." They, themselves, joined the *Allianz* Church. Yet after several years they were also baptized in the river and accepted into the Mennonite Brethren Church. Both congregations had united into one. This made the entire family happy and one in the Lord.

In 1910 our brother, Bernhard, travelled to Germany and studied for two years at the *Allianz* Bible School in Berlin. He wanted to prepare for the Gospel ministry. Somewhat later he was married to Anna Thiessen, also a believer, the daughter of Klaas Thiessen. They established their own household and moved onto their own farm. The joy of being together was not for long. When the war began in the fall of 1914 he, together with many others, was called into service. He worked as a ranger in the Koltubanka forest, district of Busuluk in Samara, about one hundred verst from home.

He was released from service in 1917. During his absence his wife had deployed prisoners of war on the farm.

They had two children, Erna and Kolya. They began farming again and tried to forget about the war. The revolution brought them new difficulties. In 1921 bandits held up the entire family. They were locked in the basement and robbed of everything. They moved in with the other family members until 1923. Both of his parents died of typhus in 1922 and Bernhard Bargen bought his father's farm.

Before the war,he was already ordained as a minister of the Mennonite Brethren Church and worked among the youth. For several years he was also a Bible teacher in the village of Lugowsk together with the minister, Kornelius Klassen. When brother Abram Martens, the leader and elder of the Mennonite Brethren Church, became ill (he had a stroke) brother Bernhard Bargen was elected as leader.

16

Then the emigration began. He said, "I cannot go and leave the flock alone." In 1926 we left for Canada and have not seen each other since then. In 1929 when many from his locality and church left for Moscow and congregational life virtually ceased— the church had been turned into a theater— he and his wife decided he should go to Moscow. He would try to get exit visas and after a week his wife and children would join him. When she arrived in Moscow, Bernhard Bargen had already been arrested by the GPU and imprisoned. She was promised emigration to Canada if she signed a paper stating she was a widow. She refused and together with her children was forcibly repatriated to Samara.

After four years, her husband returned as a cripple on crutches. While felling trees in exile, he had broken a leg and remained lame ever since.

For awhile he was a sheepherder in the village of Koltan. After the family's return they had bought a small farm. We received a letter from him at this time. He wrote that he took his children's clothes along to the field in order to help with the mending. His wife was not well at the time.

On January 24, 1935, he was again sent into exile. His wife died three weeks later and his children remained behind without a mother. Loving and concerned friends looked after them.

He was released after three years and married a widow, Lena Wiebe. A few weeks after the wedding, he was again arrested. We do not know what he experienced in exile or whether he is still alive. Only eternity will answer some of these riddles.

I should like to cite several excerpts from one of his letters. It will give us a deep insight into his suffering, struggles, and also his firmly rooted life of faith.

Koltan, Neu-Samara
June 25, 1929

We wish you much blessing in your lovely worship services. We see from your letter that you are happy there and we are happy for you. How I would like to visit you and also your services. We can still hold our services according to our custom but we do not know for how long. (The church had already been turned into a theater during the fall of that year). We can feel

17

the reins being steadily tightened.

Many of the Russian brethren who held leading positions have been exiled, imprisoned, etc. From the city of Samara, alone, eight or nine brethren have been sent to the various remote corners of Russia. The Lord will find work for them. Some have been sent to the far north, some to the far east, others to the Finnish border, and even the cold, swampy taiga is to be populated.

Recently, I received a letter from brother Kliewer, the leader of the Russian congregation in the city of Samara. He had been free until now but has been arrested and imprisoned. In the near future, the lot of believers will be a very difficult one.

We are taking everything into account. We are in God's hand. I often think of Psalms 1 and 2. May we stand the trial and be a light that shines at the right time and in the right place. The church of God is being tested. Faith is there but it has not proven itself, and these are tests for its veracity. And if the Lord finds us worthy to put us to the test, then we owe Him thanks! But we will have to learn this first. The accuser of the brethren (Revelation 12) is still at work but soon the Church of God will occupy those heavenly regions and Satan will be cast on to the earth. Jesus sees this in Luke 19:18 and also in John 12:31. We do not have to look for any signs; the coming of Jesus can occur at any moment.

Perhaps the Lord will leave us at our post for awhile. I certainly feel weak and inadequate in these evil times. And if the Lord finds us worthy to remain in our work, then we want to submit and suffer. May the dear Lord give us the necessary strength!

So much for the letter.
The Lord found his servant worthy to take upon himself the suffering of Christ. The apostle Peter speaks of this suffering in 1 Peter 4:12-13.

Do not be surprised, dear friends, at the fiery test that is coming upon you, as if you were experiencing something unheard of. Instead be joyful that you are sharing to some degree the sufferings of Christ, in order that at the revealing of His glory you may be full of joy.

Mrs. Justina Thiessen
Coaldale, Alberta

18

Peter J. Baergen
Friedensdorf, Alexanderwohl, Kleefeld in the Molotschna, Minister

He was born in the village of Friedensdorf in the Gnadenfeld district in 1881. He also attended the village school here. He was baptized in the Mennonite Church in Rudnerweide. He married Agnes Unger, a young lady from the neighboring village of Alexanderwohl. Soon after that he became a member of the Mennonite Brethren Church in Rueckenau. He continued to live in Alexanderwohl where, in time, he purchased his wife's family farm.

The Rueckenau congregation elected him as a minister and he served both there and in the neighboring Gnadenheim congregation for many years. He had a severe physical disability and, from time to time, he was subject to epileptic seizures which made his work difficult. Later he was completely freed from them. They had prayed a lot for healing.

He wished to emigrate to Canada. Initially, he wanted to go to Batum where many of our refugees were and where many experienced great difficulties, especially through disease and death. Most were forced to return to their homes completely impoverished. Several families were almost entirely wiped out.

In retrospect, Baergen was very thankful that the Lord had prevented him from fleeing. Even later, he could not leave. He had sold his farm but could not get the necessary papers. He had to remain behind and bought a farm in the village of Kleefeld. Because he was a minister, he lost his civil and voting rights and, as such, was expelled from the village. He had to settle upon the barren steppe amid great difficulties and without any means. They were very poor.

His suffering did not end. In 1936 he was arrested by the Reds and imprisoned. With the German advance in 1941-42 all men were deported eastward on foot far beyond the enemy lines. Because one leg was incapacitated, he was not included in the transport but left lying helpless by the roadside. He made his way back and in the process fell into German captivity. They soon freed him and allowed him to return home. When he arrived there, he found no one. His family had been deported—

no one knew where. Only strangers now lived in this locality. He then went to his home congregation in Gnadenheim and was able to serve this congregation throughout the German occupation.

When the great retreat to the west took place he and his entire congregation fled and came to Warthegau, Poland. Here, together with others, he developed a vital spiritual ministry. Congregations were organized, ministers elected and ordained. Souls were converted and baptized.

Then when the Russians approached, another headlong flight commenced. Many, overtaken by the Russians and the Poles, were taken into captivity. Among these was the minister, Peter J. Baergen. He and his co-worker, Gerhard Thiessen of Alexanderwohl, were taken by the Poles and, in revenge against all that was German, shot. They rest somewhere in Polish soil. No one will be able to discover their graves. Thus, these valiant soldiers of Jesus Christ await the resurrection morning. None of the next of kin here in Canada know what happened to the family.

When Peter Baergen was still serving the churches during the difficult time in the old homeland, he had to visit almost all the villages on foot. His injured leg hindered him severely. One day, he received an invitation to conduct a funeral. Mrs. Heinrich Pankratz in Alexanderwohl had died. He could not make the journey by foot. The horses had all been taken into the collective, no one had a horse for private use. What now? He asked the young brother Nicolai Goetz of Friedensdorf, who lived in Alexanderwohl at the time, to go there and conduct the funeral in his place. The brother was happy to do this service for the Lord and left for Alexanderwohl. After the funeral the Poles took this brother, Nicolai Goetz, behind the barn of H. Pankratz and shot him. A tragic death for a courageous hero of faith.

Around 1931 no ministers were active in the villages and no services were held. Peter J. Baergen had to work in the collective on the onetime farm of Vollwerk. Rations were denied him and still he had to work. They received no bread, only a soup with potatoes or millet. Amid such hardship, they struggled for their existence.

Johann Becker
Minister and Teacher
Prangenau, Gnadenfeld District, Molotschna

The teacher and minister, Johann Becker, came from the village of Franztal where his parents lived and where he also spent his childhood and early school years. Franztal and Pastwa were the two villages located on the extreme east end of the Molotschna villages where the holdings of the colonies ended in a land point. When these two villages entered into a conversation, one usually, jokingly, added, "The world there is nailed shut with boards or plastered shut with pancakes." After this came Russian villages like Tchernigowka, Njeljgowka and others. If Mennonites and their families wished to go to the Azov seaport of Berdyansk by rail, in order to bathe in the sea or eat grapes, they first drove to Njeljgowka. Generally, this rarely happened. Most Mennonites, especially the older ones, rode on the train for the first time when they emigrated to America. "Riding the rails" constituted an unnecessary luxury.

Our writer, J.H. Janzen, erected a memorial to the village of Pastwa in his small book, The History of Philosophy. He knew this village well for he had been a teacher here.

Our dear father and colleague, Johann Becker, came from this region. One could rightfully ask, as Jesus' disciples did long ago, "What good can come out of Nazareth?" And yet it has been God's style to select what is little or nothing in this world in order to put to shame the things which are something. This was certainly the case here. Johann Becker became one of our capable teachers and one of the most successful evangelists in the Molotschna villages.

After he completed the village school, he attended the high school in Gnadenfeld where the old teacher, H. Lenzmann, imparted wisdom to him in his unique way. He came to Halbstadt one year later than the author, around 1902, and studied for the teaching profession under the well-known teachers, Wilhelm P. Neufeld and Kornelius Bergmann. After [completing] the teacher's exam, he came to the two-room school in Conteniufeld, where he worked for several years with his colleague, Heinrich D. Penner. Then he was invited to the village school in

Prangenau where he worked until 1922, when the Reds expelled him from the school, because he was already a minister at that time.

He was already converted to the Lord as a young single man and joined the Evangelical Mennonite Brethren Church in Lichtfelde, which was not far from his place of work in Prangenau. As a teacher, he was well liked by the children and by the village community. In Prangenau, he became the successor to the old teacher Peter Peters, who came to Canada. Peters, after a lengthy career as a minister and farmer in the Mennonite settlement of Gem, Alberta, died in that locality.

The author and Johann Becker were often in contact. The author was a teacher in the neighboring village of Friedensruh. He married a year later than we did, namely in 1909. His wife was Justina, the daughter of the minister, Heinrich Wiens of Steinfeld. The Lord granted them a number of children, five sons and a daughter. They had a happy family life.

When brother Becker was expelled from the school he completely dedicated himself to the work in the churches. His congregation had elected him as minister several years earlier, and he was able to work with great blessing for many years. He was then appointed itinerant minister by the churches. He worked as an evangelist among the villages of the Molotschna and the Lord blessed his ministry. Souls were converted to the Lord and believers experienced a revival. Among the congregations, it was customary that the brethren travelled by two in accordance with the example of Jesus: "He sent them by twos." The brethren, Johann A. Toews, Johann Peters, Jakob A. Loewen, worked together with him, as did the author on several occasions. The Red government wanted to neutralize the influence of the minister-teachers but accomplished the exact opposite. Now these brethren, who were free [of other duties], travelled about and proclaimed the Gospel with great success. The congregations supported them materially. For example, a house was bought for the teacher, J. Becker, in Prangenau by the Missions Committee so that the need for housing was dispensed with. Brother Becker also made mission trips outside of the boundaries of the Molotschna Colony.

When the great 1920s emigration to Canada began, the Becker family wanted to emigrate for the sake of their children.

The serious eye disease, trachoma, delayed them too long. When their eyes had healed they could no longer leave: the Red government had closed all the borders for emigrants and they had to remain in Russia. For a time, they continued to work in blessing among the churches. But not for long.

The following events are related by a nurse in the Muntau Hospital. This is sister Agathe Loewen who came as a refugee to Berlin and from there has resettled in Paraguay. Today she is in British Columbia.

His dear wife already died in the Muntau Hospital in 1926. That was a terrible loss. He mourned for her deeply. His orphaned children nevertheless needed a mother and so in the summer of 1927 he married Margaretha Dick from Herzenberg, a nurse in the Muntau Hospital. Now to the satisfaction of all involved, the great void had been partially filled.

Agathe Loewen further relates:

At that time I was also present at the wedding. Later I had opportunity to meet him and also visited them in their home. I treasured him as a brother in Christ and liked to hear him preach. Once I was also present in a smaller circle of brothers and sisters when he studied the Lord's coming with us.

The last time I saw him and spoke with him for a few minutes was shortly before Christmas in 1934. He had come to Halbstadt in order to obtain a [travel] pass. This meant that he wanted to disappear from the Molotschna and from the eyes of the myrmidons of the law. I was at work at the time and he only told me that his situation was serious and that he hoped to get his pass in January. Then we said goodbye, never to see each other again.

He did not collect his pass. We soon heard that he and brother Daniel Reimer, son of Adolf Reimer, the evangelist among the Russians, were in the Halbstadt prison. Then we knew what we had to do! We prayed much for them; now and then we were also able to extend a kind service, which was not without danger to us. During that time we were able to richly experience God's help.

The greatest difficulty came in the beginning of May 1935. We supported the family in so far as the Lord gave grace. The end came here in Halbstadt after a long and painful hearing. The result: eight years in exile! What the brother experienced in terms of physical and mental suffering did not become public knowledge. Only eternity will reveal what this meant in terms of inner struggles and crises.

We tried to comfort the severely tested family through letters. There were manifold storms and difficulties. The last letter from exile was filled with forebodings of farewell. Brother J. Becker was soon allowed to go home—into the heavenly fatherland. Barely three years had gone by and all was over. Only the Heavenly Father above, and those who have experienced it, know what passed during that interval in terms of hardship and suffering.

It was not easy for the family: the first wife left five sons and one daughter; then there were two boys from the second marriage. The oldest son Hans lived near the Amur; the second worked at the Dnieper power station. Both looked after the mother so that she suffered no want. The second married a nurse and lived in the city of Berdyansk.

Mrs. Becker and the four other boys and the only married daughter, Lenchen, were forced to begin a long journey in 1941. Since then we have heard nothing from them. We can only pray for them and commit them to the heavenly father.

This is the report of the nurse, Agathe Loewen.

Brother J. Becker was a dear friend of the author. For years, he was his bosom companion and faithful co-worker. He was especially supportive during the years when I was the leader of the church in Lichtfelde. Later, he himself became the leader of the Evangelical Mennonite Brethren Church. When I left he gave the farewell sermon to a very large audience. How I sorrow for you, my dear Jonathan, and for your family in exile. Thank God there will be a reunion and a time of eternal joy and bliss where there will be no more sorrow and when God shall wipe away all tears—even those of our exiled and decimated families.

Kornelius P. Bergmann
Teacher, Worker Among the Russians, Writer

The teacher Bergmann was the son of the minister Peter Bergmann in Ladekopp, who belonged to the Mennonite

Brethren Church. Kornelius, himself, never joined it, though inwardly he identified with it and readily participated in its services. For a time, he even attended regularly, especially during his stay in Rueckenau.

He was my teacher during the years 1901-19 when I attended the pedagogical classes in Halbstadt for two years. I must say he was a teacher by the grace of God. I have never known anyone who was such an enthusiastic teacher, and his preparatory students, the future teachers, were also instilled with this enthusiasm. He could excite his students for the teaching profession like none of the other teachers. When it came to German literature, he spoke so passionately of the German poets and their works that we participated wholeheartedly and read the German writers intelligently. Thanks to his efforts, the library possessed a large holding in German literature.

And when he taught methodology and pedagogy and told us about Pestalozzi, Kehr, F. Pollack and others, our hearts warmed in our bosoms and we did not find studying difficult. If I think back on my teachers, I have to confess he was the most important of them. Beside him stands the deeply pious teacher of religion, Wilhelm P. Neufeld, who later emigrated to America. Neufeld died in California shortly after he visited Russia during the famine in 1922-23.

Later we worked together as colleagues in the Molotschna Mennonite Teachers Association. He can probably be designated as the main founder of the association which began in Rueckenau in January 1906. He worked to establish a rich and varied teachers' library. He participated in all aspects of the teacher conferences, especially the debates and the critiques.

He was also a writer of some scope. He wrote the booklet "For Those Becoming" (*Fuer Werdende*), an excellent instruction for young emerging teachers. He also wrote on behalf of animal protection. He was a special friend of nature, especially the world of birds. During his leisure time, he roamed through field and meadow with his gun in order to collect rare specimens for mounting and use in nature instruction. How enraged he became when he heard of bad boys who tortured animals! Woe to these evildoers if he got a hold of them. He often wrote under the pseudonym, C. Orosander.

Everyone who loved and honored him was sad when his work was interrupted by a lengthy illness.

During his active years, he published many articles and essays in papers which most of us read, like *Friedensstimme*, *Botschafter*, *Odessaer Zeitung* and others. At times, he could be very sharp in his criticisms, especially when he sought to rectify the political, social and ecclesiastical evils of the Mennonite world. He often spewed fire and brimstone, yet one felt the pain of his heart: he loved his Mennonite people and was zealous on their behalf. He had to endure many a counterstroke but that did not silence him. He struggled courageously for the truth.

He remained a staunch opponent of the great emigration to Canada which began in 1923. He felt it unjust that so many teachers and ministers were leaving Russia. Not long before my emigration in 1926, he wrote a critical letter to me and other ministers in which he described us as hirelings. Now that our long awaited freedom had arrived at last, it was our duty to remain and use all the opportunities for mission work, especially among the Russians. He felt we were fleeing into "dollar land" where we, as a people, would drown in materialism! Was he all that wrong? God protect us! The religious freedom he hoped for also did not materialize as he, himself, later experienced. Instead of freedom there was prison, exile and death! And yet our dear teacher and brother remained a hero of faith until his end. He faithfully endured and in exile gave his life for his master. His reward will not be withheld from him. Honor such men (Philippians 2:29-30).

His equally capable wife, whom we learned to know as a serious Christian, stood faithfully by his side as a silent partner until his death. During his fifteen-year crippling disease, she made great sacrifices in caring for the sometimes impatient patient, without murmuring or complaining. For those of us who knew and respected her, she has an important place in all our hearts and our memories. They had no children but, for a time, had an adopted daughter, Leni.

Mrs. Kornelius P. Bergmann was an Ida Staschau from St. Petersburg. Her mother was a widow. They had moved there from Germany. Mrs. Bergmann was very talented and a master at handiwork. Before her marriage she was an employee of a shoe factory in St. Petersburg. She was Lutheran and played the foot organ in her church. Her minister was Arndt. The teacher, K.P. Bergmann, learned to know her in St. Petersburg and married her. She was a beauty among the women and a helpmate of her husband.

Abram Boldt
Sparrau, Molotschna

He and his family lived in the village of Sparrau where he had a farm. In 1930 they, like many fellow sufferers, had to leave their home and farm. Though innocent, he was put in prison where he languished for a considerable period. For a time, the family went to Memrik where Abram Boldt's daughter lived; it was the Pauls family.

After a year of painful experiences in prison, Abram Boldt was released and joined his family in Memrik. In 1933 the daughter returned to the colony and found a position in the Konteniusfeld collective farm. The parents soon returned and were able to move into their old house in Sparrau. They did not like the separated family life and moved to Konteniusfeld where they bought a small farm in 1937. Now they were united with their children. Mrs. Boldt died in the following year (1938). Thanks to their diligence and their Christian walk, the Boldt family was highly respected in the village.

We younger girls (a Thiessen daughter from Konteniusfeld is reporting) felt ourselves drawn to them by a higher power. They gave us something the world did not. How happy we were in the fall of 1941 (when the Germans arrived) that our visits to the Boldts no longer had to be secretive. We sang Christian songs and our thirsty souls were edified by the Bible studies and the conversations of our brothers and sisters in the Lord. We will never forget the day when Mr. Boldt shook our hands in farewell and admonished us to remain steadfast in faith and not to neglect our prayers.

Since by God's grace Mr. Boldt was the only minister that was left, he felt called to serve the entire congregation on Sunday. He always fulfilled this obligation. He was always happy that God gave him the strength to serve us. The congregation was constantly amazed and happy that the Lord had made him

27

such a talented minister of the Word. Our young hearts clung to him. When he introduced young people's meetings and youth instruction in 1942, the young people attended with great enthusiasm. On Pentecost of that year, he baptized twenty-one people and accepted them into the church. Justa Rahn and I were among them.

Since our village was privileged to have a minister and the neighboring villages did not, he made it his obligation to serve them with the Gospel from time to time. The seed which he had sown soon produced fruit. Not long after, he began to instruct the youth in Sparrau, Rudnerweide youth had to come to Konteniusfeld for instruction every Sunday. On Sunday afternoon, he drove to Gnadenfeld and served there. They were unforgettable times for all of us. On Pentecost, in 1943, he baptized one hundred souls and added them to the church. He was tireless in his work for the Lord.

All this ended in September 1943 when we had to leave our homes. If someone had to be buried during that long difficult journey, Mr. Boldt was again prepared to offer a word of comfort for those who remained behind.

Things became very difficult in the spring of 1944 when we arrived in Poland as refugees and were scattered to the winds. Yet God held him and us in His faithful hand. When Sunday came we all walked the twenty kilometer stretch to hear the precious Word of God from his mouth. We had worked hard for six days, but that did not stop us. It is indescribable how he comforted us with the fullness of God's promises. Then we could again take up the difficult weekday work and the struggle for existence. The love which the Boldt family showed the congregation was also reciprocated by gifts of love from the congregational members.

If we could not come on a Sunday, we visited by letter. This continued until January 1945 when all contact was broken by the terrible unrest caused by the advancing Bolshevik troops.

Since the fall [of Germany] all contact between us and the family has been lost. We do not know whether they are alive or not. We assume that since they lived next to a forest and a lake and since contact with the city was difficult, they remained where they were and fell into the hands of angry Poles or the Russians. They either perished or were sent back into the suffering of Siberia. God knows.

My last and finest memories of them are from our last visit. He mentioned that the forest air was good for him and he felt better than he had in a long time. In my mind I still see him walking in the forest holding conversations with God.

Isaak Boldt
Paulsheim, Gnadenfeld District

He was born in the village of Paulsheim during the 1870s. After completing the village school, he took classes to prepare for a teaching career with Peter Siemens, the well-known pedagogue for advanced studies. Many young men in the Molotschna received their further training through him. During a fire in his house, he (Siemens) was so badly burned that he later died.

Circumstances nevertheless forced I. Boldt to give up his ambition to become a teacher and remain at home. In later years, he selflessly offered evening classes to the young people who had finished the course in the village school. They were well attended and the participants furthered their general education by sharpening their oral and written skills.

After receiving instruction, I. Boldt was baptized upon his living faith by the elder of the Margenau Mennonite Church and accepted into the congregation. Later, together with the teacher Julius Thiessen, he was called to the ministry of the Word. Brother Boldt completely dedicated himself to his calling. In an open and free manner, he preached the truth which had liberated him and so sought to serve the living God.

In his preaching and in his personal work, he pled for a decision and a decisive commitment to Christ. He was willing to bear the dishonor of the cross and witnessed the inner crisis of many a heart. Through his witness in preaching and counselling, brother Boldt was able to become a catalyst to salvation among the village young people so that lost ones were converted to the Shepherd and Bishop of our souls. In his pastoral ministry, he sought to take account of all believers, regardless of which group they belonged to, so that none remained behind. Together with Julius Thiessen, who was a teacher in the

29

village of Paulsheim for many years, he introduced Bible studies into his home village. It was noticeable that God's blessing rested upon these [studies].

When the great revival occurred among our people after the terrible Russian Revolution, the seeds which our brothers Julius Thiessen and Isaak Boldt had spread began to germinate. The Lord gave grace and many a soul found salvation in Christ. Not long after, the minister I. Boldt joined the Allianz congregation in Lichtfelde. On his farm, he erected a meetinghouse where services were regularly held. All church groups worked together in a brotherly fashion. It was the time when the farmers no longer had any horses, for they had been taken by the Reds and the various warring factions. The people could no longer drive to the more distant churches and so, meeting halls, to which the village inhabitants could walk, were opened in almost every village. Ministers from the various church groups served at these worship services.

The minister Isaak Boldt remained in his home village until May 1931 and still managed to pursue his calling, which was difficult and dangerous amid the changing circumstances of the time.

Then he and his family had to walk the way of which the poet says, "The pilgrimage of this time has many rough ways and only heroism of faith leads to paths of peace." They were sent to Tscheljabinsk, a city in the Urals. Here there were various mines where the prisoners, with very meager rations, performed hard labor. The family could not stay together. Father Isaak Boldt was taken from here and sent to Archangelsk. How he arrived there and how he looked is described by the minister P.C. Heidebrecht from Gnadental who, together with his wife, was also in exile in Archangelsk.

When Isaak Boldt arrived he was near death. He was so weak that he could hardly stand and so emaciated that they hardly recognized him. At that time, he had been exiled for five years. He gradually recovered and after several years returned to his family. It was not for long. Isaak Boldt and his son Isaak were again arrested and torn from the family. Where to? No one knows. This is the last information about him.

His son–in–law, Woelk, was also a minister of the Evangelical Mennonite Brethren Church.

This brief biography comes from the pen of his fellow citizen in Paulsheim, the minister Gerhard Dirks of Namaka, Alberta. In Russia, he was a teacher in Fuerstenwerder, Molotschna. The author also knew the Isaak Boldt family as well. I was able to speak at their silver wedding and also spoke in Paulsheim in other services, especially during the time of revival. In brother Isaak, I had a faithful co-worker in the Paulsheim congregation (1925-26), which was associated with Lichtfelde. May the Lord reward his faithful servant and his pious family according to their service (I Corinthians 3:8).

Abram A. Braun

Our father, Abram A. Braun, was born in Gnadenfeld on March 15, 1880, the son of the teacher Abram Braun. At the age of seven, he entered village school which he completed in five years and then entered the Gnadenfeld High School. He graduated in 1906 and went to the Apanlee estate, district of Melitopol, where he was active as a private tutor among the Mennonite estate owners. At the age of seventeen,he became the secretary in the district office of his hometown. Over the years, he became full-time secretary and treasurer. He remained in this post as long as the district office existed, that is until 1921.

On June 6, 1905, he married Maria Rempel from Gnadenfeld, who later became my mother. He became the conductor of the Gnadenfeld Church choir shortly after the wedding and led it until 1930. In 1901 he was enlisted in the Phylloxera Commando on the southern coast of the Crimea where he fulfilled his state service. Since the work in the vineyards was only done in summer, he worked there for three summers. In winter, he was at home and worked in the district office. During WWI he was again conscripted in the fall of 1914 and was located as a forester near the lovely city of Aluschta on the south coast of the Crimea. He returned home just before the revolution.

My father was elected as a minister by the Gnadenfeld Church in 1925. I can still precisely remember how seriously and earnestly my father regarded this election. He struggled for a long time, for he knew the great responsibility associated with the ministerial office. I was not a church member at that time but learned this from the conversations of my parents. I can remember how seriously father took the matter as if it happened today. He was ordained by elder Abram Klassen from Neu-Halbstadt, together with Karl Nachtigall and Heinrich Unruh. In the Gnadenfeld Church, he served us with God's Word between 1926 and 1930, though not without encountering obstacles and difficulties. He had to give up his position in the district office for it did not suit the officials to have a minister in their midst, especially since father had great influence among the people. He was deprived of his voting rights as were we. I was expelled from the agricultural school. Father could not occupy any public post.

With God's help we managed to stay above board. I cannot remember that father was ever discontent or that he ever complained that if he had not taken on his pastoral role things would have been easier.

In the summer and fall of 1930, the interrogations began in the village office. They wanted to persuade father to lay down his ministerial post. He was taken there on several occasions. It was always the same: renounce your faith and everything will return to normal. Father remained steadfast. In October 1930, things became serious: one assessment of grain and money after another; one more capricious than the one before. After we had swept the floor clean of all our provisions (everything we had gathered for the winter) and after we had paid our third assessment, the fourth assessment was levied. With it, came a commission which listed an inventory of our property. This robbed us of the possibility of selling anything to pay for this assessment. When we could not pay, a judicial seizure was made on November 4, 1930. Our furniture was taken out and auctioned off to the Russians at ridiculous prices.

When this difficult day ended, we sat in our empty house with no clue as to what to do next. A friend of father's came to us and warned us not to remain in the house any longer if we valued our freedom. Late at night, father went to find transport to take us and our few possessions away. At three a.m. Mr. Neufeld and his horse came and took us— father, mother, my sister and I— to Mr. Doerksen in Nikolaidorf. I think I will never forget the helpfulness and the willingness with which they aided us— they and other dear people— to overcome the first difficult period.

We drove on from Nikolaidorf and finally came to Halbstadt. Here, too, we were lovingly received by our relatives, the Heinrich Brauns, the Abram Klassens and the dear friends, Abram Letkemanns. Elder Abram Klassen gave a short sermon on the eve of our departure and prayed with us. Friends had also collected sufficient money to buy our tickets to Suworowka, Caucasus. We had only brought twenty-five rubles from home. When we arrived in Suworowka, we were lodged with our relatives but only temporarily for they all lived amid very modest circumstances. Finally we found a room where we could live. We could not, however, find employment, for everywhere in our papers was stamped the fateful word "disenfranchised." We often did not know how we would pay for our bread. We, nevertheless, found that the ancient God still lived. We received packages with foodstuffs from completely unknown people. Often when mother said, "Today we have nothing left, I can give you nothing more," the door opened and help arrived.

During all this difficult time, father did not speak one negative word. His faith in God sustained him in many a difficult hour. Our brother, for whom things became too hot in Gnadenfeld, left his family with his parents-in-law and came to us. We finally found work at the railway station as day laborers. The three of us— father, my brother and I— walked three kilometers every morning and carried corn from one granary to another. In the evening we came home tired. We nevertheless earned enough to send my brother to the Kuban when we heard from our relatives about the project granted the Germans there.

He brought us good news. "We could all find work there though finding accommodation was still difficult."

Mother, my sister and I stayed on in Arival, that was the name of the village near Suworowka, while my father and my brother travelled to the project near Kropotkin. After two months, we also came there and lived in a sheepherder's hut. My brother was also able to bring his family and so, we were finally all together.

Father then got the position of chief controller and we

were given a respectable house. We lived there in relative peace and security from 1931 to 1936. Gradually, a number of families came together in that locality who, like we, were homeless. We gathered to sing lovely choir songs and to hold our worship services.

After 1933 the old troubles began again. Father had to experience many difficulties. Finally, in 1936, the director of the Soviet enterprise, which had been organized from the liquidated German project, said to him, "It is time that you, Abram Abramovich, disappear from here. I do not want you to be arrested. You have always served faithfully in your position and you should be allowed to leave here unhindered."

Mother and father again had to pack their coffers and search for a place in the wide world where they could find lodging.

They were talked out of the idea of returning to Gnadenfeld enroute. Instead, with an address in their pocket, they travelled to the city of Kirow, province of Smolensk. Father found a position in a factory, and after several months, we moved there. Here too we had to struggle to survive, but father never spoke a word of discontent. Indeed he often had to comfort us. Even when my brother was arrested in 1937 and his wife and five small children remained behind with us, father always had a cheerful word for them. Often he said to us, "When will this sense of foreboding leave me?" He constantly felt that he would also be included among the many who were torn from their families. He always sensed this pressure and when he was arrested on February 12, 1938 his premonition was fulfilled.

He was in the Kirow prison for several days, but all our efforts to bring him food and clothing were futile. He was soon transferred to another prison in the vicinity of the city of Brjansk. At the train station he had left a little note with one of the guards. He wrote us that we should not despair, that the One who counted every hair on our heads, who fed the birds of the field, would not forget us or him. We should trust Him when we did not know where to turn.

In the last prison, we were able to give father some laundry and write a short note to him. Father confirmed its receipt and nodded a short greeting. They kept him there until August 1938, when he was then taken to Smolensk. We were also able

34

to bring him a few small things there. All our efforts to obtain an interview with him were rejected. When I was again at the Smolensk prison in September 1938, I was told that father was no longer there and that I should await further word from him. Our waiting was futile and once more I set out to learn something about his fate. After much travelling back and forth and running from one place to another, I finally found out that on September 9, 1938, father had been sent to a distant prison camp. Upon my comment that if father could write he would have done so long ago and that he probably was not permitted to do so, the official in charge only shrugged his shoulders and scornfully remarked that this might well be the case.

Since then, we know nothing about father. Is he still alive? Will we ever see him again? God grant it!

Here follows a eulogy from his friend, Jakob A. Neufeld of Gnadenfeld, Molotschna, presently (summer 1947) in Celle, Hanover, Germany.

Allow me to add a few supplementary sketches to the portrait of A.A. Braun, briefly sketched by his daughter and covering the last years of his life.

A.A. Braun was my co-worker in the Union of the Citizens of Dutch Lineage from November 1922 until 1926. He was an elected member of the executive committee and was active as secretary and treasurer of the Gnadenfeld district of this union. I learned to know and appreciate him in this capacity. With a calm reflectiveness, he worked amid the prevailing economic uncertainties and the haste of creating a new organization in that unstable, fluctuating time where one could always count on surprises. A.A. Braun, with his intelligence and genuine Christian lifestyle and with his steady disposition amid [situations of] constant flux, worked as a business leader in the union. His conscientiousness, his diligence, and his punctuality were exemplary. It was not without good cause that he enjoyed the complete trust of the executive and also the Mennonites of the twenty-seven villages in the Gnadenfeld district . . . .

During the famine in 1921-22, Abram Abramovich was already an active member of the relief committee of American Mennonite Aid in the Gnadenfeld district. In addition to his secretarial duties he had ample opportunity to make his influence felt, calming restless spirits, comforting and encouraging the despondent, correcting with calmness and love the contentious and narrow-minded. His work there was certainly to the blessing of the Gnadenfeld inhabitants. By nature Abram Abramovich was not a businessman. He had much more understanding for cultural affairs. He was deeply concerned about the welfare of the schools, namely the Intermediate School and the newly founded Agricultural School in Gnadenfeld. He was also concerned with the medical care of the Mennonite population of the district.

As a member of the executive committee he had to take issue with the various economic and business questions as well as projects of the union which, as already mentioned, was a daring and risky affair during that unstable and lawless period. The calamity facing the Mennonite population as well as the will to survive demanded undertakings and measures whose [long range] implications could not be underestimated at the moment. It was Abram Abramovich with his reserve, his cool detachment and farsightedness who often advised caution, calm reflection and moderation. In the course of four years, he faithfully and conscientiously carried out his duties as a member of the executive and as secretary and treasurer. The life span of a national Mennonite union with its agendas was rather restricted under those conditions. As soon as Soviet power stabilized and a swing to the left began, pressure mounted on the union. After it was liquidated the hunt for its former executive committee members began. Now Abram Abramovich as well as I and others had to pay for our "illegal business activities with a lengthy imprisonment," which was preceded by painful interrogation.

During this period of captivity (1928), I never heard Abram Abramovich utter a single word of complaint or accusation. In this very different, humiliating and depressing situation, for which all agreed he was the least to blame, he always remained the gentle, loving and very calm fellow sufferer. His entire disposition was tuned to accept everything as from God's hand. That was a great blessing to me as one who was a good deal younger and needed someone to lean on . . . .

Since 1925 Braun had been elected as a minister of the Gnadenfeld Mennonite Church. He was not spared from the chicaneries of the Reds. But even in this difficult and turbulent time, A.A. Braun always remained the calm, reflective, friendly, dutiful man of the church, the family, and the state. In this grave and disconsolate time, he was able to aid many a person in the congregation by word and deed. Secretly and unobtrusively, in order not to be associated with him, the distressed sought him out. His orderly family life, his gentle humor which he never lost, his even temperament, his calm manner—all this generated trust and suggested to his fellow man that all was well.

During the last years before his forced flight (1930), he was active on his own small farm. It served him rather well in spite of all the agitation and political pressures against all private enterprise. On the side he faithfully carried on his pastoral ministry which, because of external pressures, was generally minimal at that time. He persisted though he knew what the consequences might be. When this was no longer possible— he had been divested of home, farm and personal property (as we read in his daughter's report)— he felt compelled to take up the pilgrim's staff together with his wife and two daughters. He left his beloved congregation and village of Gnadenfeld and went into an unfamiliar, distant region.

In abject poverty, he moved from place to place and struggled to support his family. Only those who have been in similar situations can appreciate the difficulty, the immeasurable tragedy of such a situation for a settled, peace loving family. He never even returned to his home for a visit, though this later became possible. Probably he couldn't bear to do it. After seeking peace, security, and work in that unhappy land for several years by moving to and fro with his own and his arrested son's family, he was taken from his family and imprisoned by the GPU.

After lengthy, difficult interrogations and journeys, which weaken and crush a man, he was sent into exile, broken in body and soul. It is likely that he has long since died in the difficult circumstances. . . . His grave site is somewhere in the endless forests of Siberia.

His wife, now a gray-haired seventy-year old, and two daughters, together with the family of his exiled son were rescued in the spring of 1941 in the region of Smolensk by the advancing of the German army. They are now under German care. With a few interruptions, they have been in a refugee camp for five years and can hardly wait for the day when they will be reunited with their relatives in Canada or the U.S.A.

Jakob A. Neufeld
Celle, Hanover, Germany
Summer, 1947

Peter P. Bueckert
Minister
Schoenberg, Old Colony

He spent his entire life in his home village with the exception of three years of service in the Azov Forestry and later during WWI as a medic on the train of the All-Russian Zemstvo Union. In 1908 he was baptized upon confession of his faith in the Neu-Osterwick Church and so became an active member of the Chortitza Mennonite Church.

In 1913 he married Anna Isaak, daughter of Abram Isaak and his wife Anna (nee Froese). Their marriage was blessed with three children, two sons, and a daughter. He was a farmer and in 1923 bought a fine farm. Though the rest of his family preferred to go to Canada, he wanted to stay in the old homeland. Three of his brothers—Johann P. Bueckert of Gretna, Abram P. Bueckert of Gnadental and Jacob P. Bueckert of North Kildonan, Manitoba—have been in Canada since 1924-25. A sister Margaretha, Mrs. Gerhard Braun, remained in the old homeland.

The later lot of both families was a very difficult one. It is briefly described in the following lines as a loving memorial in the annals of Mennonite martyrs.

Brother Peter Bueckert was elected as a minister in 1926. It was already very apparent that the office of a minister brought with it the great danger of falling into the bad graces of the Communists. The brother allowed himself to be inducted into the office in spite of this and fully gave himself to the service of his master. The ranks of the religious workers were steadily depleted. When others no longer pursued their calling because they were hard pressed, he repeatedly undertook lengthy foot tours as far as Neuendorf and Chortitza (eighteen and fifteen verst) in order to preach or fulfill other official duties. It almost seemed as if the government wanted to overlook him since he was highly valued as a cabinetmaker and carpenter. Yet in the end, Schiller's words applied to him as well: "Quick misfortune's arrow flies." (Und das Unglueck schreitet schnell!)

Brother Peter was imprisoned in Alexandrowsk by the

Reds on September 29, 1936. He was held here for some time without learning the reason for his incarceration. His dear wife visited him there several times and brought him food. One day when she returned, he was no longer there, and she could not find out where he had been sent. She was unable to learn any more about him outside of the fact that he had perished miserably in the far north from the effects of hunger and mistreatment as a slave. Until this day we have not been able to learn if he was deserving of a grave or where it might be located.

On August 8, 1937, the Reds also sent Bueckert's oldest son Abram to northeast Siberia, where he remains to this day—if indeed he is still alive. Abram's wife with their ten-year old son fled to Germany and [from there] went to Paraguay with the [ship] "Volendam." Peter Bueckert's second son Peter, age ten, lay sick at home with a fever while his mother had to work in the collective. Delirious as the result of the high fever, he left his sick room, and before anyone could stop him fell into the well and drowned. The widow was left with only one daughter. When the German army retreated, she also took flight and came to Germany. She was sent back to Russia by the Reds where, together with other residents of Schoenberg, she worked as a stevedore in a port on the Volga near the city of Tscherepowetz in the Wologoda region. From there, we received a letter from the sister-in-law, our brother Abram's widow. She wrote that she had been in the hospital for some three weeks with swollen legs and feet. She had lain at home in bed the previous month. She wrote that she soon hoped to go home. We are not sure what she meant by this. Did she mean the heavenly home or simply returning to her daughter in the workers' barracks? Her daughter is working. Woe to her if she is unable, for if one does not work one does not eat.

In a few short sentences, she reports that our sister Margaretha, Mrs. G. Braun, whose husband is in Germany, was shot on her way from Germany to her place of exile. We know that her youngest sons, ages nine and thirteen, were sent away, but no one knows where.

Very briefly, let us describe the terrible fate of this family. Gerhard Braun and his wife Margaretha (nee Bueckert) stayed in Kronstal with their family. In 1923 they bought a farm and moved from Neu-Chortitza in Baratow. One daughter, Helena, was active as a nurse in a Russian hospital. When the front retreated (1941?), she too was forced to withdraw and has not been heard from since. In 1943 the Brauns and their family, including three married daughters and their husbands and children, fled to Germany where they were finally settled in Sudetengau. First their son, Gerhard, was drafted into the German army as well as their son-in-law, Janzen. Both vanished. Very recently, we learned that the son-in-law is a prisoner of war in France, but his wife had died. On May 3, 1945, our brother-in-law, Gerhard Braun Senior, was also called into military service, but on May 7 the Russian army was so close that all had to flee. The German army collapsed and G. Braun, like others, fled. He wanted to reach his family, but that was not possible for they already were in a concentration camp.

From this camp our sister Margaretha with daughter Anna, age eighteen, two sons— Hans, thirteen and Peter, nine— as well as her oldest daughter and her husband and four children were deported. They were loaded [onto trains] during the last half of the month and sent into exile. Anna was very ill at the time and remained behind in a hospital. She remained there for several weeks, and when she recovered she fled to Germany. She walked thirty miles a day for more than a week and managed to get behind the English lines. Here she found her two sisters and her father and informed them of the experiences of her mother. According to our information, brother Braun had travelled over 2,000 miles on foot and by bicycle in search of his family until he finally found his daughter. I, then, had the difficult task of informing him of the death of his wife, our sister. It would not have been so difficult if she had died a natural death. We still do not know why she came to be regarded as a criminal and had to die a violent death by execution. Various thoughts have gone through our minds. Among other things, we wonder if she may have wanted to take along her boys and struggled unto death on their behalf. Perhaps, someday, we will hear something about this. Our prayer is that God will protect the orphaned boys, and that they will learn to love God and the dear Savior as their mother taught them and not apostatize; that, if God wills, they might someday be united with their father and their family. Nothing is impossible with

God, not even this.

The report of the death of our sister, Mrs. Margaretha Braun, was brief and to the point: "Your sister Margaretha Braun was shot on August 19, 1945, enroute to this destination. I know no further details. We mourn the terrible fate of our sister and her loved ones. Yet we are confident that even if this brutal, godless power robbed her of this natural life, she has found a higher, better life through her Savior which no enemy power can assail. Bless her ashes!"

P.S. Our sister Margaretha was born on September 2, 1892 in Schoenberg, Chortitza Colony. She was baptized in the church in Neu-Osterwick in 1912 and married in June 1913.

Johann P. Bueckert
Schoenwiese, near Gretna, Manitoba

Philipp David Cornies
Teacher, Poet, Public Worker
Molotschna, South Russia

His father was David D. Cornies. His grandfather was also David Cornies, an older brother of well-known Johann Cornies from Ohrioff, the great organizer and reformer among the Mennonites of south Russia. Philipp D. Cornies had inherited something of this genius. At first, his father lived in Spat; his mother was born a Wiebe. Philipp D. Cornies was born here around 1884 or 1885. From Spat, his parents moved to Borongar, also in the Crimea. His mother died here when he was twelve years old.

He now came to his aunt, H. Cornies, in Ohrloff where he received his further training and education. His father, usually known as *Ohm Doaft*, was rather unsettled. As one of his friends wrote of him, "He was everywhere and nowhere at home."

After completing the village school in Ohrloff, Philipp Cornies attended the high school there. It was often called the "Association School," since it was founded and supported by an association of school friends. Here the author, who spent two years there, learned to know Philipp. He was always one grade ahead. He had a very good head on his shoulders and learning presented no difficulties. From here, he went to Halbstadt where he attended the pedagogical classes for two years and prepared himself for the teaching profession. He always did very well in his exams.

In the fall of 1902, he accepted his first teaching position in the village Klubnikowo in Neu-Samara. Previously in school and even now, he was an enthusiastic advocate of sport: gymnastics, swimming, running, etc. He conditioned himself so well that he was not easily susceptible to colds or other illnesses. For example, while in Halbstadt, he swam in the Molotschna River when there were still ice floes. He and his colleague, Abram Jantz, took off their clothes on the ice and jumped into the icy waters. He suffered no ill effects. When he was in Samara where the winters are especially cold, he slept near the open window and in the morning shook the snow off his blanket. In this manner he hardened his body. He possessed enormous physical strength and challenged anyone in the [wrestling] ring or in a race.

Here in Samara, he found his life's partner in Louise Penner of Lugowsk, Samara. That was in 1905. Soon after, he moved to the Molotschna and became a teacher in the village of Rosenort where he stayed as long as the Bolsheviks tolerated him—until about 1922-23.

The marriage was childless. Later they took in two orphans and adopted them. Philipp D. Cornies was an outstanding teacher and educator and had the highest respect from both children and parents. In the teaching circles, he also enjoyed general esteem and love. Between 1908 and 1918, the author was able to work with him in a school district which stretched from Ohrloff to Rueckenau. His colleagues received much stimulation from him. Later, he became a member of the Molotschna Mennonite Teachers Association. He was its chairman, active in the production of a new grammar book, head of the education exposition held in Rueckenau, etc. Possessed with a healthy sense of humor and a sharp mind, he was busy everywhere.

He was also endowed with a poetic mind and from time to time produced poems and essays of sterling quality. One of his poems appeared in the local periodical, *Aufwaerts*, published

42

at that time by Kornelius G. Neufeld in Dawlekanowo. The poem was also called *Aufwaerts*. The poem, "John the Baptist's Death in the Fortress of Machaeus," was especially gripping.

During WWI, Philipp Cornies had to enter state service together with all the other teachers. He worked the entire period as a medical orderly caring for the sick and the wounded. Then he resumed his old teaching position. He frequently served with the proclamation of the Gospel, but did not allow himself to be ordained for this work because he believed it was not his real calling. He and his wife had joined the Mennonite Brethren Church in Tiege, but he had an open heart for all believers. His sermons were substantive and highly regarded. He mastered the Russian language especially well and made significant contributions in this area.

After the fall of the tsarist government, the revolution and the reign of terror weighed heavily upon the Mennonite villages. In the colonies, there were all sorts of "Red elements" among the small number of proletariats. In the village of Rosenort, there was a certain Neufeld who terrorized the farmers in the village and beyond. When the Germans occupied the Ukraine in the summer of 1918 and stayed for several months, all these tormentors fled. Only Neufeld and two of his comrades had missed the chance to escape. Now, heavily armed, they waited in a house in Blumenort for further developments. The young men of the Kuruschan villages wanted to disarm these three bandits but feared to approach the building. They asked the teacher Cornies for advice. He sent the young men home and went to the house unarmed. He managed to persuade the three to lay down their weapons and surrender. Cornies gave them a guarantee that they would not be killed. When the Germans later placed them on trial after their denunciation, Philipp Cornies intervened on their behalf and saved their lives.

When the Reds again took control, Philipp Cornies together with Jacob Cornies of Ohrloff was arrested with many others and taken to Halbstadt and incarcerated in a cellar. Five of his fellow sufferers were taken out and shot, among them Franz Willms, the director of the Old Age Home in Kuruschan, the gardener Gaede from the same location (who was also the village mayor) and three men from the *Selbstschutz*. This was on November 10, 1921. The two relatives of Cornies were soon

43

released.

Philipp Cornies was soon taken and placed before a People's Tribunal in Gross-Tokmak. The trial lasted for three days and he was accused of anti-Soviet activities. He gave such a powerful defence oration that all present were impressed and he was soon freed. Perhaps the man he saved— as well as the poor— interceded for him.

He was arrested one more time. Since he was no longer a teacher, he and his family went to Ohrloff-Tiege where they moved into a modest house. Here, he became an assistant to Benjamin Janz, his former colleague from Tiege. They headed the Union of the Citizens of Dutch Lineage which worked towards the economic reconstruction of the Mennonite colonies. The statutes of the union had been approved by the government in Charkow. On another level, B. Janz worked for a Mennonite emigration to Canada consisting in the main of Mennonite refugees, which partially succeeded. B. Janz, Abram Fast the secretary, and several other workers like Jakob Thiessen left the Red empire before the doors closed. Others, however, like Philipp Cornies, Peter Nickel, and Jakob Neufeld were taken by the Reds and suffered a great deal.

His brother-in-law Jakob Boese— his wife and Mrs. Cornies were sisters— reported that Philipp Cornies was arrested once more and taken to the prison in Melitopol. There he endured mistreatment and torture. He was forced to promise that he would not emigrate but help with the economic reconstruction of the Soviet state. (When I said goodbye to him and his wife in his house in Tiege in May 1926, he said to me in confidence, "Brother Toews, you and your family can emigrate, but I am bound by my promise. I have to stay." He said this with a sad voice. I was cut to the heart to hear this from my long-standing, trusted friend and colleague.) Mrs. Cornies was able to visit her husband in the Melitopol prison. Until he was sent elsewhere, she walked from Tiege to Melitopol several times and brought him food from good friends in the Molotschna villages.

When the union was dissolved, all workers were placed before a court, condemned, and sent into exile. Previously Philipp Cornies had the post of agricultural advisor in Melitopol district. He had to establish butter and cheese factories in the various villages. Even here, thanks to the machinations of secret agents, he fell into disgrace. In order to save himself, he fled to Sofiewka in the province of Jekaterinoslaw. For a time, he lived at the station Lasowaja. Here evil fate once more caught up with him and he was arrested, put on trial, and exiled to Solowoki on the White Sea. He was to have spent five and a half years there.

His wife and their two adopted children, a son and a daughter, moved to Einlage. Mrs. Cornies died here. Mrs. Franz Wall (nee Ediger) of Muntau looked after her during the last days of her life.

Their two adopted children came to Germany as refugees. A sister of Philipp Cornies, Mrs. Cornelius Toews, has gone to Paraguay.

Before Philipp Cornies was exiled he spent some time in prison in Ekaterinoslaw. Here his daughter from Einlage managed to visit him several times. Mother and children worked at the Dneproges power station in order to earn their livelihood.During each visit the daughter brought clothing and foodstuffs for the father. One day, she received notification that he was no longer there; he had been exiled to the north.

Martin J. Derksen
Businessman, Farmer and Minister
Blumenort and Rueckenau, Molotschna, South Russia

His brother, Gerhard J. Derksen of Yarrow, British Columbia provides the following account of his life, work, and suffering.

His parents were Jacob J. Derksen, Schoensee, Molotschna. His mother was called Anna, nee Janzen. Our parents moved to the Crimea as a young couple. They settled in the village of Saribasch. My brother, Martin, was born on January 25, 1870 and attended school there. As a fifteen-year-old lad, he entered a business in Tukultschak, which belonged to C.F. Thiessen. They were the parents of the teacher, F.C. Thiessen, presently of Abbotsford, British Columbia. After three years, he accepted a position in a business in Halbstadt.

After one year, he entered the business of Gerhard Klassen of Blumenort, Molotschna. Here, he was active for twenty-five years and contributed substantially to the expansion and prosperity of this grocery and dry goods business. After he served there for three years, I came under the guardianship of the Gerhard Klassens (thanks to his intervention) in Blumenort. I was twelve years old at the time. Here, we were together for more than twenty years.

My brother, Martin, and his wife were converted one night during 1900. When I came into the business in the morning, he said to me, "Gerhard, my wife and I have received forgiveness of our sins." I stood as if struck by lightning. Finally, in my embarrassment I said, "Today, I'm going to the fields with the servants to plough." After this I went into [a period of] self-examination but only found peace after several months. This caused a great deal of commotion among the wealthy people. We both belonged to the Lichtenau Mennonite Church and had been baptized by elder Jakob Toews. When missionary Johann Fast, who was on furlough from the Island of Java at the time, heard that we had turned to God, he visited us. Soon thereafter, he began to hold services in the school and a revival occurred in Blumenort and the vicinity. Even Jakob Horn, an ordinary shoemaker in Blumenort, did a great work in the region. Later, under assignment from the local church, he worked with great blessing in the villages of the Molotschna through his home visitations and personal work. Sinners also found peace in the village of Ohrloff and in the high school located there.

In our innocence (or inexperience?), we and several other brethren tried to reform the Lichtenau Church for some three years. In 1903 we were baptized in Rueckenau by elder David Schellenberg and accepted into the Mennonite Brethren Church. This created a tremendous ruckus in our home. Mrs. G. Klassen, my stepmother, had already moved to Bergfeld to be with her children. She was ill for many years and had to spend each winter in bed. I had to come to mother and tell her of my conversion. She had also experienced this and had an understanding of spiritual matters, but she lacked spiritual nurture.

When the bloodbath in Blumenort occurred in the fall of

1919, I had been with my parents-in-law, Mr. and Mrs. Heinrich Gossen, for some time. My brother, Martin Derksen, had miracle of miracles, moved to Rueckenau fourteen days earlier. He had bought a farm from Peter Braun, which had formerly belonged to Franz Martens. Otherwise, he would certainly have been the first victim. They were herded into the cellar of our house. Hand grenades were then thrown through the cellar window which killed several and wounded most. The bodies were then taken to the yard and hacked to pieces.

Later, the entire farm and the large buildings of Gerhard Klassen's business were demolished. In the search for money, even the foundations were dug up—naturally in vain.

In 1926 brother Martin Derksen sold his lovely farm in Rueckenau to the dentist Abram P. Fast from Blumenort. He wanted to emigrate and even wrote to his four brothers in Canada that they should expect him in the near future. It never came to that. The family of Martin Derksen had a son, Gerhard who, because of a disease, now suffered from mental illness. He needed extra guarantees in order to enter Canada. These were delayed. In the interval, Martin Derksen was taken to the district capital of Melitopol and put on trial. He, nevertheless, had friends among the Red officials who had done business with him earlier and had learned to know him as a reliable man. These intervened on his behalf and he was not executed but had to serve as watchman for the Red officials. There were quite a number of our people who sought refuge and food here. Among others, there were the two widows of brother Adolf Reimer and Heinrich Enns. The blind sister, Maria Regehr, from Blumenort was also here. This older sister with her childlike faith was well-known among the believers' circles in the Molotschna and was a great blessing to many young and older people.

It cannot be established how long Martin Derksen remained in Melitopol in the service of the Reds nor what happened to him after that. We again found him in Warthegau among the many refugees from Russia. The minister, Jakob Loewen, a son of the well-known Jakob A. Loewen, writes of this period:

I have been deeply saddened by the fact that Martin Derksen, formerly of Rueckenau, has had to walk the difficult

47

road of suffering in his old days. I could relate many an experience to you of how the ministers and churches of our Brethren and Alliance congregations from the Molotschna have found each other and worked together in Germany. I had been separated from my home the entire period. Now we met each other again after eighteen to twenty years. Sadly, there were only a few: the Gnadenheim [congregation] with its ministers Peter Bergen, aged sixty-three, and Gerhard Thiessen from Alexanderwohl, aged seventy-two; the Rueckenau Brethren Church with brother Martin Derksen, aged seventy-four, and Johann Harder from Fuerstenwerder, aged thirty to thirty-five; the Lindenau Church with brother Ballan and brother Nicolai Enns, Tiege, aged fifty years. To think that this was our entire staff, yet you cannot imagine how happy, courageous, and active these few were. Brother Martin Derksen was not yet ordained but he worked with great wisdom, forethought and blessing in his last days.

Professor B.H. Unruh tried to help us get the rooms necessary for our religious life through the Hitler government. Unfortunately, the district leader in Warthegau, Greifer, forbade all religious activity. All efforts proved fruitless.

Soon, I stood at the head of all religious activities. Everywhere our dear choristers sang from the [songbook] *Liederperlen.* The hearts of sinners cried to God. But there was no room [available]. Brother H. Ballan had hardly begun to preach when it was forbidden by the local commander. We gathered in Nessau at the home of the Rempels (from Schoenau), but immediately the local commander notified us that he would eradicate this sect activity. Again, I wrote to Professor B.H. Unruh of the compelling of God's Spirit. The dear old professor tried everything but without success. But God gave grace and, here and there, we found grace with God and men, but without official permission. In Nessau, I went to the Lutheran pastor, who had regard for us Mennonites, and asked for a church room for our services on Sunday afternoon. Permission was gladly given. Similarly, they also had a small room in Maasburg, where the Rueckenau Brethren Church led by Martin Derksen resided. The Gnadenheim Brethren Church, whose members were scattered about Litzmannstadt, gathered in homes, here and there, according to old apostolic fashion. It was not easy for the old, brother Peter J. Baergen, then sixty-three years of age, to visit the congregation on foot, which was scattered nine to eighteen kilometers apart.

One day, I received an invitation to attend a ministerial ordination in the Gnadenheim Church. I went and found brother Ballan there as well. Today, I cannot describe to you under what impoverished conditions the dear, brother Baergen lived—in a word, it was very modest. Yet all was overcome through Jesus Christ.

The ordination festival was glorious. The two choirs from Gnadenheim and Margenau sang. The dear, brother Gerhard Thiessen, aged seventy-two, who had been deacon in the local church for many years, and brother Peter Koop were inducted into the holy service of the Lord. Brother Ballan and I spoke. The congregational meeting which followed proceeded with great blessing. Yes, dear one, even if the time in Warthegau was a short one, it has left a spiritual imprint even to this day. I still receive letters from those who have been scattered far and wide who always mention this time. In Germany, we do not find the brotherly love of the saints.

Concerning himself, brother Isaak J. Loewen adds,

Currently, I am working for P. Blank as a hired man. They are Catholics. How I feel the stigma of being a hired man. In my isolation, I write letters to the lonely and abandoned. A sister wrote to me, "Even if no one here sees us, or knows us, we are known to the Lord."

During the flight brother Loewen was separated from his family. He writes,

As of February 17, my dear wife and son find themselves in a camp in Czechoslovakia and are awaiting transport to the American zone. Until then my family and I are living in the hope that we will soon be reunited.

So much for the report of J.J. Loewen. But what happened to the people in Warthegau and especially brother Martin Derksen? Is it not amazing how believers in foreign lands, constantly in flight and besieged by fear, were so concerned about the spiritual welfare of the scattered flock? Though they had suffered under the Soviet regime for more than twenty years, they kept the faith and when it came to building the Kingdom of God, they energetically set to work. Don't they put to shame many a Christian, even entire churches in America, in which the spiritual life is often so weak? The poet is correct when he sings, "For sorrow shall prove me, and draw me closer to Him." The intense spiritual life and activity in the churches in Warthegau came to a sudden end. The Russians came steadily closer and only at the last moment, when it was too late, were the inhabitants allowed to flee. This created incredible chaos. Many refugees were separated in the confusion, others fell into Russian hands or were crushed in battle by the Russian armored columns. The old ministers, Peter Baergen and Gerhard Thiessen, fell into Polish hands and were mercilessly shot.

Martin Derksen and his family and H. Ballan were taken into Russian captivity and forcibly transported back to Russia. They did not return to their former home in Southern Russia but were sent to cold Siberia—to Irkutsk on the Sea of Baikal, far, far in the east. One letter to his brothers in Canada arrived from there, in which he reports that they are living in the midst of the primeval forest. The children have to do heavy forestry work and receive enough to eat so that they can get by. The old parents and the sick in the camp cannot earn anything and have to starve. They have no means with which to buy bread. They urgently request not to be forgotten in their great need and ask that food be sent. Unfortunately, until now, it has been impossible to send any kind of help either from Canada or the United States since Russia has closed all borders and allows nothing in, not even letters.

His brother, G.J. Derksen, adds the following,

My brother, Martin, was deeply pious. He led a godly life. Personally, he was of much help in my spiritual life. Whether he is still alive today I do not know. We think he is. One son in Russia was mobilized by the Red government as a laborer and then disappeared without a trace. One daughter, Mrs. F. Steingart, died in Rueckenau. [His] son Peter, who married missionary Abram Friesen's daughter Mary, came to Canada and died in Ontario after some years. The oldest daughter, Annie, Mrs. David Boschmann, currently lives in Niagara-on-the-Lake, Ontario. Her husband is a teacher at the Mennonite High School.

In January 1948, the news reached the author that Martin J. Derksen died in the Lord in Siberian exile on February 14, 1947. His fellow sufferer in exile, Franz F. Krueger Junior, formerly from Rueckenau, writes,

We have lost a great deal, especially me. He was my best friend and my brother in the Lord. We buried him according to our custom. We read God's Word and sang songs.

50

His wife, Mrs. Mathilde Derksen, who had shared his exile until now, travelled to the Samara Mennonite Settlement together with another woman after his death. The journey was a difficult one and after several weeks of illness she died in April 1947. How quickly she was able to follow her dear spouse into the eternal home where there will be no more sorrow. Again and again, during the flight, brother Martin Derksen cared for the children of God. Now his pathway once more led into exile (Irkutsk). In all likelihood, God had work for him among all the disconsolate there.

David Jacob and Katharina Dick
Apanlee Estate, South Molotschna

David J. Dick: estate owner; model farmer; school supporter; philanthropist; and friend of the poor and of missions— a true Christian.

He was born on June 29, 1860 in Rosenhof, district of Melitopol, province of Taurida, south Russia. This farm was also known as Brotsky. Here, he received his early education and then went to high school in Gnadenfeld, which he completed in three years. He became a member of the Mennonite church in Petershagen near Halbstadt. On October 21, 1887, he married Katharina Schmidt from Steinbach, Molotschna. She was the daughter of the well-known Peter Schmidt. She was born in Steinbach, on November 15, 1865 where she also attended village school.

After the wedding, they lived with her grandmother, Mrs. Peter Schmidt, in Steinbach until 1894. Then they moved to their inherited estate, Apanlee, where they lived in great affluence until their death in October 1919. In 1898 they were converted through God's grace and the ministry of the itinerant minister, Jakob Quiring. At the request of the Mennonite conference, he was active in many congregations and became the guide to Christ for many people. From this time onward [their] life belonged entirely to the Lord and His service. They served the Lord with gladness and love.

David Dick was a farmer, body and soul. His farm was a model of organization. He was especially interested in first-class breeding cattle which he imported from abroad. The nearby Mennonite villages in the Molotschna Colony purchased many of the offspring for their use. D. Dick enjoyed this and was happy that he could contribute to the improvement of cattle and horsebreeding. He was always kind and understanding to the many workers and servants on the estate and was universally loved and respected.

He severely condemned the ever-increasing number of Mennonites who went into business, many of whom also suffered ignominious bankruptcy. Though he was offered many good opportunities along this line, he remained true to his calling as a farmer until the very end. Again and again, he warned and admonished his children, eight daughters and three sons, not to enter into business, industry or commercial ventures.

His main ambition after his conversion was to live and work for his Lord. At his instigation, a so-called "fellowship of believers" was founded which the people of Steinbach, Juschanlee and Apanlee as well as many believers from the Molotschna Colony joined. This was simply a broad-minded alliance [of believers]. One remained a member of the local congregation yet desired to nurture one's spiritual life in a special way through fellowship around the Word, communion, and work for the Kingdom of God. The services were held monthly on an alternating basis at each of the three estates. Ministers from the various churches were invited. Among the outstanding adherents of this movement were the ministers Jakob W. Reimer, Peter Penner, Jacob G. Thiessen, Abram Nachtigall, Isaac Ediger, Peter Riediger, Jakob A. Loewen and many others. The following estate owners took a special interest in the work: Heinrich Guenther of Juschanlee, Peter Schmidt, Jakob Dick and Nicolai Schmidt of Steinbach, together with brother D. Dick and Jakob Sudermann of Apanlee. It was an energizing movement which spread blessing. It did much for the spiritual life of the Molotschna and also went far beyond its borders.

On the other Sundays, family services were held on the estate. A sermon was read in the morning and a Bible study was held in the afternoon, in which the entire household and even the German domestics participated. On such occasions, forty to fifty persons gathered at the Dicks. Ministers and teachers were a special concern of father David. Special ministerial and teacher's courses were held alternatively on the estates Apanlee, Juschanlee and Steinbach in order to lead the participants deeper into God's Word. For this purpose, gifted ministers and workers from home and abroad were invited to present ongoing lectures. These workers came from our own midst or from Switzerland, Germany, England, and the Baltic states. I will name a few of these workers for the Kingdom of God: Jakob Kroeker of Germany, Peter Unruh, Peter Riediger of Berdyansk, J.W. Reimer, Professor Stroeter whose favorite theme was "Kingdom and Church," Fritz Oetzbach, small in stature yet great in faith, Dr. Baedecker, Rev. Broadbent from England, Adam Podin, the prison minister from the Baltic states, Baron Uexkuel, also from there, tent missionary Jakob Vetter and others. The Bible courses were usually one week long. All the guests and participants received food and accommodation. This meant a great deal of work for the dear housewives, their daughters, and the domestics, but the sisters did this work joyfully as unto the Lord. Mrs. D. Dick participated regularly in all these activities. All ministers and teachers were invited without regard to their affiliation. [In these meetings], the truth of the notion of the unity of all believers was reinforced in many of the hearts of the participants. The author had the privilege of attending number of such Bible courses and savored the blessings in large measure.

Brother David Dick was also the founder and initiator of the first Mennonite Tract Society in Russia. He was the chairman of the society for the entire period until 1914 when WWI broke out. He worked steadily on behalf of this cause. Many tracts in the German and Russian languages were distributed by him and other members between 1904 and 1914. The German tracts came mainly from Germany while the Russian ones came from the printing firm "Raduga" (rainbow) in Neu-Halbstadt. At the beginning of the war, this activity almost resulted in his exile to Siberia, ostensibly for injurious [religious] activity. The Lord did not allow this to happen and he could remain at home. The tract society, however, ceased to exist like many other organizations among the Germans. I think only of the Molotschna Mennonite Teachers Association, which was also dissolved. I was a member of both organizations. All the materials prepared by the tract society carried the logo "God is Love." The society dues were three rubles.

Between 1904 and 1910, D. Dick was the president of the

Mennonite Forestry Service in Russia, in which our young men fulfilled their state service with forestry or other useful work. He was faithful and conscientious in this task and was loved by young and old. He was especially concerned with the salvation of the youths in the forestry service. He looked for faithful, pious forestry managers who were everywhere installed as chaplains and administrators. In addition, he also made sure that itinerate ministers, who were especially blessed by God, visited the forestry stations and held evangelistic meetings. During that time, there were great revivals among the recruits and many of our fathers dated their conversions from that time period.

Brother Dick also made major contributions to our people in the area of education. In 1906 he and the minister Jakob Esau of Lichtfelde contributed more than most towards the establishment of a high school in Alexanderkrone. During the entire period of its existence, he assisted the school by word and deed. The school faced many difficulties, even from the government, but our men persevered. It was due to government pressure that the school was later transformed into a business college. Dick remained the chairman of the school board until the Red government took over such schools during the revolutionary years 1918-20 and used them for their own purposes. Then brother Dick had nothing more to say in school matters. One of the first teachers at this school was Isaak P. Regehr, who remained there almost until his emigration to Canada. Then he became a teacher at the Bible school in Herbert, Saskatchewan.

The School of Commerce in Halbstadt was also deeply indebted to Dick. He gave much time and effort to this new project. Initially, he was a member of the school board and later became the chairman. B.H. Unruh, now in Germany, was one of the first and best known teachers of this school as was Abram Friesen, who with Unruh was a member of the study commission which prepared the way for emigration to Canada. D. Dick was a schoolman in the best sense of the word. It could be truthfully said of him that "He loved his people and he has built the school for us." With thankful hearts, we want to erect a memorial to him for later generations.

All our benevolent institutions enjoyed his favor and his

material support. Whether it was the school for the deaf in Tiege, the orphanage in Grossweide, or the hospitals in Muntau and Ohrloff—all received his wholehearted patronage. When the institution "Morija" was founded in Neu-Halbstadt for the training of nurses, he had to be involved, if not as chairman of the benevolent society in question, then certainly as an active and desired member.

He was above all concerned with the well-being of the poor. When it was time to establish a new Mennonite settlement, the poor settlers knew to whom to turn for assistance, which took the form of an interest free loan or an outright grant. His Russian neighbors also frequently took advantage of his good heart and his widely known spirit of benevolence. No poor man, provided he was honest, knocked at his door in vain. He could not say no. If a poor man lost his cow or his horse there was always a helping hand in David J. Dick.

That was also the reason why Mrs. Katharina Dick was beloved among the poor Russians of the region. Many Russian villages lay very close by. During the unsettled years of the early revolution when many estates were burned down and the murderous bands were everywhere, not one hair on their heads was touched. The surrounding Russian villages took them under their protection.

During the Bolshevik period, brother Dick was arrested and imprisoned, but his Russian neighbors came before the court with 7,000 signatures and he was released. Similarly, he was released from Red captivity on two other occasions. Later, the good reputation of the parents often benefited the entire family. The saying, "The parents' blessing builds houses for their children" applies here as well.

David Dick did not accumulate riches but used them in every conceivable way for the cause of God's Kingdom. When Dick died he gave his eldest son, Jakob, all the books and accounts. To his amazement, the son found that there was almost no money in most of the banks, in spite of the fact that the net income during the last years was around 150,000 rubles. When he died, Dick said to his son, Jakob, "Don't call in any of the loans, take only what they give you." Many were indebted to father at the time. He never charged a poor man interest. Both husband and wife tried to apply in deed the word of the

Holy Scripture: "Do not forget to do good and be generous for with such sacrifices God is well-pleased" (Hebrews 13: 16). In this pursuit they were one. This was also the reason they stayed on their estate during the time of anarchy when everything was helter-skelter. They had a good conscience before God and man. They were not afraid but placed their complete trust in the Lord.

During Christmas Eve in 1905, when there was widespread unrest, the Kleefeld choir with its conductor and teachers, Isaak P. Regehr and Aron A. Toews, drove to Apanlee in order to sing some comforting Christmas songs under the bedroom windows of the families, Dick and Sudermann. It was a beautiful sound on that lovely Christmas night. The carolers were invited into the house by the Dick family and offered tea and all sorts of lovely Christmas cookies. They mentioned they had anticipated evil visitations many a night and this night visit with its beautiful songs had been a great comfort. That was a godly service according to James 1:27.

And yet these philanthropists had to die a terrible death. Who can fathom the way of God with the children of men, especially with His saints?

The oldest son tells us the following about this incident.

On October 16, 1919 (O.S.), during the period of total anarchy, six heavily armed robbers came into the house around ten o'clock at night. They had come from a great distance and had been attracted by the prospect of great booty. They stole everything which had not already been stolen. Then they placed mother, father, my brother Hans, our manager, and me against the wall of one room and demanded money. When the robbers burst into the house, the Lord had wonderfully allowed the six sisters and the five domestics to hide and so find protection amid this deadly peril. Since we had no money— it had all been taken earlier— one of them counted to three and immediately two of them who had loaded their weapons fired. Father fell to the ground, but mother remained standing with a body wound. While the murderers were reloading their guns for the second time, I rushed through the door where they were standing and escaped. One bandit fired after me and hit me in the knee. I, nevertheless, ran into the field and hid. I remained a cripple for the rest of my life for the knee remained stiff. During the confusion, the manager and brother Hans opened a window and escaped. Mother also wanted to flee but received one shot in the leg and the third in the head. She fell down dead. Father pretended to be dead. They shot at him but missed, and so, father lived for another twenty-four hours. The doctor later established that the first shot had penetrated the liver, stomach and lung. The doctor only arrived after eighteen hours. During this time, father experienced terrible pain and anguish. Yet we children thank God that he could live for a time. The experience will remain unforgettable. His last words were, "Don't despair at the very end." Thus the deaths of our beloved father and our unforgettable mother.

"Blessed are the dead who die in the Lord. "

Heinrich H. Dirks
Minister of the Gnadenfeld Mennonite Church

Heinrich Dirks, the last minister of the Gnadenfeld Mennonite Church, Molotschna, south Russia was born on February 18, 1872 on the Island of Sumatra, East Indies at the mission station Pakanten. His father was the missionary Heinrich Dirks, from Gnadenfeld and his mother was Aganetha Dirks (nee Schroeder) from Mariawohl, south Russia. His parents were sent out in 1869 by the Netherlands Mennonite Mission Society, which was also supported by the Russian Mennonites, and they founded the mission station Pakanten. Heinrich spent his first nine years there. In 1881 his parents and the children returned to Europe due to the ill health of the mother. At first, they came to Holland, then later to Gnadenfeld, south Russia. The Gnadenfeld Mennonite Church elected missionary Heinrich Dirks as their elder and so Gnadenfeld became the future residence of the family Dirks.

Here their son Heinrich first attended the village school. His teacher was Heinrich Janzen. Then he entered the high school there. Here his teachers were Wilhelm P. Neufeld in religion and German, David Dick who instructed mathematics, etc. and the [native] Russian, Porajkoff, who taught Russian language. After he had completed this school with good grades, he prepared for the teacher's examination, which he also passed with ease. In his twelfth year, he gave his heart to the Lord. At the age of seventeen, he received holy baptism upon [confession of] faith. Since he perceived an inner calling to become a worker in the vineyard of the Lord, he decided to study further.

He received his theological training at the Missionary School at Barmen, where his father had also been educated. He obtained the funds for study from the widow, Mrs. Peter Schmidt, in Steinbach. His teachers were Dr. August Schreiber and P. Kraft, and in medicine the health inspector, Haeusner. He entered the Missionary School as a first-year student in the fall of 1890. He returned home in 1893 in order to present himself for state service. Every young man in Russia had to present himself at age twenty-one. He was then examined to determine whether he was physically strong enough for this service. The unfit and those who had family obligations such as being the only son in the family were exempted, while the others had to serve. If one drew a high lot one was occasionally exempted, if enough recruits had already been accepted. He [Dirks] served his state service as a teacher, which was allowed by the government because of the shortage of trained teachers.

For two years, 1893 and 1894, he was a teacher in the village school in Ogus-Tobe in the Crimea. Between 1895 and 1905, he was a teacher of religion and German language in the newly built high school in the village of Neu-Schoensee in Sagradowka. The Gnadenfeld Mennonite Church had already elected him as minister in 1895. He was ordained on Ascension Day of that same year by his father, elder H. Dirks. He was thus a teacher and a minister with more than ample work for his Lord and Savior.

Since he was subject to nervous exhaustion, the elder H. Dirks could not fulfill his dual role of elder and itinerant missions minister without additional help. Therefore, in 1905, his son, H. Dirks, gave up his teaching position and at the request of the congregation became his father's assistant. He kept the church records, accompanied his father on mission trips, and did most of the correspondence. Since he was not married and had no family to support, he purchased a small farm (*Halbwirtschaft*) with his savings consisting of 32 *dessiatines* of land, a house, yard and garden. This allowed him to serve the church without renumeration. For ten years he was an indispensable help to his ailing father, who died on February 18, 1915 (O.S.). Mother had already died on August 26, 1911 (O.S.).

In the spring of 1915, at age forty-three, the minister Heinrich Dirks had to enter state service. He was sent to the south coast of the Crimea with other men and youngsters where they worked in the forests and the gardens. Even during this time, he worked for his Lord by bringing the glad tidings of Jesus to the Tatars and the Gypsies. In 1917, he returned to Gnadenfeld. Once more, he took up work in the church.

In 1922 his land was confiscated by the Red government, because he did not farm it himself. Until now, he had given half of his land to a good friend who had a large family. With the loss of his land, H. Dirks became destitute. He, therefore, petitioned the district court to grant him and his sister, who looked after his household, a piece of land. Thereupon, these two people were granted eight *dessiatines* of land.

H. Dirks associated himself with several farmers, all of whom had become impoverished. They worked the land collectively. It was a paltry effort since the draft animals, the horses, had been taken from the farmers and many had only an emaciated cow to pull their wagon and their plough.

Since ministers lost their civil rights and were disenfranchised, he again lost this land in 1929-30 when the collectives were founded. His land, home, yard and garden all went into the collective under the name of his sister who had not been disenfranchised, because she declared herself willing to work in the collective.

His yard and barns were used for a large collective pig farm. H. Dirks had become a poor man. The heavenly Father nevertheless cared for him. He could still manage, though not with any overabundance. His sister had several sheep. When necessary, wool could be sold or exchanged for foodstuffs. At times he received some food from good friends, so he did not starve.

Though he was completely impoverished he was still highly taxed, and it was difficult to collect the money on time. Late payment always resulted in an escalation of the tax. Repeatedly, he was called before the village council and asked to renounce his ministerial position. He was not only to publicize the renunciation of his ministerial post in the local Red newspaper but also to renounce his faith in God and declare that everything he taught and preached was erroneous. He freely and openly declared he could not do this. He was then told that he would always remain poor. If, however, he took the appropriate action he would receive a good position, for they needed intelligent and educated men. After such discussions, he was always sad when he came home.

The Lord God, in whose service he stood, granted him the strength to remain steadfast and true to Him. He continued to preach God's Word in the church on Sundays, at weddings and funerals, and on other occasions in the homes. His brothers and sisters were often ordered to renounce him and to evict him from his quarters. He was pictured as a dangerous man who agitated against the Soviet government. The brothers and sisters naturally did not do what was demanded of them. They lived in love under one roof and did not think of renouncing him.

The year 1936 arrived. A tax of 17,000 rubles was levied upon the church. Since the congregation could not pay such a high sum, the Reds confiscated the church. The congregation was dissolved. The minister Heinrich Dirks was sternly forbidden to preach. The young people who had received baptismal instruction could not be baptized.

Heinrich Dirks now travelled to the Don Basin to stay with good friends for a lengthy time. He returned home after several months where he was happily received by his next of kin. He no longer made visitations. Whoever wished to visit him came to his room.

On June 10, 1938 he was arrested and taken away by auto. He was imprisoned in the city of Dnjepropetrowsk for three and a half months. He was condemned for spreading political-religious propaganda and sent to a distant camp in the far north. His next of kin never received a letter from him; he was, naturally, not allowed to write. A Russian who returned from exile, secretly visited his next of kin and brought the news that minister H. Dirks had become seriously ill in the spring of 1939 and died in the camp. The Russian also reported that he had been together with many of our men in the north and added that the old man simply had not been able to make it.

Aron A. Dueck
Teacher, Minister,
Member of the Commission
for Church Affairs

He was the son of the honorable Aron Dueck family of Prangenau, Gnadenfeld district. His parents had a farm on the street very near to the school and on the right side of the small Juschanlee River. Here, Aron Dueck spent his childhood and youth and attended the village school where P. Peters was teacher for many years. Then he went to high school in Gnadenfeld. From there, he came to Neu-Halbstadt and completed the two-year pedagogical course. After completing the teacher's exam, he accepted a teaching position, but I'm not sure where.

He soon came to Margenau and accepted a position as teacher in the newly constructed village school. Here, he remained until his exile in 1931. In his younger years he came under the strong influence of atheistic friends, but by God's grace, he was converted and became a zealous and faithful servant of the Lord.

He found a faithful partner in the believer, Ida Regehr, who steadfastly stood by him until his early end. She was the daughter of the minister Peter P. Regehr of Margenau. She was a member of the Mennonite Brethren Church, while he was and remained a member of the Mennonite Church in Margenau. The Lord blessed the marriage with two children—a son, Theodor and a daughter, Vera. In school, Aron Dueck did a thorough job. He had a good mastery of the Russian language and possessed a very buoyant spirit, which made him very popular with students and parents. The author was a teacher in Rueckenau at the time. One summer, we decided to take a trip to the city of Berdyansk on the Sea of Azov with the older students. This trip was very interesting for our students. It was the first time they had ridden on the train, seen the ocean, swam in it, and watched the great ships. That was still in the tranquil time before WWI when the Mennonite colonies stood in full bloom, when progress was discernible at all levels.

How different things became later! In the long run, Aron

Dueck could not stay in school. The Margenau Mennonite congregation elected him as minister, and he completely dedicated himself to this shepherd's role. It was soon a question of being either a teacher or a minister, not both. No minister (cult servant) was tolerated in the Soviet school. When brother Dueck was confronted by this choice, he decided to follow his ministerial calling and gave up his beloved teaching position, fully aware of the consequences. It became difficult to make a living, since ministers received no salary from the congregations.

As a minister, he was disenfranchised and deprived of his civil rights and, therefore, had no employment possibilities. Mrs. Ida Dueck, herself, writes of this to the friend of her youth, Elfrieda Friesen, daughter of B.B. Friesen, Vancouver, British Columbia. In the old country, these two were intimate friends and had worked in the Sunday School together. Now their paths had separated. Ida Dueck with her husband and two children was in exile, and Elfrieda Friesen had emigrated to Canada with her parents. The report of Mrs. Dueck follows. After the customary introduction she writes,

I want to describe the difficult circumstances in our home [village] during the recent past and our resettlement away from there. Lately, the situation for the disenfranchised and especially the ministers has become very difficult in Soviet Russia. Last year (1930), we were already assessed such high taxes that we feared the worst. Since we had accumulated some savings in the better years, we were able to escape once more. The following winter was a very difficult one, but we remained in our house and kept our cow. During this year, however, the taxes were so frequently levied and were so high that we finally had to give up. All our remaining possessions were confiscated and, after a time, everything was sold. They left us an old kitchen table and two wooden chairs. We did not have to sleep on the floor for long. Our parents, the Peter Regehrs, lent us the necessary furniture and we could remain in our house. I found it most difficult to lose the cow, for the children needed the milk so badly. The Margenau residents were all very helpful so that we did not suffer much. In spring, my husband searched for work but was rejected everywhere because he was disenfranchised. Finally, he found a position in the "white earth pit" near Hierschau as an illegal worker; virtually all the workers were the "disenfranchised." For my husband, it was a difficult, unaccustomed work, but he was happy that he had found a job. It was ten miles away, but he came home every Sunday.

On one such occasion, my husband was arrested. He had spent Sunday with us and wanted to go to his place of work early Monday morning. During the night, armed men burst into the house, chased him out of bed, and took him with them. It happened so quickly that he could not even say goodbye to the children. We remained behind as though stunned. We were not told the reason for his arrest nor where he was taken to. In the morning, I learned that the same thing had happened at the Johann Heidebrechts. My husband and 300 others were put in a barn in Halbstadt, naturally under heavy guard. It was so crowded that they had to lie with their heads against the wall and with their legs sprawled over each other. They received no bread or other sustenance. We had to look after all the prisoners' needs. The distance was over twenty verst; it was not always easy to get everything there on time. There was another great difficulty; we carefully saved [the foodstuffs] at home and when we brought them the prisoners did not get everything. The guards kept the best things for themselves. Those were five difficult weeks. We feared the worst, but what that would be no one knew.

Once, I awoke during the night of Saturday-Sunday and heard loud talking in front of our house. I realized that I and the two children were being carefully watched. It was a sad Sunday for us. In the afternoon, we were officially notified that we and the children were to be sent to the north. I could only take as much along as we could carry. You can imagine that it was not much: empty straw sack, a pillow for each, the essential under-linens and clothes and a few provisions. It was during the night of June 23-24, 1931 that we were taken by box wagon to the Stuljnewo station near Waldheim, accompanied by armed riders (just like dangerous criminals). Our men had already been brought from Halbstadt to Stuljnewo. It was a joyous, yet sad reunion. There were such heartrending scenes. We were so densely packed next to one another that we could hardly move. We lay down and perspired. There were many Bulgarians in addition to the Germans. (Generally they had been well-off and so were treated as kulaks.)

We travelled for eight days. During this entire time, we were only allowed to get out twice. We begged the guards to let us out more often, since some already had swollen feet, but to no avail. We did not know our destination and received no answer to all our inquiries. We felt like fools, travelling and travelling without knowing where to. As we journeyed through the Ural Mountains we saw wonderful regions and large evergreen forests. In spite of all the difficulties, the children had a good time; children are children and don't worry too much about things.

63

So much for the letter from exile.

In a second letter from Kir-Sawod, dated January 28, 1932, Mrs. Aron Dueck reports that they have sent the children home to the grandparents. The authorities had announced that all children under fourteen could leave their place of exile and return home, if they so desired. The parents found this separation from the children very difficult, but they thought more of the welfare of the children than their own. The only brother of Mrs. Aron Dueck, Peter Regehr, made the long journey from Margenau to the place of exile near Kir-Sawod in order to get the children. In the city of Tscheljabinsk, some ten verst from Kir-Sawod, he was arrested and put in prison. He managed to send word of his situation to his sister and brother-in-law. Oh, how they prayed for his release in the camp so that the old parents would not be robbed of their last support. The Lord heard their prayers and, after one month, he was released. One Sunday morning, he suddenly appeared. What joy! During his four day stay in the camp there was much conversation. Peter Regehr had brought along some warm things: a snug down-filled quilt, a coat, felt boots, etc. Since it was more than -30 Reaumur they were very thankful for these. It was hard to say goodbye. In addition to the two children of the Duecks, Regehr took along ten other children from the exiled Mennonite families. How the parents missed the happy interaction with their children, but they knew they were safe in the care of the dear grandparents. A lively correspondence ensued. That was still allowed at the time; later it was forbidden.

In that same letter, she adds,

Formerly, we would not have thought it possible that we could live in such an impoverished state. We live in an earth hut. In one corner, posts are stamped into the ground. Thick, unplaned boards lie on top. We sleep on these. Then we have a very simply fastened together table and a short bench without a back— that's all our furniture. A family, Isaak Sawatzky, from Tiege, together with their two children, also live with us. The boards on which they sleep are located only a few steps from ours. There are no internal walls. There is seldom a quiet moment. The only door we have leads directly to the outside. When we open it, the cold streams in like white steam.

The food is as poor as the accommodation. The state of our

health leaves much to be desired. I was recently examined by the doctor and he diagnosed malnutrition. Little wonder! Many are eating horsemeat. Therefore, we are so happy that you want to send us a package. We don't want to beg, but it would help us so much.

In the third letter, Mrs. Dueck thanks her friend for the parcel with its precious contents, and the children send their thanks for the pictures. The cold during February and March as well as the snowstorms were unrelenting, but the letter of March 10, 1932 closes with the words, "Do not lose hope, spring must come."

The weakened physical state of Mrs. Dueck could not, in the long run, overcome the deprivations of exile. Not long after, she succumbed to the hardships and went to her grave in the virgin forest.

Her husband, Aron Dueck, was freed, and he returned to Margenau and married a Justel Heidebrecht. The family Heidebrecht lived in Margenau as refugees. Earlier, they had lived on an estate near Gaitschur.

Later, brother Aron Dueck was once more exiled to the north. There was no further news from him.

The old parents, the P. Regehrs, had been expelled from their farm and lived in a small house belonging to their children, the Aron Duecks.

After the completion of this portrait of Aron Dueck, I received a letter from his nephew, Isaak P. Regehr from Margenau, who has come to Canada from Europe as a forestry worker. He provides additional information about the fate of the family of the minister, Peter P. Regehr of Margenau, Gnadenfeld district, Molotschna. He is the grandson of this minister. He writes as follows:

My grandfather, Peter Regehr, died in our house in 1933 in Margenau as the result of starvation. He was also buried here. It was a very large funeral for he was generally beloved and the entire region had come to his burial.

Grandmother died in our home during the summer of 1935 and was buried in the Margenau cemetery. Aunt Ida—Mrs. Aron Dueck—died in northern exile during the fall of 1932. Uncle Aron Dueck visited Margenau in 1934. During the summer, he married Justel Heidebrecht and then returned to his place of exile with the two children, Theo and Vera. Vera soon became a teacher and Theo a [truck]driver. Uncle Aron Dueck was a teacher until 1937, when he was again arrested and sent to another location in the north. Since then, we have heard nothing from him. We only know that he had to leave alone. His wife and children remained at the old location until 1939. Since then, we know nothing of them. My father—Peter P. Regehr Junior—was arrested at work on May 20, 1938. He was taken from home by two militiamen and, since then, we have heard nothing.

My oldest brother was sent to Siberia in 1941. I had to drive cattle to Taganrog (a city on the Don River in the south) to prevent them from falling into German hands and so did not get to Siberia. During the German occupation, I was conscripted (March 1942) into the German army.

On September 11, 1943, our villages were ordered evacuated and after many hardships I arrived in Warthegau near Litzmannstadt on March 18. My brother, Gerhard, died enroute near the city of Uwranj. My mother came to Germany with Mariechen, Sara, Kaethe, and Kornelius. I was home in July 1944, and since then have not seen my loved ones. I was still in correspondence with them in November 1944. After the surrender, I was captured by the Russians but secretly fled to Germany. I found none of my loved ones. Through others, I learned that most refugees were captured by the Russians in February 1945 and sent to Siberia. My dear mother and siblings were among these.

The wife of my oldest brother, Anna Toews, had lost her mother and her son, Peter, aged eleven, during the flight. My sister, Mariechen, lost her two children, Heinz, aged five, and Hilda, aged three, during the first day of the flight. She reached Brandenburg all alone and was apparently captured by the Russians and sent back into misery.

And so, I have lost all my loved ones and stand alone in this world. At first, I came to the camp in Cologne and from there to Gronau. From Gronau, I had the great privilege of leaving for Canada as a forestry worker. God be praised and given honor, glory and thanks for this. We are thirty-one Mennonite men here and work in the forest everyday. We are, undeservedly, well-off.

Bernhard B. Dyck
Co-elder of the Evangelical Mennonite Brethren
Church in Rosental
near Chortitza, Old Colony

Bernhard Dyck was born on November 30, 1881 in Hochfeld, Nikolaipol Volost, Jekaterinoslaw where he lived uninterrupted, until his attempt to emigrate in the year 1929.

He attended school for nine years. He gained the very extensive knowledge which he commanded by reading all the books he could get his hands on. He spent four years in the forestry service and was manager (as such, he was the assistant to the chaplain) for three of those years. These four years of service were of considerable importance to his spiritual development.

In 1907 he married in Hochfeld. In 1909(?) he was elected to the ministry by the Nikolaipol Mennonite Church, at that time still subordinated to the elder of the Chortitza Church, Isaak Dyck.

In 1912 he went to Berlin where he attended the Allianz Bible School for one year. Here he received much spiritual instruction for his later work as minister of the Gospel.

Between 1914 and 1917, he was a medical orderly on the trains of the All-Russian Zemstvo Union. After the war, in 1920 he joined the newly founded *Allianz* Church in Rosental and henceforth led the segment of this church which established itself in the Nikolaipol Volost.

In 1929 many members of the *Allianz* Church, together with their leading ministers, left for Moscow in order to emigrate. He and his family were among these. His destination was Canada and the way there had been cleared for him. The night before the departure of the first emigrant train from Moscow he, together with his son Bernhard, and many other leading men, was arrested by Soviet authorities. His family was sent back to the south, while he was held in Moscow for a month. What it means to stay in those terrible Lubyanka and Butyrka prisons for a month and be tortured day and night, only those who have experienced it know. He was then transferred to Charkow, the capital of the Ukraine. There his case was brought to trial. It was accompanied by painful interrogations and a complete disregard for all human rights. The court sentenced him to three years hard labor in northern Russia, ostensibly for initiating emigration.

On March 26, 1930 he arrived in Kandalakscha, district of Murmansk, on the Kola Peninsula, where he was to work as an orderly in a hospital. Here, his situation seemed bearable; however on December 8 of the same year, he was brought to the Island of Solowoki where he had to spend the rest of his captivity. From here he wrote to his friends, "Now I have fallen among the murderers. Pray for me."

After two years, he was promised his freedom, if he would bring his family and settle on the island. He did not take up this offer.

On July 3, 1932 he was released "for good behavior and hard work," four months before his sentence expired.

After a difficult journey— at the beginning of his trip, all his things and food were stolen— he arrived home on July 12, with his [hair] greying and in poor health. Because his stay in Hochfeld might have inopportune consequences, he left the same year for the settlement Arkadak with his wife and smaller children. He was rearrested on April 1, 1933. After two weeks, he was freed and expelled. He was forced to return "home." Destitute, he found temporary refuge in Schoenberg, Chortitza Volost.

His brother, the poet and writer, Arnold Dyck in Steinbach, Manitoba from whom I have most of this data, concludes:

> From here (Schoenberg), I received his last letter dated November 3, 1933. No further information has come either from him or from someone in his family. From other sources, I have learned that he was again arrested and exiled again. Where? I have never learned. Why? From private reports, I can only conclude that it was related to the tireless pursuit of his ministerial duties.

> Bernhard Dyck suffered severely during his incarceration:— bodily— from hunger, cold, and the extremely difficult work; — psychologically— from the hopelessness of his own situation and that of his family, which was totally destitute. This was apparent from the reports of his fellow sufferers. He never mentioned anything about his own suffering to his loved ones, who began to view this as a symptom of a nervous disor-

der. That is the way I knew him from earlier days. He never complained but bore his suffering silently and patiently, turned inward.

Reverend Abram Froese of Oak Bluff, Manitoba, his former co-worker in his home church, adds the following dimensions to his life story.

Peter Penner from Arkadak reports: "Reverend Bernhard Dyck here makes his livelihood as a tinsmith and shoemaker and continues to preach as he always has. That was already the case after his return from his first exile on Solowoki [Island]."

Later they report from Schoenberg: "Here, too, brother Dyck pursues his handiwork. While he does not preach publicly, he proclaims the Word at Bible studies and at the Lord's Supper, from which we derive a great blessing." An even later report reads: "Bernhard Dyck preaches the Word to us every Sunday, and we derive a great blessing from his work."

Even here, his stay was not long. He soon had to flee but was soon arrested and brought to the prison in Alexandrowsk. Here, his wife and friends visited him frequently and brought him provisions. One day, when his wife wanted to visit him, he was no longer there. He had vanished without a trace, and since that time there is no further information. God alone knows his fate.

Isaak Dyck
Elder
Chortitza, Rosental, Chortitza

He was the elder of the Mennonite Church in Chortitza for many years. He was the son of elder Gerhard Dyck of the same locality. His wife was Margaretha Hamm. As a young couple they moved to Grossfuerstenland, a Chortitza daughter colony. He was a teacher in Michelsburg for three years. Here, he was also called into the ministry in 1876. He then became a farmer by purchasing one of the many farms which was being sold cheaply by the owners emigrating to America.

After six years, he was called to the Anadol Forestry Service as a chaplain and manager. This was a completely new branch of Mennonite activity in Russia. He remained at this responsible post for six years; then, after a fifteen-year absence, returned to his home village of Rosental.

After the death of elder Heinrich Epp, he was elected as elder in 1906 and served as such for over thirty-three years. With advancing age, his hearing declined and, in 1922, he installed his successor, Peter Neufeld, as co-elder.

He was president of the Committee for the Support of the Forestry Commandos and also president of the Chortitza High School Board. He was repeatedly elected to the deputations sent to St. Petersburg to make representation to the government on various matters. His intuitive sense and his clear, sound judgment usually assured him success.

During war, revolution and civil war, those in public positions and those who had regional influence were hard pressed. He was also targeted, and during the worst confusion, he was forced to flee and hide for some six months. When he returned after a half-year absence and witnessed the devastation wrought by bandits and ravaging disease, his spirit was broken.

The new circumstances and the expanding spirit of disorder and violence exhausted him. It was a difficult choice as to whether or not he should join the emigration to Canada. The ill health of his wife and the love for his church persuaded him to remain and end his life in the setting where he had worked for so long. An overwhelming homesickness filled his soul during his last years. He wished to join Him whom he had served so faithfully for many years. His longing was fulfilled on August 24, 1929, and he was buried on August 27.

His life's partner followed him into eternity, a year and seven months later. Margaretha was over eighty-one years old. She, too, had a great yearning for her heavenly home.

Their daughter, Mrs. Peter Klassen of Hanley, Saskatchewan relates the following incident from the life of her dear father during those troubled times.

This episode occurred in 1919, when the Makhno bandits entered our villages. A German lad went to Makhno and said, "Do you know why the White Army is so powerful against you? Elder I.G. Dyck is praying for it." This was oil poured on the

71

fire. Armed men were immediately sent out to find this man and bring him to the bandit leader in camp. They did not know our father personally and the people who were questioned did not give father away. Warned by good friends, he went to his brother-in-law in the neighboring village. It was not long before riders were searching this village for father. He was standing in the yard observing this activity when a wagon filled with bandits came racing into the yard. "That must be him, yes that's him," they shouted. Father quickly went behind the barn when a fellow came running from the other side, "Where are you man, where have you gone?" Father was astounded and was about to ask, "Are you looking for me?" He distinctly heard a voice say to him, "Don't speak. I have blinded his eyes." Father observed him very closely and later related that the eyes of the bandit were rolling about crazily, like those of a wild animal, but that he had not seen him. This made father so trusting that he turned and walked into the house, even though there were bandits there.

Meanwhile two years had passed. My husband and I and our family had moved in with my parents so that they should not be alone. It was a winter evening when I and my sister Anna and the children were sitting in the "little room" patching. The door opened quietly and in stepped the unkempt boy who had caused my parents so much grief two years ago.

"Can I speak with Mr. Dyck?" he asked.

I took him to my parents' room. He stood at the door and said, "Mr. Dyck, will you give me a piece of bread."

"Is that you, Abram?"

"Yes," he answered.

"And you are coming to me for a piece of bread?"

"Yes, who else would give it to me?" he replied.

Father winked at me and said, "Give him what he wants."

I can see his very sad countenance in the face of such shamelessness and heartlessness to this very day. Hunger hurts and the great deprivation had driven the lad to us. Father had not allowed himself to become bitter on account of his meanness. He probably thought of the words of Jesus, "If your enemy hungers, give him to eat . . . ."

Alexander Ediger
Elder
Schoensee, Molotschna

Alexander Ediger was descended from an educated family in Berdyansk. He was born in 1893. His father owned a printing press and for a time was the Danish Consul [in Berdyansk]. His mother was the daughter of the wealthy Berdyansk mill owner J. Friesen. The Edigers were a prominent family and their three sons grew up in a cultured and, by Mennonite standards, rather worldly atmosphere.

A. Ediger received his elementary education through a private tutor who did not neglect music. He became a piano virtuoso. Later, though he could not sing well, his choir prepared complicated songs and cantatas with the help of the piano. After the completion of elementary school, he went on to high school. I learned to know him at this time as I was attending Neufeld's secondary school in Berdyansk. He was very gifted and possessed a friendly, affable temperament. After completing secondary school, he attended the historical-philosophical faculty of St. Petersburg University. Following his graduation, he went abroad and spent some time in Berlin and Vienna. I don't know whether he continued his studies there. I lost track of him during the war and the revolution which followed. I heard from him again in 1923 when the Schoensee Church in the Crimea called him as their minister. I was very surprised to hear that Ediger was a minister. While still in Berdyansk, neither he nor any of his friends would ever have expected this. Yet he came to Schoensee with his young family. He had married in the Crimea. With his friendly disposition and his earnest, heart-searching messages, he soon won the hearts of all. He was ordained as minister the same year and about a year later was ordained as elder.

During this time I, too, was elected as a minister. I worked with A. Ediger and became a close friend. I once asked him what had brought about the great change in him and what had motivated him to become a minister. He told me that God had spoken to his heart during the difficult experiences of the Revolution. Then, too, his believing wife had influenced him to choose the Way of Life decisively and to dedicate his talents and energies to the affairs of God's Kingdom. His wife was a Dueck daughter from the Crimea, a sister of Jakob Dueck of the Tent Mission who, together with others, was murdered by bandits in a Russian village.

For some years, Alexander Ediger worked in the Schoensee Church with great success. He was assisted by a number of young, newly elected ministers. There was a refreshing growth and maturation in the church. A revival took place and many committed themselves to the Lord. Regular services, Bible studies, and youth meetings were held in all the villages of the congregation. On certain Sundays, the entire congregation gathered in the Schoensee Church, insofar as the great lack of horses allowed this. The level of singing reached a new high; cantatas and oratorios were sung in the Schoensee Church. Unfortunately, this was the last bright flicker of the candle before it was completely snuffed out. The powers of darkness were already at work destroying and suffocating all religious life in Russia.

On the day that I left for Canada in April 1926, a meeting of the Commission for Ecclesiastical Affairs was held in Ediger's home. (He was the chairman of the commission.) He nevertheless accompanied me to the Tokmak station. When we parted he said, "God willing we will soon see each other again. I am also coming to Canada." But his Master had different plans for His servant. The way of persecution and the way of the cross had been selected for him. At the end of this way, a martyr's crown beckoned. He was arrested in 1929 and imprisoned in Melitopol for a while. He was then released. Not long after he was exiled to the Murmansk region, close to the Polar Sea. He developed heart problems because of his difficult experiences. Thanks to a letter (which was possibly sent to authorities), his situation temporarily improved. He even thought of bringing his family. Since then, nothing can be learned of his fate. One can almost certainly assume that he, like many others, sealed his faith with his death.

H. Goerz
Arden, Manitoba

A Letter from Exile

Encouraged by brother B.B. Janz, I should like to publish a letter from Alexander Ediger, which he wrote from exile to my brother Johann Goerz, then a young minister of the Schoensee Church. The letter has no date and does not indicate the place of writing. If I remember correctly, it was sent to me in 1934. My brother managed to stay home and serve the church for an amazingly long time, but was then taken from his young family and sent to Siberia where, and I cannot assume otherwise, he gave his life for his Lord.

We all remember A. Ediger so well. He was widely known for his striking personality, his high education, his courageous witness for his Lord, and his membership on the Commission for Ecclesiastical Affairs. We heard that he was exiled to Murmansk in the high north of European Russia, on the coast of the Arctic Ocean. The letter is probably written from there.

My dear brother and friend!

I wish you and your house the peace of God and the inner fellowship with our Lord and Savior. It is Pentecost and towards evening I walked into a Russian church and attended the festive service. The singing in the high vaulted room was beautiful, and the quiet reverence which permeated the large assembly was especially soothing. I thought of the song, "He is always there if one desires Him." What a comfort it is that we can always have Him, regardless if we are in the North or the South, free or captive, together or all alone.

"Jesus Christ, yesterday, today and the same forever."

Do you know that during this time, I have met many a dear fellow believer. You can imagine what this means to me in my situation to converse with such a person and mutually strengthen one another in faith. Not long ago I met a dear Lutheran brother here in the far north, whom the Lord had led into deep ways. We greatly strengthened one another through mutual encouragement. He let me read a poem which has remained in my memory. A tired pilgrim is on the way to his eternal home. He has been enroute for a long time: the sun is hot and his limbs ache. The large cross which he carries on his shoulders presses upon him. "Oh, if only the cross was not so heavy," he sighed. As he walks along, he suddenly sees a saw lying beside the road. Wait a minute, he thinks, I can make my cross lighter by cutting off a good-sized piece. No sooner said than done. He continues on his way with his shortened cross and finally reaches the city towards evening. Oh no, a deep wide moat surrounds it and a bridge is nowhere in sight. The pilgrim takes his cross and tries to lay it over the moat but it is too short. He needed exactly the length which he had sawed off. How sad, so near and yet so far from his goal. So, tired pilgrim, do not saw off your cross, patiently carry it further for your Savior, Himself, will help you. You will soon reach the eternal city and then you will rest with God. Thank God, there is still a rest for the tired people of God.

Then I met a dear young brother from Konteniusfeld who, in spite of difficult circumstances, has remained firm in the faith. He has been separated from his family and church for years. I often have to think of Elijah and his feeling that faith no longer existed. Yet I am convinced that God has many thousands even here. Yes, the Lord knows His own and the hour is nigh when He shall come and call them by name. I firmly believe He is near. This has become a blessed assurance for me. Joyously, I look heavenward and my heart calls even louder, "Come soon, Lord Jesus."

How are you, my dear brother? How do you like your work? I am so happy that you can work. I pray to God for you, that He may protect you and fill you with much wisdom and power. As far as I am concerned, I know I had to walk this path. The Lord had to lead me this way, it meant only good for me. They were often difficult times and I have seen hunger, cold and nakedness in abundance. And yet, looking back on my pathway, I can honestly say, "Bless the Lord Oh my soul and forget not all His benefits." I have often had to think of a text on which I once spoke: the Lord does not protect from suffering, but protects in suffering. You know as long as one does not suffer one fears suffering and thinks one will not be able to bear it when it comes. Yet when one is suffering one begins to experience the comforting and helping hand of God. How meaningful that Word from Psalm 23 has become: "Yes, though I walk through the valley of the shadow of death, I will fear no harm, for Thou art with me; Thy rod and Thy staff, they comfort me."

I spent six days with my loved ones. They were lovely days, but how quickly they passed. Now I am alone again, but hope that I am soon in a position to bring them here. I thank you from the bottom of my heart that you visited them. When my family wrote me about it, it seemed as though you had visited me. How often I think back to the time when you and other dear brethren came to me and how we prepared [for our tasks] and mutually edified one another. In my spirit I often walk through the villages of the Schoensee congregation, stop before each home, and think of its occupants and of what we experienced together. What a beautiful time it was when many a soul came to the Lord. How well our Bible studies were attended and how they united us!

How are you getting along in your work? How was your Pentecost [celebration] in Schoensee? Were you able to give baptismal instruction to the young people? On my journey I met two young people from Wernersdorf. I was so happy to see them. It seemed like a bit of home. I was so thankful that God granted me this opportunity. Will we see each other again? I would like this but is it possible? Many people have departed from us during this time and I, too, was near leaving. Now my health is somewhat better, but I will never get completely well for my heart is in bad condition. But what difference does it make? I'm going home to the Father's house.

"To wander silently in pilgrim's garb
'Til God calls to a better land
Redeemed am I, at home above
With Jesus journeying happily from here."

Supplement

Mrs. Kaethe Ediger came to Canada early in 1949. She now personally reports the most significant experiences in her and her husband's life.

My dear husband was exiled to the White Sea Canal in 1932. He was charged with organizing the emigration of the Mennonites. After he was released in 1935, he only spent a few months at home. Our son, Harry, was especially close to his father at this time. It was almost as if he sensed that he would soon lose his father. Even now, my heart still aches when I think how he never let him out of his sight.

One evening the already familiar agents of the GPU again arrived. They took my husband with them and not long after I was arrested.

Both of us were sent to a concentration camp in the Far East called Bamlag, I for five years, my husband for seven. I took our poor children, Dagmar and Harry, to our relatives, Heinrich Edigers in Simferopol. Before we left on our journey, they offered to release my husband, if he renounced his faith.

My husband would not hear of it.

The journey took one month. For the first two years after our arrival in Bamlag, both of us could work in the office. After Kirow, a high official in the Soviet government was assassinated, the treatment of exiles became much worse. Political prisoners like us were no longer allowed to take any responsible jobs. As a result, I became a cleaning woman and my husband had to supervise a group of men working on the railway which was being constructed.

In 1938 we were permanently separated. My husband was brought to the city of Swobodnj (Freedom) -—what irony! Here he was imprisoned. He sent me a card from there in which he pitied me, for he sensed that I would remain alone. Since then I have received no sign of life from my dear husband.

When I was released in 1940, I wanted to go to my children. They had moved to St. Petersburg, since my brother-in-law Heinrich Ediger of Simferopol had also been arrested. The children were accepted by Theodor Ediger, my husband's brother, who lived in St. Petersburg. Unfortunately, they could not remain with him for long since he and his wife were also soon exiled.

I was forbidden to live in St. Petersburg since I had been labeled "politically unreliable." I settled in the country near St. Petersburg and so could visit my children from time to time.

When the Germans marched into Russia, the front came between me and my children, and I have never seen them again. My greatest concern is that my children be saved and not only they but all the loved ones who are suffering in distant Russia. It is so difficult to live a life of faith there. My greatest joy is the hope that the Lord will soon return.

Your sister in the Lord,
K. Ediger

Heinrich J. Enns
Minister of the Mennonite Brethren Church in Alexandertal, Molotschna and Evangelist among the Russians

His father was Jakob Enns, minister of the Mennonite Church in Rosenhof, which belonged to the Schoenfeld Mennonite Settlement. Together with the minister Kornelius Epp, he served the church there for many years. Jakob was well-known beyond [the confines] of his own congregation, since he was also an itinerant minister. He received his training for the ministry in the Allianz Bible School in Berlin. They lived on the estate Tiegenhof.

It was here that his son Heinrich was born on July 31, 1888 (O.S.). He had five siblings: the other six had died in childhood. He also attended elementary school here. He later graduated from the Halbstadt High School. He grew up in a Christian home which certainly had an influence on his later spiritual development. In later years, he could not point to the exact time of his conversion, yet he showed his commitment through his life.

When the war broke out in the fall of 1914, he and his brother Gerhard were sent to an army hospital in St. Petersburg in order to serve the wounded and sick among the soldiers. During his free time here in St. Petersburg, he had the opportunity to become acquainted with the leading workers among the Russians: Adolf Reimer, Rev. Kargel, J.B. Neprash, J.S. Prochanow and others. Here, he visited the services of the Russian evangelical Christians. This contributed considerably to the fact that he, himself, went into this mission after the war ended. Towards the end of the war, he and his brother served as medical orderlies in Sarkoje Selo (summer residence of the tsar). After the revolution of 1917, our believing brethren in the service founded a Christian Soldiers Union with the object of carrying on missions among the soldiers in the army. The two brothers, Heinrich and Gerhard Enns, were also among these workers. In 1918 brother Gerhard Enns was baptized by immersion in St. Petersburg.

In addition to the German language, brother Gerhard

Enns had a thorough grounding in the Russian language. At home on the estate, he always had the opportunity to interact with the Russian servants and workers, and during the war there was the contact with Russian soldiers and officials. In this fashion, the Lord prepared His servant for His later service.

After the war Jacob Dick, the preacher and evangelist among the Russians, founded the Tent Mission (*Zeltmission*) in order to carry the Gospel to the various Russian villages and cities. The long-awaited and desired religious freedom had finally arrived, though it was of short duration.

Brother Heinrich Enns and his sister were totally involved. Quite a number of young heroes of faith united from various congregations. Russians, Jews, and Latvians were also participants in this new mission endeavor, as Russia called it. In Germany the evangelist, Jakob Vetter, had begun [this sort of work] earlier.

Here brother Enns also learned to know his future wife, Katharina Janzen of Alexanderwohl, Molotschna, whom he married soon after. They lived in the village of Alexandertal and joined the Mennonite Brethren Church there. The Lord granted them five children.

In the meantime, the entire family of Jakob Enns had to flee from their estate near Tiegenhof, since the bandits plundered and robbed everything. Many were murdered at that time (1918-19). They lost all their possessions and henceforth were completely impoverished. The mother had died earlier. The father and his family found refuge in Halbstadt, Molotschna. Here he died on December 3, 1919 and was also buried. Of his children, only one son, Gerhard Enns, who was mentioned earlier, came to Canada (Kitchener, Ontario) with his family. During his last years in Russia, he lived in Kleefeld, Molotschna where he was conductor of a choir for a time.

Through the richly blessed work of the Tent Mission, the Gospel of Salvation penetrated many a dark place in southern and central Russia. Many souls found peace. Little wonder that the enemy soon offered opposition. It was during the time of the civil war. Anarchy ruled everywhere; no one was sure of his life; yet, unafraid, the brothers and sisters of the Tent Mission continued to work. When a group came to Dubovka (Eichenfeld) one day, they were attacked by an organized band of murderers and brutally slain. Four brothers and two sisters lost their lives. Even the founder and leader, the real soul of the mission, brother Jacob Dick, died a martyr's death here. He, nevertheless, had the opportunity to preach the Gospel to his murderers before his death.

Now brother Adolf Reimer took charge of the orphaned mission in a special way. He gathered all the workers and founded the so-called mobile Bible School or Bible Course, in which the workers were led deeper into the truths of the Holy Scripture. Our best men from the ministerial ranks were elected as teachers for these courses. Because the times were already difficult, this group moved from place to place, supported by the free-will offerings of the brothers and sisters in the Lord in these localities. A strong interest in missions was awakened in many. During these years of revolution and civil war, more was done for the spread of the Gospel by the various Mennonite groups than ever before. But this flowering of missions did not last long. Soon every type of missions activity was forbidden under threat of the death penalty. Many ministers and other religious workers were brought before the courts and sentenced, some to prison, others to exile.

The Heinrich Enns family had been totally impoverished by the circumstances of the times: the children suffered from malnutrition and clothes were not available. In spite of all this, Heinrich Enns remained a courageous and willing worker.

He worked among the Russians and Germans. After the death of Adolf Reimer in 1921,the minister and evangleist who was the greatest Mennonite worker among the Russians, Heinrich felt himself called by God to be Reimer's successor and worked untiringly until his end.

Amid many difficulties and dangers, he visited the Russian churches far and near. He was especially concerned with healing the many quarrels in the churches. The Russian congregations were young and inexperienced in church work. Furthermore, they had no educated ministers and leaders, and that caused many a difficulty. Brother Enns helped them as best he could, just as his predecessor Adolf Reimer had done. But the communists had had their eyes on him for a long time. In order to put an end to his activity he was arrested and brought to trail along with many others.He and his entire family were deprived of their civil rights and sentenced to five years in prison at hard labor and another five years exile outside of the Ukraine.

Brother Enns managed to flee. He came to the Caucasus. Here,he was happily received by the brothers and sisters and simultaneously found a refuge. Many others of our ministers and workers were there. Here,too,persecution began after a few years, and no one was safe any longer. Brother Enns wanted to bring his family here. There was more food here than in the Molotschna and the Old Colony because the front had not remained here that long and because the region had been spared by robber bands.

What to do? Secretly he made his way home and came to the village of Rudnerweide. His family came here with the object of returning to the Caucasus. It was not to be. As a result of the difficulties associated with his long flight, he became ill with typhus. Soviet authorities soon heard about this, and before long the family which had hosted them received strict orders to expel these people from their home. As a ministerial family, they were disenfranchised and without civil rights and so had no right to stay in the village. If the hosts did not comply, they, too, were threatened with expulsion.

What now? From sympathetic people, Sister Enns managed to borrow a wagon with a horse. The deathly ill brother was placed upon a bed of hay, the five children were seated upon the wagon and so, sister Enns, with her sick husband and the small children on the wagon, led the horse to the village of Mariental. They could find no hospitality; everyone feared expulsion. At the end of the village a brother, Abram Loepp, came to the street and invited them inside ". . . until the police throw us both out." The dear brother Heinrich Enns went home after an impoverished and difficult life, yet one rich in work and blessing!

There were new difficulties for the sorely tried sister. The village Soviet of Mariental did not allow the body of the deceased to be buried in the church cemetery. In the fourth village, she finally got permission to bury her husband. It was Alexandertal, the village in which they lived for so long. Here lie the two faithful workers among the Russians: Adolf Reimer and Heinrich Enns. Both are buried in the cemetery of the village of Alexandertal, their earthly remains awaiting the resurrection morning, that great moment when the trumpet of God shall sound to awaken their corruptible bodies to eternal joy and bliss.

And what of sister Katharina Enns in her bitter sorrow? Not long after, the widows of both of these men received the order to leave the village of Alexandertal with only as many goods as two hands could carry. The mothers took their children by the hand and during the cold month of January walked the long way to the city of Melitopol sixty-five verst distant—and that with six children. How long must the path of suffering have seemed? Many a sigh, many a soul's cry of distress must have been sent up to God. But no one had pity on them. They only found temporary shelter and board among the Russian brothers and sisters in the city. It was not to be for very long. They had to leave here as well. Where to now? The two fellow sufferers moved from place to place until one day sister A. Reimer collapsed on the way and died. God, our Lord, alone knows what happened to sister Enns. We cannot understand how He reigns. Someday, one will see what He intended. In Hebrews 11 we read of the suffering of the saints: "the world was not worthy of them" (as. 38).

The information was provided by the minister Heinrich Goossen, Manitou, Manitoba and the brother of H. Enns, Gerhard Enns, Kitchener, Ontario.

Supplement

Mrs. Heinrich Enns lived in the district capital of Melitopol for a considerable time and found kindly accommodation among the Russian believers there. For a time, she worked in a canning factory. Later, she was removed and had to help pave the stone road leading from the large factory village of Waldheim to the station Stuljnewo. Here, the disenfranchised and those stripped of their civil rights had to perform hard work without pay, toiling only for the scanty daily bread which was sparingly rationed.

Mrs. H. Enns was only of a slight stature and the work of carrying and dragging stone required more than her strength.

83

Once again, she came to Melitopol. Her daughter, who had been trained as a nurse, had to accompany a transport of men sent from the south to the north for forced labor in 1941. Since then she vanished without a trace. With the approach of the German army during the same year she, herself, (Mrs. Enns) and her four children were deported to the distant east.

The minister and evangelist, David Reimer of Alexandertal, also lived in Melitopol at that time along with the blind brother Tjahrt, with his wife and two children from Grossweide.

They, too, experienced the same fate. All left blessings among believer circles in Melitopol and also in the Molotschna villages.

Heinrich H. Funk
Elder
New York, Ignatjew Settlement, Ukraine

H.H. Funk was born in Neuenburg, Chortitza district, Old Colony in the year 1880. His parents were both pious people and though they were not wealthy, gave their children model training and education. Heinrich experienced a cheerful, happy childhood at home. There were eleven siblings in all, eight sons and three daughters. After Heinrich and his twin, Peter had completed the village school they, thanks to the urging and pleading of the village teacher, went to the high school in Chortitza. They were among the first to leave Neuenburg for further training. Though it was difficult for the parents, they willingly made the sacrifice. They were eager students. They breathed the air of a healthy family atmosphere and a cheerful, buoyant spirit prevailed in the Funk family. There was a great affinity among family members. They loved to socialize and were loved in the community. A model order and an energetic spirit of work characterized the entire farm. Five of the sons received advanced education.

During the third year of high school, Heinrich contracted a bad cold which settled in his lungs. He had to withdraw from all youthful activities. This withdrawal had a deep effect on his entire later life. He was always aware of the lonely and the sick and felt compassion for them.

The paths of the twin brothers separated after leaving high school. Heinrich Funk went abroad to study theology and Peter Funk went to a gymnasium in Jekaterinoslaw to study law. The two brothers carried on a regular correspondence; neither of the brothers undertook any venture without consulting the other. With the support of the churches, Heinrich Funk came to the theological institute in Basel, Switzerland. The beauty of the Alps made a lasting impression on the enthusiastic young student. He was loved by his fellow students and made friendships with people who would henceforth influence him.

Once abroad Heinrich Funk completely regained his health thanks to the change in climate, lifestyle and complete contentment in his work. He returned home as a healthy young man. He was now prepared to take a position as a teacher of religion and German language in a high school. Since such a position was not available at the time, he became the head teacher in the school at Schoenhorst.

Soon a new high school was built in New York in the Ignatjew settlement. He received a position as a teacher for German and religion and worked here for almost twenty years. Now his wishes were fulfilled and he had achieved his goals. In New York, he also learned to know Sonja (Susanna) Rempel and with her founded his own home. It was a lovely, cheerful place. Funk and his wife were attractive personalities, both in body and soul. Mrs. Funk possessed a lively, cheerful nature and managed to run a well-appointed and generous household. Four children were born: two girls and two boys. Heinrich Funk was elected as a minister of the local Mennonite church. He distinguished himself by his enthusiastic instruction in German literature and by the rich content of his sermons. He possessed a strong sense of duty and an ardent love for everything noble and beautiful in life which was associated with the divine. Many a member of his congregation experienced his refreshing spirit and his generosity during his counselling sessions.

This idyllic family life and this ministry of blessing would come to an end with one blow. When WWI began in 1914, H. Funk, together with many other ministers and teachers, had to enter state service. Funk survived the time of war and revolution rather well. Now he could once more work as a teacher and minister, but heavy pressure soon came to rest upon him. The elder of the New York Mennonite Church, Abram Unrau, became old and ill. The congregation elected H. Funk as his assistant. He experienced many things during this period. Only few of them were happy. He was often arrested and spent days in prison. Soviet authorities finally presented him with an alternative: either he would remain a teacher and give up his ministerial office or he would give up his teaching position. H. Funk selected the latter. He left the teaching profession with a heavy heart and totally gave himself to the work of the church. During this time, he took over the office of elder, since his predecessor A. Unrau had to completely withdraw because of the weakness of old age. Now his pathway of suffering really began.

At that time, there was a determined exodus to Canada and as the ranks of the congregation thinned, Funk's family was also gripped by the desire to emigrate and flee the worry-ridden life in Russia. Funk could not easily decide whether it was his duty to bring his family to safety and follow the church members who had already left or to stay and continue to shepherd the congregational members who remained behind. For years, he suppressed the desire to come to Canada and faithfully continued in his office as elder.

By 1929 circumstances had worsened sufficiently, so that it became clear that any regulated congregational life was out of the question. It was the last chance to emigrate. Funk even managed to get his exit papers. They planned to depart by train on November 4 and Funk and his family were excited at the prospect of finally leaving. On the evening before they were to take the train, he was arrested and led away.

Here is an excerpt of a letter of his wife to her sister in Canada.

It was several hours before the train was due to leave. The baggage was at the station, our house was already locked and we, with our hand luggage, were at our neighbors for supper and to say farewell. These had been difficult days and Heinrich was tired. He had lain down for a brief nap. Then the police arrived, inspected all our baggage and Heinrich's papers, arrested him and took him away. The same evening on the very train which we were to take he was taken to _____?

He was kept in prison amidst the worst conditions for over four months. When he finally came to trial, he was exiled for eight years to the far north. The charge was that he had agitated for emigration especially since he himself had sought to emigrate. The family remained behind without its breadwinner and lived in an empty house, for the furniture and everything else had been sold.

Funk had been sent into the regions of the pine forests in the not-so-distant north. His wife and children were especially worried about his generally fragile health. He had suffered from a lung ailment while young, and they feared that he would not survive the vicissitudes of the concentration camp.

After an eleven month absence, it became possible for his wife to visit him. She found that he had been given lighter work because of his health and that he was keeping rather well. She was most impressed by his deep faith in God.

She wrote:

> Heinrich has such courageous faith. I was amazed, and happy. In every letter and on every occasion he sent encouraging and comforting Bible citations for those persons for whom he cared. These are the Bible verses he pointed out: Psalm 46; 126; 23; 90:1; 91:121; 37:5; Matt. 11:28; John 11:40 and others.

> Here is a short letter he sent to his relatives in Canada, including his mother-in-law, when he was out of exile.

> Your loved ones far, far away! A heartfelt thanks for your thoughts. I was often encouraged in difficult times when I remembered that your hands were lifted up in intercession for me. This visitation is difficult but it comes from God. He can change all things. He can also grant us a reunification even though the future currently looks so dark. The bread of exile is bitter, very bitter, but there is Psalm 46:8! We have experienced some evidence of His help and benevolence. God be with you! How are you dear mother and auntie? How often we think of you. God protect you and allow us to meet again, if not here then there.

> In heartfelt love,
> Heinrich

His situation in the work camp worsened. There were reports that he suffered from scurvy because of the salted meat. His elbows and knees were swollen and filled with water.

When he wrote this, he did not know that at home his wife had died. He had been sent 600 verst further north and so the news did not reach him.

A letter sent to Canada by his brother reflects the deep sorrow on the occasion of Mrs. Funk's funeral.

She was buried on the following day. As the sun began to set, many wreaths decorated the grave around which the children cowered. Little Heinz's heart wanted to break and he literally had to be pulled from the grave site. There was certainly no lack of participation, but how different it would have been if Heinrich had been present. Those who were left behind had no point of focus, even Sonja in her coffin seemed so lonely and abandoned.

His daughters married during his absence without the benefit of father's and mother's blessing. The sons-in-law, to the joy of the father, were stalwart Mennonite men. The happiness of the daughters did not last long. Both men came to a terrible end. The daughters again stood alone in the difficult struggle of life.

During the last period of his exile, H. Funk was attached to an American geological mission making a research trip in northern Russia. Here, he recovered somewhat.

After a seven and a half year exile, he was allowed to return home. What a reception. His wife was not there to welcome him and his children were scattered far and wide. For a time, he stayed with his niece Anna Janzen, nee Wiebe. Then he began his long journey to his second oldest daughter who had moved to a city in central Asia. Here, she had obtained a position as a teacher. Her husband was also exiled. The exhausted father, thanks to the loving care of his daughter, had barely begun to recover when she too was taken from him by death in 1938. She died during childbirth. According to another version, his dear Else died from a fever infesting the region and succumbed in spite of all the efforts made by the doctors and her fellow teachers. The teachers were very fond of her and, as a result, she had managed to get her father a position as secretary in the high school where she worked. They lived together in a small room where the broken father, after much deprivation, suffering and sorrow, once again experienced a child's love, compassion and care.

Now the old man again stood alone trusting God. It is believed he travelled to Leningrad to his other daughter whose husband, according to rumor, was shot by the Soviet government.

In 1940 the old, sickly man was again exiled. He was sent to an island together with his brothers, the lawyer Peter Funk, Hans Funk, and Gerhard Funk. (Some say he joined his brothers in exile voluntarily.)

When his wife had visited him in his first place of exile, she described him as thin, old and grey. Therefore, there is little hope that he is still alive. One almost wishes that the much tried pilgrim had gone on to his hope and reward.

The above information comes from the brother of elder H. Funk, Jakob H. Funk of Leamington, Ontario and his nephew Heinrich D. Dyck, principal of the Mennonite High School in Springstein, Manitoba.

Herta, the daughter of elder H. Funk, is currently in Germany as a refugee and adds a few details about the last years of her dear father. He studied together with Dr. Benjamin H. Unruh and in one of his letters, Unruh calls him his bosom friend. Here is Herta's report.

Father left school in 1925-26. As far as I know, he wished to go overseas but was elected elder and then felt obligated to stay. He found it difficult to leave the school. It was with a sad heart that he saw the students passing by or listened to conversations about the school. The school authorities did not like to see him go. They tried to keep him through various means but for him the matter was decided. He said he could live with the separation of church and state but when they demanded he promote anti-religious propaganda as a teacher he left the school. So father remained behind in New York as minister and later elder.

At that time I attended a technical training institute and know little of father's difficult struggle until 1929. It was not his style to speak much of difficulties and about the most difficult, the many visits of the three letters -- GPU -- he could

say nothing. (All who had anything to do with the GPU were forbidden to speak.) You know father and know that he did not
break his word. He never spoke about things which could not
be spoken about.

In 1929 there were various circumstances which had a
direct bearing on Papa's life. First, a large portion, perhaps the
greatest portion, of his church members left for Canada and so
he did not feel so obligated to remain there. Then there were
family issues as well. In the seventh grade Elsa was one of the
best or the best in her class. She received a report card with
outstanding marks but with the observation that she stood
under the influence of a religious family. These words blocked
any chance for a job. She could neither enter a school nor find
work.

Simultaneously, I was expelled from the technical institute, that is, I was given a "free" choice to leave. I had to
either denounce my father or leave the institution. This happened two months before my training was complete. I only had
to do my practicum. And so, I left empty-handed, without a
diploma. For four years father struggled to supply the means
for my schooling. He was almost the only one who had to pay
tuition because he was disenfranchised. The two of us were
home without any prospect of income or a position. This
bolstered father's decision to emigrate.

I remember that father was often interrogated and that he
always came home exhausted. He never told us anything. He
kept his word.

Two days before we were to leave, he was again taken late
in the evening. To our joy, he returned by three a.m. This time
he even told us a few things. He was asked why he wished to
leave and he gave the reason cited above. They tried to persuade him to stay but soon realized that his decision stood.
Then they said goodbye and wished him a good journey.

In a somewhat optimistic mood, we prepared for our departure. (The rest is in the earlier report.) For four months he was
imprisoned in the district capital. Once a week we could bring
him food. I was also able to visit him several times, naturally,
under supervision. How it hurt to see father's pale face behind
the bars and to hear the haunting creak of the heavy iron doors.
He was arrested on November 4, 1929, then sentenced to eight
years in concentration camp in February 1930. I was lucky
enough to spend a half an hour with him before the train left.
He still did not know his sentence and only told us that they did
not read him a list of accusations as in the case of others. Tact-
fully, I let him know that he was sentenced to eight years. He

90

became paler but controlled himself and calmed me down. Whether three or eight years was immaterial, he thought he would barely survive three years. He hoped they would release him since they had not read any charges against him. Then he left. The rest [of the story] we know.

Martin M. Hamm
Minister
Zagradovka, Province of Cherson

My father, Martin M. Hamm, was born on February 1, 1869 in Jeletzk near the Sea of Azov in south Russia. His father was the head herdsman on an estate. His mother was a Cornies daughter. Not long after, his parents moved to Schoendorf, Borosenko settlement.

He wanted to train as a teacher, but was unable to do so because his father died prematurely. Instead, he had to stay with his mother and look after the family farm. He was already converted in his youth which, considering the circumstances of the time, was in itself a wonder of God's grace. Eagerly he began to witness for his Lord, not only among the Mennonites but also among neighboring Lutherans. Though he experienced much opposition some were converted to the Lord. The public opinion of that day held that, in view of his youth, he had gone too far. As a result, he had to endure much misunderstanding and animosity.

In 1908 he was baptized in the river by the minister Jakob Martens, later of Ufa. Not long after, he joined the Evangelical Mennonite Brethren Church in Sagradowka, where he and his family had moved. He had married earlier and found a faithful wife in sister Helena Penner, Schoendorf. That was in the year 1894. The Lord blessed this marriage with seven children. His home church elected him to the ministry and also ordained him. His work also included other villages in the colony. He also went on mission journeys to the Old Colony, the Kuban and Suworowka. He enjoyed attending the Christian conferences in the Molotschna which were held by believers of the various churches under the leadership of the ministers Jakob W. Reimer, Peter Riediger, and others. Ministers from abroad

91

like Dr. Baedeker, Professor Ernst Stroeter and others presented lectures. He always came home refreshed and continued to work energetically.

Who would have guessed that his life and work would end so suddenly? He was not even fifty years of age when his life was taken by a murderous hand. It was on December 1, 1919 when an attack by the Makhno Band suddenly befell our home village of Schoenau.

Several days earlier, other villages of our settlement had been overrun and many lives had been lost. The rumor had spread through the villages that the Makhno Band had left and the danger had passed. On the Saturday before his death, the teacher of the village school, Jakob Peters, came to my father and asked whether a Sunday morning service would be held in spite of the unrest. He answered, "Yes, when the Lord ploughs so deeply we must plant the seed of God's Word as best we can." The attack came early Sunday morning. Father and many others fled the village. Just outside of the village, they fell into the murderers' hands.

Even in his hour of death, he thought of the welfare of other souls. In his last hour his son Franz, who had been captured with him and witnessed everything that happened, was converted to the Lord. He marvelously escaped a terrible death somewhat later. He (father) also comforted the other death candidates. When they began to attack him with sabers he, with the open Bible in his hand, declared, "For me to live is Christ and to die is gain."

He did not fear the gruesome death. Soon thereafter, his spirit departed and the bloody body lay on the ground.

He now looks upon Him who died for him, whose message of the cross was so precious to him, and which he felt was worth preaching to others.

Abraham Harder
Grossweide, Molotschna, South Russia

Since June 20, 1906 our parents, the Abraham Harders, lived in Grossweide where they established a home for orphaned children. The number of children grew steadily.

During the famine winter of 1921-22, there were some eighty children. Together with the personnel and the family itself, there were some 104 inhabitants. The Soviet government viewed our institution as a government institution and already took a hand in its internal operations in the summer of 1921. In February 1922 a teacher was sent into our orphanage to take control. After she had observed the operation of our institution for two weeks, she demanded to be driven to Tokmak. In my presence, she told the director of education that she could not take control of Grossweide, since this would mean the ruin of the institution. She was not in a position to supervise its operation along its present lines.

We remained [relatively] undisturbed until November 1922, though we had to endure various chicaneries. The religious instruction of children was forbidden as were prayers and the singing of Christian songs. A communist education of the children was initiated. We could not accept this. When we openly declared that our conscience was bound by God's Word and that we could not give up the Christian training of the children, the government sent us both a *politruk* and a communist as a teacher. The latter was a former Mennonite who sought to harass my parents in various ways. First my dear wife and I had to clear our room, then my parents had to do the same. All the personnel left the institution, since no one wished to work under the new administration. Only twenty-two of the eighty children remained. The others were taken out and cared for by relatives or other Mennonite friends. In this way, a number of them came to Canada. The twenty-two children were soon taken to the government institution for German children in Prischib and Russian children were brought to Grossweide. It was soon noticeable in the institutional administration that others were in charge. The motto "Eben-Ezer" on the gable of the large house was soon taken down. The two pump organs soon were literally in pieces. Drawers from the linen closets were used as feeding troughs for the horses. The central water heating was not functional until the next winter. There was dirt and filth everywhere. It was very painful for the parents to witness this destruction.

For sixteen and a half years the parents, trusting in God, did the work committed to them. They gave their best years, their strength and energy as well as all their possessions. Now the work they held so dear was taken from them and they were sent away. There were difficult struggles and an inner search for understanding. The faithful, heavenly Father did not forsake them.

Together with my parents, we moved into the former teacherage, where my brother and his family already lived. He had earlier been expelled from an institution for Russian children in Schoenau. Even the child care workers, who otherwise had no home, came there for the winter.

Father was repeatedly interrogated by a *troika* (three-man tribunal) and threatened with exile and death, because they wished to label us counterevolutionaries. The Lord helped, wonderfully, during this time of great fear.

In June 1924 we moved to Canada in the hope that our parents and siblings would soon follow us. Things turned out differently. Our brother-in-law, H. Dueck, emigrated to Mexico and later came to Canada. In the fall of 1924, my brother Abram Harder and family travelled to Germany and then to Paraguay because he felt the way to Canada was barred. My parents lived in Grossweide until the late fall of 1924 and then became the house parents in the senior citizen home in Kuruschan for two years. The P. Kaethlers moved with them in order to help with the work, but left for Canada in October 1925. In the fall of 1926 my parents gave up their work in the senior citizen home and moved first to Rosenort, then to Rueckenau. Here, father became a deacon in his old age. My parents wanted to end their days here, especially since my oldest sister Anna, in spite of all efforts, could not get permission to enter Canada because of her poor health.

One Sunday morning in 1931, father was taken out of the worship service. Communist authorities took everything away from them except for a few clothes and bed linens. Our parents had to tighten their belts even more. Since exile usually followed such confiscation, our parents packed what had been left and fled to the Crimea. Brother M. Derksen took them to the station during the night. The Lord was gracious. They found a warm welcome from my sister and brother-in-law, the Jakob Janzens, whose small house now became their home. Their tranquility did not last long. After only four months, in May

1931, the Jakob Janzens and their five children were sent into the swampy virgin forests near Archangelsk. My parents were taken along but after three days at the station were allowed to return to Spat. They were not allowed to live in the house of their children. There was no room for them in the village. They were given an earth hut just outside the village which had been a chicken barn. They moved in and lived scantily from the little which father and my sister Berta could earn. They, nevertheless, lived in steadfast fellowship with the Lord. Children and friends helped with gifts from abroad. How poorly they fared is illustrated by the fact that they went to the fields to gather wheat ears for bread as well as dried manure on the pastures for winter fuel.

After a very long illness our dear mother, believing in her Savior, died in that earth hut near Spat in July 1936. She went home like an exhausted, homeless pilgrim. There, she will be with the Lord at all times and no one will evict her. Father was very lonely now. He had almost no brethren with whom he could fellowship. He often visited other Christians in their homes and prayed with them. There were no longer any services.

A few months after mother's death, in September 1936, my youngest sister, Berta, married a K. Harder from Tsche-Tsche near Kurman Kemalschi. Father moved there with Anna. My brother-in-law Kornelius was an orphan and had two younger siblings. Father became the head of the house.

When Berta and Kornelius' first son was several months old, a new calamity struck our loved ones: Kornelius was arrested and vanished without a trace. Berta had to look after everything. She worked in the *Sovkoz* and received her small rations. These had to do for four, since Papa and Anna were disenfranchised and deprived of civil rights. They could obtain no ration cards and, at the market, the prices for products were very high. Father tried to earn what he could. He made chick cages for the hatchery, wooden barrels, etc. as his strength and [available] raw materials allowed. He even made toothbrushes for the store. The family here tried to help out, but our money did not go far since all dollars had to be sold at the government exchange rate. Even though life was very marginal when it came to food and clothing, our old father had a bountiful inner life. Again and again, God spoke to him in marvelous ways. His letters of the time speak of his inner fellowship with the Lord and mention repeated answers to prayer in the little things of life. Our father never lost faith in his heavenly Father in spite of the difficult pathways into which he was led. In response to our inquiries, father, in one of his last letters, cited the verses from Hebrews 10:37-39 as an indication of his inner feelings. That remained his position to the very end. The last news from our dear father reached us in March 1941. Since then we have learned that he and the sisters together with little Rudi were deported to Kasakstan in September 1941. All further information is lacking. Father was seventy-five years old at the time. Is he still alive or is he with the Lord? We do not know. We have committed him, who was not only a father but a friend and guide to me, and the sisters as well as all other siblings to the grace of God . . . .

Johann A. Harder
Yarrow, British Columbia

Heinrich Harder

He was a teacher but also a minister of the Molotschna Evangelical Mennonite Brethren Church, whose meeting hall was located in Lichtfelde. He, himself, came from Neu-Halbstadt. His wife Helene was a daughter of the widely known teacher, minister, and poet Bernard Harder of Halbstadt. She also possessed outstanding poetic gifts. Many a fine poem of hers has appeared in our periodicals. I can still remember one of her poems which appeared in the Mennonite papers under the title *Lose Blätter* in which she portrayed the lot of the scattered Mennonite refugees in a most gripping fashion. This family unfortunately had no children, though both loved children intensely. Later they adopted a daughter called Njuta (Annie) who gave them much joy.

Heinrich Harder possessed a good pedagogical training and was a teacher for many years. His longest stay was at the estate Steinbach on the Juschanlee River. Here lived the well-known families Peter and Nicolai Schmidt, Jakob Dick, Klaas

Schmidt, the family Regehr and others. The school was only small, but the teacher Harder completely dedicated himself to his profession. He had a very friendly manner which attracted people, yet he possessed a very steadfast character. In the school district stretching from Steinbach to Mariental he, together with his colleagues, was a regular participant in the teacher conferences and contributed much to their vitality. His colleagues included Abram Janz, Elisabethal; Johann A. Toews, Alexandertal; the teachers Boese and P. Toews, Schardau; Abram H. Harder, Pordenau; Peter Wiebe and Abram Nickel, Mariental.

During the German occupation in the summer of 1918, the teacher Heinrich Harder celebrated his twenty-fifth jubilee as a teacher. The author, at the request of the Molotschna Mennonite Teachers Association, presented the jubilee address utilizing the text, "A laborer is worthy of his hire."

He left Steinbach and accepted a teaching position in Sparrau when Steinbach was largely depopulated by the Bolsheviks and a communist children's home was established there. Since he was also a minister, he had to give up his beloved teaching position because of pressure from Soviet authorities. The family then moved to Neu-Halbstadt, where he had been appointed as minister of the Mennonite Brethren Church. The services were held in the so-called *Vereinshaus* (Association House), where the services of other Mennonite groups were held as well.

Almost all of the ministers had emigrated or fled and so, he had much work in the congregations. He did not labor in peace for long. As a minister, he was soon disenfranchised and deprived of civil rights. One high tax assessment followed another and soon he was obliged to leave his post. He and his family moved to the Memrik region. The meetinghouse in Halbstadt was closed and turned into a high school gymnasium.

Here (Memrik) they were very poor. Finally H. Harder found a position as night watchman at a government project. Later he was sent to the high north together with all the other Mennonite inhabitants near Memrik. All reliable information has been lacking since then.

Postscript from May 1948.

We have just now received further information about the last years of the whereabouts of the Heinrich Harder family. At the beginning of the 1930s, they had moved to the Russian village Borisowka, in the region of Stalino (Jusowo). Other Mennonite families were also living here: the deacon Abram A. Dick and family from Lichtfelde; the Andreas Buller family from Waldheim; Flemings and Woelks from Rudnerweide and others. Hans Buller, the son of Andreas Buller, had married H. Harder's adopted daughter, Njuta. They lived together with their parents and spent several happy years there. In March of 1935, they wrote that they still felt secure, as if protected by a rocky cliff. Materially, they were not too badly off. They had their so-called family evenings (they were not to be called services) where Mennonite families came together and edified themselves through the Word, and with song and prayer. They were always happy when the day off stipulated by the government fell on a Sunday. They were still celebrating birthdays together and a lovely Bible verse was the usual birthday gift.

In August 1935, Njuta wrote to Canada noting that the help from the dear friends of their parents had kept them alive. They were only lacking in lard. Mother was becoming steadily thinner and their earnings only bought bread. During this time, Heinrich Harder found a position as a teacher of German in a ten-class school. He was highly respected in the school and the director of the school often came to visit him. Previously, he had been employed as a night watchman by a nurseryman. In 1935 they celebrated Christmas with the Abram Dick family, and they even had a Christmas tree. The teacher H. Harder had brought a number of books along. These were circulated and there was a good deal of reading.

Yet on April 30, 1936, Heinrich Harder and his son-in-law, Hans Buller, were arrested and imprisoned. The charges were probably related to the holding of religious services. They loved to sing the songs of Zion and that had not gone unnoticed.

In June 1937, they were freed but they did not say why. At that time it was dangerous to write or receive letters from abroad.

In one letter from that time, they mentioned Acts 8:3 where we read, "But Paul made havoc of the church and, forcing himself into homes and dragging out men and women, he put them in prison." They also mention the song, "Master the tempest is raging."

In March 1939, H. Harder lay seriously ill in a hospital. He suffered from a stomach ailment, and his wife had heart problems. They recovered and during this year they, together with their children, were able to move into their own four-room house. Dear friends lent them the extra money. They were happy together. They planted vegetables and flowers near the house. Then came WWII and all the German settlers were forcibly deported to Kazakhstan and other places. The journey began on October 2, 1941, and on November 4 they disembarked. On December 23 and 24, the temperature stood at minus 45. Bitter misery and poverty held sway among the deportees; they were now to establish a new livelihood without any means.

Heinrich Harder and his family came here (Kasakstan?), but they did not survive for long. Both died, one soon after the other, and were buried here.

The son-in-law, Hans Buller, eulogizes his parents-in-law and especially the father. He writes to his kin, the Heinrich Bullers in Ontario.

> In the years when father still had a regular income as a teacher in the diaspora, he did much good among the poor. He possessed an upright heart, was always kind and friendly, and can right be counted among the great of our people. I mention our dear aged ones, once again, and praise the goodness of God that He has taken them unto Himself. My dear father-in-law was a great gift to me. At his table I could absorb and learn what is currently so useful to me. I still have many things to ask now that his mouth is closed forever. There was hardly a thing for which he did not have an answer. He was not a craftsman for he hardly knew how to use a hammer—but he was a teacher by the grace of God! He has fought a good fight.

Is that not a splendid testimony for one of our servants of God who breathed his last so far from home?

Peter C. Heidebrecht
Minister and Forestry Manager

Peter Cornelius Heidebrecht was born in the village of Nikolaidorf, Gnadenfeld district, Molotschna on November 20, 1868. His childhood and youthful years were spent in the parental home. He went to school in Nikolaidorf and also attended catechism instruction. After this, he was baptized in the Margenau Mennonite Church.

After age 18, he learned to become a blacksmith. At age 21, he had to enter the forestry service. He was drafted into the Phylloxera Commando on the southern coast of the Crimea. The commando had the special task of finding a harmful insect called phylloxera in the vineyards of the southern Crimea. Where it was found, the vineyards were destroyed to prevent its spread. The very finest grapes grew on that coast, and the large vineyards of the imperial house were also found here. In the summer and fall, these young men in service enjoyed the very best grapes to the full. They lived in tents because the climate was mild and, also, because they were constantly on the move.

In 1894 he married Maria Driediger from Gnadental. Shortly, thereafter, they took over a blacksmith shop and a farm in the village of Alexanderwohl. At that time, there were already Bible studies as well as vital spirituality [in the village]. P. Heidebrecht was a regular participant. After several years, he left Alexanderwohl and purchased a farm in Gnadenfeld. Here, he also did not find what he was looking for. In 1900 he moved to Dawlekanowo, Ufa, near the Ural Mountains. They rented land on an estate called Pekkar. There were ten to fifteen settler families, both Mennonites and Lutherans, and each family lived alone on its farm. The first years were rather difficult. The majority were from the south and quite unaccustomed to the climate. Here, the minister Heidebrecht had found his rightful place, as all the settlers gathered in the homes every Sunday for worship and Sunday school. Heidebrecht brought a good many books with him which helped him in his preaching. The Bible, however, remained his best teacher, and he understood it better than learned discourses. His sermons were simple and to the point, and repeatedly, he stressed the necessity of an upright life in Jesus. After two years, the settlers built a school with a teacherage. They also found a good Sunday school teacher and choir conductor in Jakob Balzer. The settlement grew materially as well. There was a special unity and love among them. P. Heidebrecht led the youth instruction for some years, while baptisms and communions were held by ministers coming from Dawlekanowo.

There were two Lutheran villages nearby. They had no regular minister. The minister Heidebrecht often conducted services there and distributed tracts and Bibles which he obtained in Dawlekanowo. This town, so to speak, was the spiritual center of Ufa.

They frequently had visitors in their home, including Molokans (a special sect among the Russians), whose land bordered on his. Together they read the Russian Bible and said goodbye with a kiss.

It was probably around 1904 when the Tatars in the region suffered great deprivtion Thanks to gifts from the Mennonite settlements to the south, products were purchased and the so-called soup kitchens inaugurated. Here the starving from the Tatar villages were fed. Heidebrecht supervised these kitchens in several villages. The Tatars liked him. He also employed some of them as workers on his farm. When a special friend among them came to minister Heidebrecht in spring and asked for seed grain, he gave him a *pud* (forty Russia pounds or thirty-two English pounds). When his wife scolded him as ministers' wives tend to do in such circumstances, he replied, "Well, God can give me so much more next year if the poor 'Achmet' (a Tatar name) cannot return it." This trust in God never left him. When things seemed dark, he clung to God's Word and God led wonderfully.

He was already active before his ordination which took place in Dawlekanowo in late fall of 1907. Then he took the position of a forestry chaplain and manager in the newly founded forestry of Schwarzwald. He had long had the desire to do more for God's Kingdom and his own people. Material concerns did not stop him, though, at times, his family worried about the future.

In January 1908, he arrived at the station Snamenka. The Russian forestry and training school was seven verst away. A Mennonite forestry was also to be built in this region. It was a magnificent, rich forest region, the trees were mostly birch and ash. Until March the family lived among the Russians, who had never seen such people before. Then the Mennonite youths who were to perform their state service arrived. During the first year, there was a great deal of construction. In September, the buildings were completed to the extent that the manager's house and the main barrack could be occupied. The young men were happy to have a roof over their heads for winter.

It was not always easy for the minister Heidebrecht. The spiritual and material supervision of such a large institution demanded all his energies. His experiences during his own time of service were a great help and his open and upright manner disarmed his opponents among the forestry soldiers. There were between 160 and 180 men at this forestry and there were many different personalities among the many young Mennonites. Often he locked the door of his room and sought help and counsel from his God. He made no distinctions. He tried to be nonpartisan. It did not matter whether the needy soul belonged to the "Old Church" or came from another camp. For him, all were disciples of Jesus who searched for and loved the truth. He served here faithfully and sacrificially until 1917. Then the time came when those of Red persuasion ruled and the spiritual leaders had to leave the forestry service.

He and his family found shelter in the village of Gnadental. He took over the farm of his parents-in-law who were still alive. The times were already unsettled but the farmers still believed that a miracle would occur and that somehow the government would be overthrown. It did not happen and the landowners had to give their lovely farms over to the Reds.

The minister P. Heidebrecht often preached in the Mennonite church in nearby Margenau. After several years, he became the leader of the congregation. Because he wanted to bring some changes into the church, the more orthodox Mennonites did not agree with him. One day at a church meeting they told him, "Heidebrecht belongs in Rueckenau, not here." (Rueckenau was the headquarters of the Mennonite Brethren Church.)

In time, the teachers who were ministers had to leave the schools by order of the Red government. The teacher Bernhard

Wiens now came to Gnadental. These two were deeply concerned about the spiritual welfare of its inhabitants. During the last years of free worship services (1925-27), the young men were encouraged to lead Bible studies and prayer meetings and to preach at evening services. The ministers, Benjamin Ratzlaff of Gnadenfeld, Isaak Boldt of Paulsheim and many others worked eagerly for the Lord in the Mennonite villages and congregations in the Molotschna. In certain respects the years 1917-27 were not the worst, especially as it concerned the spiritual life. Through His servants, the Lord instigated a great revival among some of the Mennonite settlements in Russia. A vital spiritual life reigned everywhere, and a great deal of missionary work was done, especially among the Russians. People wanted to catch up on what had been neglected for so many years.

Many Mennonites left Russia for a new home in Canada between 1923 and 1926. Among these were the two married daughters of P.C. Heidebrecht. The father bade adieu with the words, "Goodbye! If we do not see you in Canada, children, then above!"

In 1929 they paid the government twice for exit visas, but to no avail. When the great flight to Moscow began in the fall of that year, the Heidebrecht family also decided to go there. They wanted to leave the land of horror and Red terror at any cost. Their only son had died in the Far East near the Amur River on the border of China. In 1928 Mrs. Heidebrecht had lost her right arm through an accident. Both parents-in-law had died and life in Russia became more difficult with each passing year.

There was unrest in almost all the villages. Everyone left for Moscow to get exit visas, but without success. The Heidebrechts had not even left Gnadental when a government commission arrived in the village. A public meeting was called and the farmers were asked directly why they wished to emigrate. The minister P. Heidebrecht stood up and openly declared that [it was] for religious freedom since the Christian training of children was forbidden and also in order to ensure material survival, since this was not possible here.

Because he had spoken so openly, the order to arrest Heidebrecht came the next day. He was taken under guard to a prison in the district capital of Melitopol, where he remained for five months. The conditions in Russian prisons defy description: cold, damp, dirty, full of vermin, very bad and usually insufficient food. In the long run, few survive, most fade away and die. In addition there are the satanic interrogations and mistreatments.

The minister P. Heidebrecht came into such a prison. His family, though far away, supplied him with food and clothing. Together with other prisoners who, like him, were innocent, he was sent away to what was at first an unknown destination. Finally, after a long and anxious wait the family received word that he had arrived in Archangelsk on March 30, 1930. Forty-two persons had been loaded into each freight car. They were without seats or sleeping arrangements and some seventy carloads were sent [north] at one time.

They were housed in barracks, though later some with lighter sentences were allowed to find private accommodation. P. Heidebrecht, Cornelius Wiens from Muntau and a Willms were in a Russian home, ten verst from the city. They had to work eight hours a day, or they did not receive their bread ration card. The exiles had to present themselves to the administration every tenth day. It was a special privilege for them and their loved ones to have mail service. The [food] products in the north were of poor quality and difficult to obtain. The northern population was bitterly poor, hence relatives in the south helped as much as possible. Many wives followed their husbands into exile in order to ease their lot. They made great sacrifices and were true heroines.

Life was difficult. The climate was much colder than they were accustomed to and many became ill and died, especially the children. Mrs. Heidebrecht voluntarily went north to join her husband in 1931. Back in the villages, everything had been given over to the government. Everything had been taken from the farmers and put into the collective: house, barn, cattle and even the last food supplies. They stood there stripped and vulnerable to starvation.

Heidebrecht and his wife wrote a large number of letters from exile to their children in Canada. The letters were, again and again, filled with praise and thanks to God that He had led so protectively, given them health, and children as well as good friends who supplied them with their physical needs. There was no complaining or grumbling. They received parcels from a number of persons in Canada. Furthermore, most of the exiles did not work on Sundays. Though worship services were forbidden, three or four of them gathered together for edification.

The minister, Isaak Boldt of Paulsheim, Molotschna, had lived with them since the fall of 1931. When he arrived he was near death. Mrs. Heidebrecht wrote that he had barely been able to stand and was so thin that they hardly recognized him. He had been exiled for five years and his family had been sent in the opposite direction to Tomsk, far into central Siberia, where they were suffering great want. In winter they had sold their clothes in order to buy bread.

In these letters, a Peters family is also mentioned, who came from Taganrog on the Sea of Azov; Mrs. Peters was a German citizen. She survived two years on the barren Solowoki Island in the White Sea and now she was to work for three years near Archangelsk. In 1933 this woman received money from Germany to pay for the journey back to her homeland with her five-year old daughter. But this money was taken from her by the Russians and ostensibly returned. How vile!

At that time, one American dollar was worth fifty rubles in the *Torgsin*, but a loaf of bread cost twenty-three rubles, oil was seven rubles per bottle, and it was difficult to get it at that. The *Torgsin* was a business firm where one could buy food and clothing at high prices for American dollars or other foreign currency. In this way, Russia earned foreign exchange for trade, since the Russian ruble had no value abroad. The starving in Russia had to give everything they had just to save their lives.

In 1933 Heidebrecht and his wife again returned south. The village Soviet of Gnadental had petitioned for a blacksmith, who was urgently needed in the village. Heidebrecht worked here for several months. They had no home, however. Their former residence had become a day care, and Jakob Driediger's house and barn had been turned into a horse barn. In Abraham Klassen's yard, there was a cow-barn for the collective, etc. The Mennonites had all been collectivized. Only those who worked in the collective received bread. No one had any authority.

There was another purging in 1934. Again, they sifted through all levels in order to find people for slave labor in the north. Again many were exiled, even to Wladiwostock in the Far East.

Every woman in the collective had her duty, whether she had little children or not. There was always plenty of work. If someone complained, his name was soon on the black-list and that meant nothing good for that individual.

In 1934 the P. Heidebrecht family moved to the Caucasus which for some time was a place of refuge for many Mennonites from the colonies. Someone had warned them to leave the village. The same situation existed in most villages, and therefore many sought security in a distant land. Here the Heidebrechts lived in the Russian village of Ssablyi where there were approximately 180 refugee families. Some had settled permanently, others simply lived in rented accommodations. The Dietrich Wiebe family from Lichtfelde and the teacher Klassen from Gnadental were also among the refugees and lived in the mountain city of Georgijewsk. That was in 1935. Many Mennonites, here, worked in banks and businesses, and many among them had high school education. The girls worked in the gardens and hatcheries. Whoever worked had food, and most were not concerned about anything more.

There were no worship services. The minister P. Heidebrecht made many visitations. He mostly walked. He also spent several days with elder Abram D. Nickel before he died and was saddened by the elder's severe suffering.

In March 1938, the children in Canada received the last card from their parents with the request not to write anymore, for the times were becoming desperate. Again and again the old grey-haired servant of the Lord praised God for the many benefits he had received. In spite of dark and difficult days, he did not want to give up his faith.

Later a persecution broke out among the many refugees in the Caucasus. Many were arrested, sentenced, exiled, imprisoned and finally, with the approach of the Germans in 1941, collectively exiled to Kazakhstan in central Asia and to Siberia. Many families were separated and have not found each other to this very day. For many, the process was complicated by the law which forbade all correspondence.

Postscript:
The last information from Russia confirms that P.C. Heidebrecht was sent into exile in the year 1941. The children in Canada do not know where he was sent.

Heinrich and Liese Huebert
Muensterberg, Molotschna

Heinrich Huebert was the son of the mill owner, Johann N. Huebert, in Muensterberg on the Molotschna. In addition to village school, he had finished the Ohrloff High School. Later, he helped his father in the mill business and on the farm. He married a Liese F. Janzen. He was born in 1883.

Since the Huebert family was wealthy, they were singled out during the Bolshevik era and subjected to all kinds of pressure until they were completely impoverished. The sons were not spared from exile.

It was a time when all sorts of levies were being forced upon the population. If the required sums were not raised, hostages were taken from the midst of the inhabitants. They were kept in prison until the money came in. Often, they were shot in order to intimidate the population and make them compliant. One day, these communists came to the village of Muensterberg and levied a large contribution upon the village. Heinrich Huebert volunteered to go from house to house to collect the money. In the interval, they had already taken one of the wealthiest neighbors, Abram Isaak Wiebe, as a hostage and threatened to take him with them.

When H. Huebert had collected the money, he hurried into a room to count it. Already, one of the bandits was on his heels and shouted, "Hands up!" As soon as that happened, the intruder gathered up the money and pocketed it. At this moment, his sister-in-law walked by the window and when she saw the danger in which he found himself,she shouted for help. The robber vanished, as did the wagon carrying the Red soldiers. They pushed Abram Wiebe off the wagon. When they saw Kornelius Huebert standing by the mill, they shot at him.

107

He stumbled and fell to the ground but was not hit. Later Heinrich Huebert confessed that when his life was threatened, he had a great urge to jump upon his enemy and choke him. But he resisted the temptation and remained nonresistant.

He was first arrested in January 1930 and taken to a prison in Melitopol. His Bible was taken from him. He wrote, "I know that my Redeemer liveth." He was exiled to Kotlas in the extreme north of Russia. He was allowed to return home in October 1933. According to one letter, he was unable to travel because he lacked money and clothing. He, like a gypsy, had only rags on his body.

In his distress, he wrote to his brother-in-law, Gerhard H. Sukkau. Huebert later wrote his relatives in the Molotschna, "If my brother-in-law had not cared for me, I would have been lost. Blessed are the merciful for they shall receive mercy!"

His family [not only brought him] but his wife and two sons to the Caucasus. What a reunion that was!

He writes of that time [in exile]:

> I experienced many things during my three years of suffering. The difficult experiences were sometimes so deep and precipitous that one became terribly frightened.

In the Caucasus, he was first employed on the collective farm as a cowherder. Later, he became a gardener and as such had to plant five hectares of forest and three hectares of vineyards. The family made mud bricks and built a house of them. They were thankful to God for a modest home. Unfortunately, both he and his wife were ill. The doctor diagnosed leukemia. Then in 1937 he broke his leg, and for this reason was unable to earn anything. In the same year he was exiled, as was his brother Abram and many others with them.

There was no further news after 1937.

Now some information about the life of his wife, Liese Huebert, nee Janzen. While her husband was in exile the first time, she struggled to survive with the children. At times, she received help from her family in Canada, but there never seemed to be enough.

After the corn had been harvested in the fall of 1932, the authorities allowed her to glean in the fields. She and her nine-year old son went into the cold and wet fields and came home wet and completely chilled.

The gleaning brought bad consequences. During a winter house search, they found two pud of corn. On January 5, 1933, she was imprisoned in Halbstadt. The trial was held on January 12. She was declared a *kulak* and accused of having stolen corn. The severe sentence: ten years forced labor in the north and five years exile. The children apparently wept bitterly and cried, "We will die and not see mother again."

In prison, the women had to take turns making tea in a large kettle on the yard for the prisoners. On January 25, it was her turn. From that time, she vanished and was never seen again. All the police searches were of no avail. Some said she had died, others asserted that she had joined her husband in exile, still others believed she was in an insane asylum. Was it any wonder? They had taken all she had.

The truth was that she had first fled to the Crimea. She could stay nowhere for long as everyone feared to keep her. For a time, she was in such straits that she wanted to surrender to the police, but a friend dissuaded her.

Amid severe cold, she then fled to the Caucasus. She had no coat or wool jacket, only an old head covering which a sympathetic Russian woman had given her. The Lord safely led her to her family, the G.H. Sukkaus, where she was warmly received. She also found her children here. Sukkaus had got them from the Molotschna. Here, she would soon greet her husband, H. Huebert, when he returned from the first exile.

After her husband had been exiled for the second time, Liese, mother Huebert, and sister Justina moved to Memrik where, at the outbreak of the war in 1941, they were deported to Kazsakhstan with all the other Germans. Mother was eighty years old at the time. What a sad situation!

Mrs. G.J. Thielmann (nee Huebert)
Niagara-on-the-Lake, Ontario

Heinrich T. Janz
Minister and Elder
Landskrone, Molotschna

Heinrich T. Janz was born in Landskrone where his father Tobias Janz lived and operated a farm. His parents belonged to the Mennonite Brethren Church. Here, Heinrich, the youngest of the brothers, received his village school education. Then he studied in the Gnadenfeld High School and afterward attended the pedagogical classes in Neu-Halbstadt. His first teaching position after obtaining his certification was on the estate Taschtschenak, Melitopol district, which belonged to Mr. Cornies. He was a teacher here for two years. Then he went to Sagradowka and became a teacher in the village of Steinfeld.

During this time, he became acquainted with the young lady, Tina Reimer from Schoenau, whom he subsequently married. Six children were born of this union, of which two died as young children.

He then became a teacher in his home village of Landskrone, where he worked for many years (1913-24). For a while, he worked together with the teacher and minister, H. Willms, who later went to Canada and subsequently died on the Namaka settlement. Since his local congregation had elected him as a minister and because he was active in this capacity, he could not be a teacher after 1924. In the schools, the Bolsheviks tolerated no ministers as teachers. They feared any religious influence upon the children and wanted to eliminate it.

In 1928 elder Gerhard Plett of Hierschau was compelled to resign his office for reasons of ill health. At the request of the congregation, he was able to induct his younger colleague, Heinrich T. Janz, into the office of elder. He was able to lead the congregation as shepherd and bishop until 1931. Then the beautiful, almost new church was taken away by the authorities of the Soviet government and turned into a movie theater.

The last baptism in the church in Landskrone was at Pentecost, 1931. Elder H. Janz was able to baptize fifty-six young souls. He served at the marriages of many young people and also preached the funeral sermons for many, including his former elder and predecessor, Gerhard Plett.

On Sunday morning, he preached in the church and in the afternoon participated in the Sunday school, helping the young Sunday school teachers with their preparations. There was a Bible study on Sunday evenings which he usually led.

He especially dedicated himself to the youth and stood by their side during that difficult period. In 1923 his first wife, Tina Reimer, died after a three-day illness which was probably typhus. She left a number of young children behind: the oldest was only eight years of age. It was a sad funeral. An aunt looked after the motherless children until they got a new mother. H. Janz married for a second time, a Tina Ediger from Gnadenfeld. Three children were born to this marriage.

Their stay in Landskrone was not a long one. The ministers could not pay the high extra taxes which the government imposed on them: they simply went bankrupt. Janz and his family moved to the large Russian market town, Gross-Tokmak. That was in 1932.

In Gross-Tokmak, H. Janz became a night-watchman at a government project. The Janz family was very poor. Janz, like all other ministers, was disenfranchised and deprived of his civil rights. As such, he had no right to a job nor could his children attend school. For these reasons, they left and moved to the Caucasus in 1934, where many of our ministers had found refuge. The peace was short-lived. In November 1937, elder Heinrich T. Janz, together with three other brothers, was sentenced to death by a tribunal in the city of Pjatigorsk. The court proceedings lasted a week. Along with them some twenty-eight men were sentenced to longer and shorter periods of forced labor.

His fellow candidates for death were the evangelist Isaak Poetker from Wernersdorf, Johann Koop from Stawropol and Nikolai Reimer. For ninety-nine days, these brethren waited for the execution of their sentence in their death cells.

Finally, thanks to the petitions of their relatives and friends the death sentence was commuted to ten years exile. Janz came to the city of Krasnojarsk in Siberia. The last news from him came from there in March 1939. He wrote a very sad letter to his loved ones. His health was very poor; he could no longer do any hard work; he had received a posting as a watchman. His food ration was totally inadequate for his decimated body, and he suffered from severe malnutrition. He noted that if help was not soon forthcoming he would starve to death. That is the last word which his loved ones received from him.

His wife and his sister-in-law, Mrs. Dietrich Janz, were sent to Kazsakhstan. His son, Erwin, was in the Red army and came into German captivity. Then, he became an interpreter for the German army. In 1944 he managed to visit his aunt in Poland, Mrs. Maria Bergmann, the sister of his father, Heinrich T. Janz. Most of our information comes from her. She came to Germany and then Holland as a refugee from Poland and from there went to the brother of elder H. Janz, Hermann Janz of Detroit, Michigan.

Another son of Heinrich Janz, Peter, lay down on the railway tracks and committed suicide. Earlier, he had been imprisoned for two years, was released, then had to appear before the GPU again and again. Finally, he despaired of life. He had only been married for three weeks. What a sad lot!

Mrs. Gerhard H. Willms, nee Anna Dick of Landskrone and currently in Newton, Kansas, writes the following about her former teacher, H.T. Janz:

My husband and I had the privilege of being his students. He was an outstanding preacher and teacher. During 1921-22 I taught in the Landskroner Dorfschule under his leadership and there learned to appreciate him in a special way.

The author also knew and respected the dear brother and fellow colleague. We worked together for many years in the Molotschna Mennonite Teachers Federation seeking to raise the standards of our schools in the Molotschna. Later, when both of us had been forced out of the schools by the Reds, we worked together preaching the Gospel. One of the last letters I received in Russia before my departure was from brother H. Janz, Landskrone. In it he conveyed the heartfelt greetings of the Molotschna ministerial conference, which consisted of all three [Mennonite] groups, and wished us blessings for our journey to Canada. The ministerial conference was held in Landskrone in May 1926. I was sad not to be there and deliver

112

my assigned address on the Coming of the Lord. Unfortunately, this valuable letter, like so much other material, was lost in the [house] fire of March 29, 1942.

Everything ended so sadly in Siberia! Who would have ever thought it? Our younger fellow workers like Janz, Aron Dueck, Alexander Ediger and others still believed in a better future in the old homeland, while the rest of us had given up all hope and taken up the wanderer's staff. Who can blame them—or us?

"—all from these whom God so inclined, made preparations" (Ezra 1:5), that is what was said of the Jews in the Babylonian captivity. How differently God leads His own. His way is holy!

Johann M. Janzen
Minister
Memrik

Johann Martin Janzen was a minister and during the later years a longtime leader of the Mennonite Brethren church in Memrik, whose church was in Kotljarewka. He had a good education. He had completed the pedagogical classes in Halbstadt, and for many years was a teacher in the village schools of the Mennonite settlement at Memrik. I learned to know him in the summer of 1905 on a vacation trip in the Crimea led by the teacher Wilhelm P. Neufeld. He possessed a buoyant nature and was liked by all. When he became a minister, he completely dedicated himself to his calling. His work was highly esteemed. He was able to serve the church longer than any other minister, because he possessed little property. His turn eventually came, and one day he had to walk the path of sorrow. He was imprisoned and exiled and little can be learned about his further fate. It is obvious that somewhere he was silenced forever. If the evidence is not misleading, he sealed his confession of his Master with the martyr's death.

Supplement

Johann Janzen was born in the Mennonite village of Ebental, later called Nikolajewka, in Memrik, province of

Ekaterinoslaw, south Russia. He spent his childhood and youth here and also received his elementary education.

After this, he became a pupil in the Ohrloff High School in the Molotschna where the outstanding teachers Kornelius Unruh, Johann Braeul and Johann H. Janzen were active from 1899 to 1902. He then went to Neu-Halbstadt where, in a two-year pedagogical program, he completed his qualifications as a teacher. The teachers there were N. Djogtjarow, D.J. Dueck, Wilhelm P. Neufeld, Cornelius Bergmann, and others. In the fall of 1905, he accepted his first teaching position. He taught in a small commerce school on the estate of Mr. Heinrich Sudermann near the station Grischino, province of Ekaterinoslaw.

After two years of teaching, he found his life's partner in sister Martens from Orlowo, Memrik. Then he accepted a teaching position in Herzenberg, where he had the opportunity to participate in the work of the Mennonite Brethren Church. He became the conductor of the church choir and was also asked to help in the proclamation of the Word.

He left this place after two years and came to Barwenkowo in the province of Charkow. He served the Mennonite group here as teacher and minister. His work was a blessing.

During the summer holidays, he stayed in Charkow with his friend, A.H. Dick, and studied mathematics under the well-known teacher, Festa, in order to prepare himself for the private tutor examination. Festa was the son-in-law of the well-known Kharkov teacher, Nikolas Hildebrand.

With the outbreak of WWI, Johann Janzen had to enter [state] service. He was a medical orderly. As such, he made himself most useful and served faithfully.

After the end of the war, he again ministered the congregation at Herzenberg as a teacher until he had to resign for reasons of conscience. He, like so many other teachers, could no longer comply with the demands of godless school officials.

He, then, returned to his home in Memrik and, during this critical time, substantially aided the congregations in the struggle for the defense and self-preservation of the churches in the face of steadily mounting pressures from the Soviet government. He had special gifts and abilities in dealing with officials, and he spoke very good Russian. Through his pleasant manner, he could accomplish things which others could not.

Here in Memrik, he was called to the ministry by his home congregation and ordained by elder Jakob Derksen. After the latter's death, he took over the leadership of the church and effectively worked far beyond the borders of Memrik. In one mission trip, he even came to the Kuban. In the difficult years of affliction, he faithfully served the churches. In spite of all the dangers, denunciations by false brethren, and other difficulties, he stayed with the congregations until 1937.

After returning from a missions trip in the fall of 1937 and after serving at a funeral in Nordheim, Memrik, he was called to account for his actions by the government and exiled to Siberia for ten years. His wife had the opportunity to visit him in exile and brought a photograph back which clearly stands in great contrast to the photograph of his teaching years. All further information is lacking.

A.H. Dick
Winnipeg, Manitoba

Wilhelm W. Janzen

His parents initially lived in the village of Rudnerweide in the Molotschna. He was born there on December 26, 1883. His mother died not long after, and little Wilhelm stayed with his grandparents who lived nearby. Later, when his father remarried, the uncles and aunts cared for him. One uncle, Abram Janzen, became a teacher in Kotljarewka, Memrik and his nephew, Wilhelm, stayed with him until he completed the school there. Meanwhile, his parents had resettled in Neu-Samara.

Wilhelm stayed in Memrik until he married. He loved singing and music and liked to play the violin. After completing school, he was a hired hand in the village for a time. When he was twenty-one years of age, he learned the joiner's trade. He led a quiet withdrawn life and did not mix much with his peers.

Here [in Memrik], he took baptismal instruction and was

baptized and accepted into the congregation by his uncle, elder Peter Janzen of the Memrik Mennonite Church. In the summer of 1908, he and his uncle travelled to Samara to the wedding of his oldest sister. Here, he learned to know his future life's partner, and soon he celebrated his wedding with Katharine Regehr, daughter of Peter Regehr from the village of Podolsk.

One year later, the young people and their parents-in-law moved to the Mennonite settlement of Barnaul in Siberia. Here the young, courageous couple founded their home in the village of Silberfeld. The walls were built of prairie sod and the house had an earthen roof. The necessary wood and lath came from the forest some eighty verst away. A barn and a silo were also built.

Soon, came the evil war and our Wilhelm Janzen had to enter the service. High in northern Siberia, he and many other Mennonites had to cut railway ties in the forest. He remained here until the end of WWI. When the revolution erupted in 1917, he came home.

Before the war, the Mennonite congregation had already elected him as song leader, then deacon, and finally, as minister, though he did not allow himself to be ordained at that time. During his service in the north, he faithfully served his compatriots in the forest with his preaching.

In his home church, it soon became apparent that he did not completely agree with the nature of congregational nurture. He soon left and joined the Mennonite Brethren Church. Here, too, he was offered a ministerial position and soon ordained.

After the mass flight of German colonists to Moscow in the fall of 1929, people were arrested in all colonies and sent into exile. There was a widespread search for the instigators of this movement. They wished to forcibly nip in the bud the desire for foreign lands. Wilhelm Janzen was among these unfortunates. He was especially singled out because he was a minister and the spiritual leader of his people. All his possessions were listed and confiscated on behalf of the Red government. Janzen was first taken to the nearby district capital where he had to shovel snow from the streets and roadways during the winter. The food was very meager, and during the terrible cold they had to sleep in unheated barracks. Then came something even worse. He and his whole family, together with many others, were sent to the Narymskij-Krai in the far north. Amid the bitter winter cold, they had to begin their long journey into the taiga, into Siberia's immense, uninhabitable virgin forests. The small children and the possessions were loaded onto sleighs. All others had to walk the long way on foot, even the older children and the weaker women. Most of the small children froze to death and were buried in the snow enroute.

For a long time, their next of kin heard nothing from them. When the first letter finally arrived, it was clear they were in dire straits and would all starve to death if help did not arrive. Mother and siblings in Russia did what they could, but no package ever arrived. In Russia, there was much theft on both the railways and in the post office, so nothing was safe. Only one package sent from Canada via Germany reached them, but too late. When the children heard that a package from Uncle Peter in Canada was on its way they were overjoyed and said, "Now we will be able to satisfy our hunger." Yet when it arrived, they had died of starvation. The mother wrote that it might save the father who was so weak that he could only sit up long enough to eat. After that, nothing more was heard from them. According to information from other exiles, the entire family perished.

Their home was a hole in the ground with an earthen roof. On the one end, there was an opening for a window, on the other, a hole which served as an opening for a door. That was in the year 1931.

His brother, Peter W. Janzen of Springstein, Manitoba adds, "His first wife died in 1924 from typhus. Then the Lord gave him and his five orphaned children a new mother in the person of the widow, Eva Teichgroeb, who had one daughter. She shared his and the children's suffering in exile until she too died of starvation."

Abram A. Klassen
Last Elder of the Mennonite Church
in Neu-Halbstadt, Molotschna

He was born in Gnadenfeld and had high school education. He was also a graduate of the Barmen Missions School in

Barmen, Germany. For a time, he was a teacher and in 1910 became a salaried minister of the Gnadenfeld affiliate [churches] in the Crimea: Ogus-Tobe and Sarona. In the Crimea, he was also a sometime member of the school board. He had been a minister since 1895. His wife was born a Rempel from Gnadenfeld or perhaps Ogus-Tobe. He had an excellent education and was widely read. He was invited to become a teacher at the Gnadenfeld High School where he taught religion and German in the pedagogical classes. Occasionally, he served the Mennonite church in Neu-Halbstadt with his rather learned sermons.

When elder Heinrich Unruh had to resign from his position because of his advanced age and ill health, the teacher Abram A. Klassen became his successor. Those who knew him well said that he was an upright, faithful servant of his congregation. Fearless as a steadfast witness, he stood in his place and did not budge even when bandits flooded into Halbstadt.

His brother-in-law, Rempel from California, secured a free passage to America for him. He, nevertheless, told his congregational members that God had showed him his post here [in Russia]. He advised other families with small children to emigrate forthwith. He could not see well for his eyesight was poor. Even with glasses, he was shortsighted. He was almost blind at the end of his life.

When he could no longer fulfill his official duties because the communists made any spiritual nurture of the churches impossible, he moved to Melitopol on the Molotschna River, the district capital. Other church workers had found refuge here before him, like the teacher Kornelius Bergmann, the minister Johann Peters, and others. He had to experience many a difficulty in his old days, but this only brought him closer to his Lord. He was able to stay in the city for a considerable time.

One day when he was very ill, he was exiled. Because he was too sick to walk, the brutal Soviet police placed him on a truck, and so he was taken into exile. Mrs. Klassen was also with him. Elder Klassen died enroute. Recently, information has come to America that Mrs. Klassen and her son-in-law are still living in exile. Their adopted daughter fled to Germany and with her daughter is living in the American zone.

People complained that, because of his learned language,

the sermons of elder A. Klassen were often above the heads of his listeners. He used many foreign words in his sermons. I can remember an incident in a Bible study where elder Klassen was working together with a number of others. Again, there were so many foreign words which ordinary mortals did not understand. In all seriousness, one of the participants commented that he thought he was at a Bible study but did not know whether he should bring a Bible or a foreign language dictionary in the afternoon. This bothered elder A. Klassen, and he tried to speak and preach more simply, but it wasn't always easy for him. His piety, integrity, and God-fearing life preached louder than his learned words.

Elder Klassen had to seal his tested faith with a martyr's death. Praise and glory to God! Marie P. Isaak was the adopted daughter of elder Klassen and his wife. She married David Friesen who, with his son, is also in exile. Mrs. Friesen writes that she received her last letter from her husband via Canada a year ago (1946). He was in exile in Narim in northern Russia. The wife of elder Klassen was there as well. The letter contained the news that elder Abram Klassen died in a railway cattle car enroute to exile. Where is he buried? God alone knows. That was in 1943.

Since David Friesen had contacted pneumonia when the letter was written, and since Mrs. Klassen was ill as well, it can be assumed with certainty that both have died. All letters remained unanswered. The mother of David Friesen is still concerned about the fate of her son. She is waiting for an opportunity to come to Canada. Her brother, Johann P. Isaak lives in Glenbush, Saskatchewn.

Abram J. Klassen
Minister
Spat, Crimea

Abram J. Klassen was born on December 3, 1884 in Ohrloff, Taurida, south Russia. He was the son of Jakob P. Klassen and his wife Agnes, daughter of elder Abram H. Goerz, Ohrloff.

In 1893 his parents moved to Spat in the Crimea where

they had purchased a farm. A. Klassen attended the village school in Spat, and after its completion went to the Ohrloff High School where he finished the program in three years.

His God-given mental ability was well above average and he was truly an educated man. In the development of his character, the influence of his mother, who was a Christian of strong faith, was stronger than that of the schools and private instruction. She raised her children with hands outstretched in prayer and through exemplary Christian living.

His father died in 1902. Abram, as the eldest son, carried on the farm for his widowed mother and helped her raise three younger brothers and a sister. The responsibility and leadership which burdened him in his younger years helped to strengthen his character and prepared and fortified him for his struggle of faith.

In October 1903 his mother married a second time and so became less dependent upon Abram. He prepared for the teacher's examination by self-study and private instruction. For two years (1904-06?), he was a teacher in the village of Ebenfeld, district of Nowo-Usensk in Samara. He won the love of the students, the respect of youth, and the recognition of the adults and the entire community. He was remembered by all in Ebenfeld.

Then he had to fulfill state service at the Alt-Berdyansk Forestry. He held the position of a meteorologist.

In October 1910, he married Agnes A. Esau of Spat. With his young wife, he went to Barwenkowo for approximately a year to learn business in Froese's store. Then he opened his own business and commission agency in Spat which did well.

Soon after the outbreak of WWI, he was drafted and served as a medic, first in Simferopol, then in a sanatorium in Szaki, a cure resort in the Crimea.

After the war, he was elected as minister by his home congregation in Spat and ordained. He was also elected as a representative of the Crimean Churches in the Commission for Ecclesiastical Affairs.

When he was in the army medical service, he had to liquidate his business and suffered a great loss. He became a farmer. The revolution and civil war brought him, as well as many others, into financial ruin.

During Pentecost 1925, he was visited by his brother, Peter who had succeeded Abram as teacher in Ebenfeld and worked there for eight years. The Ebenfeld Church had called Peter as their minister. The brothers had not seen each other for nine years. Peter came to say goodbye for he was in the process of emigrating to either Mexico or Canada—wherever God might lead him. Peter wanted to persuade Abram to set out and seek a new homeland. In Russia, the Mennonites faced destruction and oblivion. Abram recognized this but believed he still had to fulfill a great and difficult task.

Responding to Peter's pleading and pressure at their last farewell Abram said:

Don't try to dissuade me. You must leave. The quicker you leave the better. I fear you will not cross the border for the GPU has had you on the blacklist for a long time. You have been a help and blessing to thousands of your suffering fellow human beings. You worked and struggled for your neighbor as long as you could. The Red authorities and the GPU know of you from the Urals to Moscow. Your public efforts and work on behalf of the churches and the Germans along the Volga is a thorn in their eye. If you do not vanish from the scene voluntarily, the GPU will make sure you suddenly disappear. Your role in Russia is finished. Now go while you still can!

My situation is quite different. My role in Russia is not complete, my work here not done. In fact, it is about to begin. My congregation needs me more than ever before. Should I cast my gun into the trench and flee in panic the moment when the enemy heralds the attack?

If I left the church now, you, I, myself, and everyone would despise me—and first of all my Lord and Master. I will remain at my post until my Master allows me to leave or I fall in battle for my Master. I will not throw down my banner.

Abram spoke with holy fervor, his eyes burning with noble fire and conviction. Deeply moved and shaken, Peter took his hand and pressed it firmly and warmly. "You are right, brother! Blessed is the man so occupied when his Master and General comes. God help you to complete the good fight."

The two brothers parted, never to see each other again upon this earth.

The struggle for Abram J. Klassen and his fellow minister

J.J. Wiebe from Minlartschik, Crimea began in January, 1926. Just as they were professional colleagues, they now became fellow sufferers and fellow combatants. Until Wiebe's exile shortly before Klassen's death, they experienced everything together.

They were faced with a choice: to voluntarily renounce their ministerial positions and cease all activity, thereby retaining their civil rights, or continue their work and be stripped of their rights and all possibility of making a livelihood. Abram wrote to Peter who had come to Canada in October 1925: "I will remain at my post until I hear the General say, 'Go, your work is done.'"

In November 1926 Abram wrote, "I travelled in the Crimea as a minister for one month and served all whom I could reach with the Word." The official and congregational work became more and more difficult until Abram reported on October 28, 1928:

> I and the minister J.J. Wiebe spent thirty-two days in the Simferopol prison of the GPU, because we defended forty-four young Mennonites before the authorities. In our home library you read the book, *The Spanish Inquisition.* What I suffered in comparison with that—well" the half has never been told." (A reference to a well-known Mennonite hymn: *Mir ward die Hälfte nie gesagt.*) Now my role here is finished! I have done what I could and not I nor anyone else can do more. Now I can leave, only time will tell if I really will be able to do so. If possible, get an entry visa for us.

Letter of October 5, 1929

> Thank you, dear brother. The entry visas and the tickets have arrived at *Ruskapa* here in Moscow, but I cannot leave for I am once again a guest of the GPU. Because they know I will not break my word, they have made me promise that I will not flee and have released me until my case comes to trial. What a contradiction! It defies every description. One is accused of the greatest crimes, punishable by death according to the law, yet they know they can believe and trust my word and I am allowed to go free! I can stay at home with my loved ones and only have to report to the GPU in Simferopol twice a week. According to the GPU records, I am in prison. I wonder who is pocketing the cost of my room and board! That is how things are done here.

On October 14, 1929, Abram reports extensively on the flight to Moscow: "A wild panic seized all Germans . . . . My situation is one of despair and desperation!"

The exact dates when he was again imprisoned are missing. According to later reports, what he and the minister J.J. Wiebe endured defied all description. They were accused of being the instigators of the "flight to Moscow." Klassen was interrogated without a break between twelve and nineteen hours a day. After inhuman punishments and threats came the tempting offer:

> Deny God! Admit openly that you preached a God to the stupid peasants who does not exist, so that the church could control and exploit their stupidity. If you admit this, we will give you your exit visas and enough money so that you and your family can go abroad immediately. We don't care a damn about you. You can do what you like over there but here we are concerned that your influence is too widespread and strong. If you didn't incite them, the stupid farmers would soon be convinced [to stay].

Klassen later wrote from exile that if he had publicly denied God the GPU would certainly have allowed him to go abroad. The minister Abram Klassen remained true to his God and was not a deserter. He, J.J. Wiebe, and three other fellow sufferers were sentenced to death.

On April 6, 1930, Hans Klassen reported that Abram had been sentenced to ten years exile in the high north. (I am not certain why and when or who commuted the death sentence.)

On February 2, 1930, while A. Klassen was in prison in Simferopol, his wife and children were sitting at a sparse dinner meal— poor fare was already the order of the day. Suddenly, a wild horde of GPU thugs burst into the house and chased Mrs. Klassen and her children out of the house with only the clothes on their back. They destroyed or stole everything which the family still had. Mrs. Klassen grabbed a blanket in which she wrapped her youngest son and took half a loaf of bread from the table. Now she stood on the street without sustenance and homeless, at the mercy of cold and hunger, apparently forgotten by men and God. Those who sheltered such banished and exiled persons were driven out and despoiled themselves. With no regard [for his personal safety], Hans Klassen gave shelter to his brother Abram's family.

On April 24, 1930, twenty-four Mennonite families from Spat were taken to Simferopol in order to be sent to the high north as dangerous *kulak* elements. Mrs. Klassen and her children were among these. Two days later, eight long trains filled with exiles departed for the arctic. When the eight trains had left, four Mennonite families, whose names had not been called during the loading of the exiles, stayed behind. Mrs. Klassen and her children had also remained. No one knew who had caused these families to be left behind, possibly a secret friend in the GPU.

These now received their citizenship papers and the right to collect their scattered belongings insofar as they could find them. More than half had vanished and could not be retrieved. Mrs. Klassen was also allowed to move back into her house. In the weeks following his exile sentence, Mrs. Klassen and the oldest children were able to visit A. Klassen for a few minutes and bring him food on several occasions. They hardly recognized their husband and father for he had suffered terribly.

A. Klassen's only letter [from exile] is to his brother in Canada:

> June 8, 1930 . . . I have been here in exile since May 14. When I was being sent away Agnes (his wife), Olga, and Hans were standing on the platform. I did not see my younger children again . . . .
>
> My feet and legs look like fence posts. I am ill and tired and cannot sleep in spite of hard physical labor. The nerves want to give way. During the past two years, I have had to suffer a great deal. The last seven months were indescribably painful and difficult.
>
> Today is Pentecost Sunday. I read Jeremiah 29 and 30 and Acts 2 for myself. Thank God, I still have my Bible. But tears cloud my vision and a lack of faith in God threatens hope and courage. And yet with God's help and assistance, we will also be able to bear this.
>
> My comfort: I am innocent!
>
> Help my family. Don't write to me directly. Agnes will send me your letters. I am not allowed to write from here. This letter is coming to you in a roundabout way. Adieu!

As circumstances allowed, food parcels were sent to A. Klassen from both Canada and Spat. On August 10, 1930, his wife reported, "Abram was already swollen from hunger before the first food parcel reached him. Richer and better food improved his health and made him stronger."

For months, there were no further reports from Russia. Finally, some news arrived. A. Klassen was somewhat better and his health improved. For some five months he worked in an office in the Archangelsk region near the village of Yerestnaja.

Separation from his home and family, deprivation, overexertion, and the raw climate quickly undermined his health. He had a very responsible position, for he held the keys to the money chest and kept the account books. His superiors trusted him completely. He was respected and beloved by everyone. The local population called him "little father" or "pastor."

As his illness intensified, his friend in struggle and suffering, J.J. Wiebe, visited him and comforted him. Klassen suffered two strokes. He recovered from the first one and the doctors gave him some hope that his bad cough would dissipate by spring. After his second stroke the minister J.J. Wiebe was sent to [?]. That affected Klassen severely, and he deteriorated rapidly and was brought to a hospital near Sibulon. In order to save him, the doctors, hospital personnel and authorities gave him food from their meager rations and paid for his medicine. Seriously ill, he lay in the hospital for one month.

Another fellow sufferer, Federau, wrote to Klassen's wife saying that if she wanted to see her husband alive she should come as soon as possible.

A train from the south steams in the direction of Archangelsk. Mrs. Klassen and her oldest son, Hans, are sitting in a third-class coach. All their thoughts and words revolve about the dying husband and father. Federau's letter had caused her to undertake the long, difficult and expensive journey. The train travels too slowly! Why, its barely crawling along. The station stops are endlessly long. "God, don't let us arrive too late! Let us see him while he is still alive," mother and son pray. They could get there in another three days, but the train travels so slowly and the way is so long!

On July 3, 1931 the doctors diagnosed A. Klassen's condition as hopeless. In the morning, he was transferred to the house for the dying in the virgin forest and laid upon the hard straw mattress. The house for the dying has no beds, only a platform made of thick planks and a block of wood instead of a table. Instead of a mattress, there is only a bit of half-rotted straw—there is no thought of a pillow and blanket. Those "who were breathing their last during Stalin's First Five Year Plan" did not deserve this. Here, there was no service and care. Here, one simply died!

No one stayed with the dying A. Klassen, no one gave him a drink of cold water, no one cooled his feverish brow. His fellow sufferer, Federau, checks on him from time to time, but usually finds him unconscious. He remained in that condition on July 4 and until noon on July 5, when Federau saw him alive for the last time.

In the lonely house for the dying in the primeval forest, A. Klassen is fighting his last battle. No! The battle is finished. Victory has been won. There is no dying, he has gone home to the Father.

At three o'clock in the afternoon, Federau again comes to visit his dying friend. He is sleeping softly and looks twenty years younger. Federau calls his name but receives no answer. Then he realizes that Klassen is dead.

Federau announces Klassen's death to the camp administrator and is ordered to bury Klassen. He digs the grave together with two Russian fellow prisoners. By eight o'clock in the evening a new grave mound arches in the cemetery at Sibulon near Yeretzkaja.

They buried A. Klassen far from his home, without a coffin and without a song or a prayer or a funeral sermon. It seemed he was a shovel full of dung in "Stalin's First Five Year Plan."

No! And again no! They did not bury A. Klassen—his perishable body, but not his soul and spirit. Abram Klassen's original "I," his soul and spirit, emerged as victor over Stalin, death, hell, and the devil!

Abram Klassen fought a good fight, he kept the faith, he

finished his course and, henceforth, there is for him the crown of righteousness!

Whoever dies in this manner dies well!

Mrs. Klassen and her son reached Yeretzkaja on July 7 and asked the way to Sibulon. When they passed the cemetery they saw two new graves. "Is he already under the mound?" In camp they were told, "A. Klassen died and was buried two days ago."

With the cry "Too late! Why so, my God?" Mrs. Klassen collapses. Lovingly the exiles care for her. "She is the wife of our little father Abram Jakovich and that is her son," the exiles whisper to one another. They try to help and comfort as best they can. "He was our pastor and a friend to all of us."

His wife and son kneel at the grave and cannot comprehend or understand why God leads them in such difficult ways.

After a long, difficult and frustrating return trip, they finally arrive at home. Life has lost its worth, content, and attraction for those left behind. In their quarrel with God they have only one question, "Why? Why us?" (from Mrs. Klassen's letter).

Only after some weeks did they begin to sort through the few belongings of the dear departed which the camp administration—an exception!—had returned. They wanted to preserve anything which might serve as a reminder of the loved one. They found his diary.

This proved a true source of comfort for them. The dear husband and father knew what was coming well in advance and tried to prepare his wife and children for the path they might walk so that they should not despair. Again and again, he came back to the words:

> For I know the thoughts I think concerning you, says the Lord, thoughts of peace and not of hurt, to give you a future and a hope. Then you will call upon Me and will come to pray to Me, and I will hear you. You will seek Me and find Me when you will seek Me with all your heart. Jeremiah 29:11-13

An inner calm returned and they could say, as did their dearly departed one, "If God wills I will remain silent." Their struggle for survival and their struggle against the evils of the

Red hell continued. It was incredibly difficult, yet they bravely held their stance. Their holy and lofty motto remained "As God wills."

Since 1935 there has been no further word from the family of Abram and Hans Klassen. Their subsequent fate is completely unknown.

P.J. Klassen
Superb, Saskatchewan

Abraham A. Konrad
Minister
Fuerstental, Suworowka
Province of Stawropol, North Caucasus

A.A. Konrad, son of Abraham J. and Katharina (nee Braun) Konrad, was born on June 6, 1898 in Alexanderkrone, Molotschna. He spent his childhood and youth here until he reached the age of sixteen. After he graduated from village school, he attended the business school [in Alexanderkrone]. He was converted to the Lord at age fourteen and constantly tried to live a God-fearing life. Just before the outbreak of WWI in 1914, his parents moved to the Kalantarowka settlement, province of Stawropol, North Caucasus. In 1918 he was baptized upon confession of faith and accepted into the local Mennonite Brethren church. Here, he was elected as a minister. In October 1918, his father was shot in his own home. In 1922 he married Eva, the daughter of Johann Epp, Suworowka. In 1925 they moved to a farm in the village of Fuerstental, Suworowka, where he was ordained in 1927 and elected as leader of the congregation.

In 1929 when the movement to Canada via Moscow began, he first travelled to Moscow without the family. He then returned to collect his family and emigrate. When he arrived home, he was arrested at the railway station by the GPU and imprisoned, probably in Pgatigorsk. He remained there several months before the trial. He was exiled for three years to an island in the White Sea near Murmansk in Russia's far north. He had to work in the virgin forests. Both food and clothing were poor and inadequate. He lost his toes through frost, yet bore his suffering in steadfast faith in God and encouraged his wife to bravely endure until they were reunited. The Lord granted them special grace. After two years, he was released and his sentence altered so that he could spend the last year in the south near the city of Saratow where he worked in a collective farm and was allowed to bring his family with him.

I will allow brief excerpts from his letters to speak for themselves.

He writes in November 1932:

> The family is with me. We have rather good accommodation, but I do fear the winter. I don't know what will happen. We cannot stay here. In the spring, we would like to return to our loved ones in the south, but we don't know where to go. We are homeless.

His wife writes:

> After many difficult days and years, we have finally had the joy of seeing each other again. It was such happiness, yet we still have the longing to be among children of God. The people here are very godless. No song, no fellowship gladdens our hearts. Abraham, who has lived in these circumstances for three years, would love to go back home. We have to set our hope upon Him who has cared for us so far. We beg you, if possible, to send us something. It is very difficult to beg. We cannot describe how difficult our situation is. We are tired of life and do not believe that there will be any more happiness for us in this life. But we want to trust God and await His salvation.

In 1933 they could go south. They were accepted on a collective farm in the village of Neu-Hoffnung in the Konosawod settlement, Stawropol province, north Caucasus. A few excerpts from letters:

The brother writes in April 1933:

> We are, thank God, alive and well. In February we received a parcel from you. Many thanks. If we were to describe our situation, it would be sad indeed, only a lamentation and begging.

July 1933:

The situation is such that during the period of heavy labor we have to do our work but don't get enough to eat. The most essential thing, bread, does not suffice. I operate a binder and am so weak that I can hardly manage. We are short of everything: no money; our clothes are worn out, no shelter and, on top of that, we are unable to satisfy our hunger. We are completely dependent on the help we receive from abroad.

February 1934:

We can say that this year things are not as difficult. Thank God we are not starving now. We were able to build an earth hut one and one-quarter meters into the ground. If compassionate hearts and generous hands had not helped us, we would have perished from hunger and poverty. I don't want to complain but must confess that we go about in rags. Oh how much calamity and suffering there is in our land! . . . . We are exhausted and tired of life. On Sunday we hope to celebrate communion as a small group in the neighboring village. That should revitalize us and give us courage and strength to further walk our pathway of faith. We have four children: three boys and one girl.

May 1935:

Nothing much has changed. There is no question of being out of work. There is more work than of anything else. We are eating bread but have to add corn flour to it.

His wife writes:

We are so concerned about what will happen to our children. The Word of God is not communicated to them; no services, no prayer meetings, no Bible studies, and no singing. They are indoctrinated with all that is worldly and godless. It is sad to have to write about it, but much sadder to experience it. I often think how easily it could be our turn to leave this life. One would like to be reunited with the entire family over there, where there is an end to all suffering. I also want to inform you that our dear parents (Johann Epp) and brother, David, with wife and children are again in exile.

So much of the report of the letter. The final report came via a communication from a sister, Katharina Regehr, who has recently come over. During the retreat of the Russian army, she was imprisoned and, therefore, not at home when all the

Germans of the region were evacuated to Kazakhstan in Asiatic Russia. She reports the following of brother A.A. Konrad:

> One day in 1937 the police came on the yard and arrested him. He was ordered to go to the truck which stood on the street. He is said to have cried like a child for he could not endure all the hardships once again. He had to say goodbye to his wife and children and amid tears was pushed to the truck and loaded onto it. Nothing more was heard of him. In 1941 his wife and children were sent to Kazakhstan together with all the others.

Johann Loewen
Friedensfeld, Province of Jekaterinoslaw, South Russia
Poet and Conductor

Johann Loewen came from the Jasykowo settlement. At the age of fifteen, he moved to Friedensfeld with his parents. During a period of revival led by the minister Christian Schmidt from the Kuban, he and many others were converted to the Lord. Following baptism, he became a member of the Mennonite Brethren Church.

At age twenty-one he entered state service and spent four years in the Anadol forestry. He was already poetically gifted in his younger years and composed many a fine poem. Some of his poems were later collected and printed. In the forestry service, he became friends with Heinrich Unruh who later became a missionary to India.

Soon after his service, he married the neighbor's daughter, Anna Friesen. The young couple moved to the Nepljujewo settlement, No. 1. Here they leased a farm. Johann Loewen founded a church choir here, which he led as conductor for twenty years. He was also a teacher in the Sunday school and worked with the young people.

When the revolution broke out after WWI, the neighboring Russians came and took our leased farms away. We had to move back to our home village of Friedensdorf. Things did not remain calm here either and bandits roamed about engaging in their activities. My husband fortunately escaped with his life.

131

There was a brief period of calm. During this time, my husband was again a teacher in the Sunday school and choir conductor. He was elected as district conductor and, as such, he visited the congregations and had to arrange practice sessions and song festivals with the singers and conductors. He was completely in his element. This lovely time soon came to a close. The church building was taken away from our congregation. Not long after, the services, which were held in homes, were also prohibited.

When the emigration began, my husband procured exit visas for others, yet when our turn came they were no longer available. We also did not join the group which fled via Moscow in 1929. We could not obtain tickets to Moscow. So by God's decree, we stayed in Russia.

Now the state farms were established and my husband got a position as gardener. Many *kulaks* were deported at this time, and only my husband remained of all the former farmers. The leader of the collective farm, a party man, tried everything to get rid of my husband. Three times he succeeded in getting my husband imprisoned in Nikopol, but because he was useful to the government, the court freed him each time. He had, after all, planted a large vineyard which brought the farm thousands of rubles. The enemy did not rest, however, and one night in June 1937, the GPU agents came into the house and in half an hour he was gone. Again, he came to the prison in Nikopol, but this time forever.

Soon, thereafter, our son went to bring him clothes and food but could gain no access. He was able to see his father and speak with him a week later. Father looked very pale and exhausted. During the next six weeks, they also arrested the son. On another occasion, he was visited by our daughter-in-law and our grandson, aged fourteen. After four years, this lad too was a prisoner. The same thing happened to our son-in-law.

When the daughter-in-law, Anna, went to visit her husband, father-in-law, and brother-in-law several weeks later, all three had vanished. They had been sent away, but no one knew where. Now fifteen years have passed, and we have not been able to learn what happened to them. I don't think my husband is still alive, for he was already sixty-six years of age at the time. In earlier times, he was a healthy, strong man, but during the last years his health was severely undermined, especially during his three imprisonments and the excruciating, painful interrogations connected with them. When, for example, he returned home from his second imprisonment, he was as pale as death. All he said to me was, "Now I understand the expression 'Oh hell, Oh hell, now I know you.'" My comfort is that my husband kept the faith all those years. In his farewell letter he wrote:

My dear Lena, my faithful life's partner: Why did such a hard blow, like none before, have to strike us? I have accepted my fate and have only one request of you, my dearest, and of you children. Don't take it too hard. Accept it as coming from God's hand and comfort yourself [with the thought] that we shall see each other again in heaven, to where I'm bound in steadfast faith.

To the daughter-in-law he wrote: "Dear Anna, look after mother when she is sick and weak. God will reward you!" Then he added: "Dear, poor Anna, how I have prayed for you and for you all. Do not despair. God will help. And you my dear Abram, be a faithful and good son to your helpless mother." The last words were: "I am in good spirits."

I received this letter, this last news from my husband, in the most wondrous way. He had wrapped this letter in a piece of bread and sent it to me with some other things. The prison warden did not notice it. God's ways are so wonderful. I and several others are here in Canada and the others are suffering in exile.

Mrs. Anna Loewen (nee Friesen)

Johann Martens
Elder
Einlage, Old Colony

In 1929 the dekulakization of the peasantry began in Russia. Since my father was one of these, sequential assessments were levied on him, each higher than the previous one. He made these payments as long as he could. One day he could no longer pay the assessed sum. Trying to raise the amount was useless since he would be exiled one way or another. The congregation, in order to avoid self-recrimination, rallied and paid the sum. It was useless. Not long after, in 1929, my parents were expelled from their home. In 1930 the parents and both my siblings, together with many others, were exiled to the Urals. Since I had a curvature of the spine and could not work, I was allowed to stay with my stepbrothers and sisters, because they had a name other than Martens. After a difficult ten-day journey, they arrived in the Ural Mountains near the city of Bagoslow not far from Swerdlowsk.

There they struggled for a livelihood in the vast virgin forests. Those of us who remained behind tried to supply our parents with parcels as best we could. Since a package came from abroad now and then, the government felt it prudent to send them to another location in order to lose track of them. They had to work very hard. My siblings had to fell trees. My sister, who was fifteen, rubbed her shoulder raw carrying logs. Father had to unload sacks for a time. Since the food was very scarce and his night shelter under an upturned boat was a very wretched one, he almost died. Thanks to the Lord's leading, he was able to get easier work herding horses in the forest. Since he suffered from heart and kidney ailments and the forest was damp and swampy, he could not do this for long. His legs became swollen from the wet and the cold.

He was finally able to see a doctor, but since the doctor was forbidden to declare people sick when they were really sick, this proved to be a difficult situation. The Lord wonderfully intervened and the doctor gave father a certificate stipulating that he could not remain in his present job under any circumstances. He became a bookkeeper in the camp office.

We repeatedly tried to intercede on behalf of the parents. We collected signatures, wrote to Moscow and Kiev, but all to no avail. My mother, who did not have to work, had to walk twenty kilometers to collect food supplies. One day, when she was carrying ten pounds of potatoes, she found that she could not take the sack from her shoulders since there was no one to help her put it back on. She rested by simply leaning against a tree. When she came home and put down her burden, she felt a jolt along her spine and soon after a paralysis of the right side of her entire body began. My parents had to live under the most difficult circumstances for five years. It became clear that my mother was quite incapacitated and that my father was aging. One day, they were informed that they were free to return home. Only my brother had to remain behind and is still there today. My sister escaped after eight months in exile.

My parents returned in 1936 but no longer had a home. Good friends lent them 3,000 rubles and so, they were able to purchase one half of a house.

My father did not shy away from doing any job. He did any available work during the day, and at night he was a watchman in the horsebarn of the collective farm. Since my mother was helpless, I unfit, and my sister working, father also had to do a great deal of work in the household. Every month we took a portion of everyone's earnings in order to pay off the house [loan]. It was a difficult livelihood, since the money had to be divided between living expenses and debt retirement.

The year 1938 was a very eventful one for us. My father, two brothers, and a brother-in-law were taken by the GPU on the same day. At the time, when my parents were sent to the Urals, one brother was married and the other in the Red army. For a while, the prisoners were incarcerated in Zaporozhye. We could not speak with them nor leave anything for them. We could only ask if they were still there, and we went to ask again and again. We were filled with anxiety for some people had received the answer, "He has died." One day, we got word that they had been exiled to the far north. Since then, we have heard nothing more from them. Every inquiry has proved useless. In ten years, we have found no trace of them.

We are thankful to God that He has led so wonderfully and given us a home here in the Chaco. Mother and I live with my married sister who fled earlier from the Urals. Thank God, her husband is with her.

Kaethe Martens, daughter.

Supplement
Elder Johann Martens was born on June 7, 1875. After completing village school he attended the Chortitza High

School and also took the teacher training course there. Then he attained his teaching certificate for elementary school and was a teacher for thirteen years. In 1917 he was elected as a minister but did not accept the position immediately, for at that time he was the district head in the Chortitza Volost. When the Makhno bands came somewhat later and wanted to execute him, he fled on foot to Neuendorf during the night. During that episode, he promised God that if He would save him, he would accept the call [to the ministry]. This happened not long afterwards. In 1924 Johann Martens was elected as elder of the Schoenwiese congregation. In 1927 two of his married daughters emigrated to Canada. He could not emigrate because of his crippled daughter.

D. and A. Wiebe
Gardenton, Manitoba

Kornelius K. Martens
Teacher and Minister
Member of the Commission for Church Affairs

Some sixty years ago in the town of Spat, not far from the city of Simferopol, my grandfather Kornelius Martens and his wife Helene (nee Wolf) had joined the newly established Mennonite community as settlers. They had previously lived in Wernersdorf near the Molotschna. Here their eldest son, my father, Kornelius Martens, was born on November 18, 1880. When he was five years old, my grandfather was killed by a young horse, shortly before the birth of my Uncle Abram. My grandmother continued to manage the farm. She married a second time when my father was thirteen years old and then moved to Margenau.

My father, who was very gifted, attended village school which, thanks to his teacher, he successfully completed. With financial support from a Mr. Heese, he was able to attend the Gnadenfeld High School. Since the family was large—there were seventeen thanks to the two marriages of my grandmother—father worked on the land during the summer months in order to earn money for his studies. Later, he came

136

to Halbstadt and completed his teaching training course. The most gifted and diligent students, Benjamin Unruh, who presently lives in Karlsruhe as Professor Unruh, and my father were granted scholarships to study in Germany. My grandmother opposed this plan, being of the opinion that the wisdom of this world would not be good [for her son] and could lead to pride. Thereupon, my father took his teacher's exam and went to Samara as a village school teacher. Later, he was active in Alexanderpol in the Don Basin. Here, he married Sara, the daughter of Julius Friesen, on July 27, 1903. He served as minister of the Mennonite church in that locality and extended himself on its behalf with little regard for himself or his position. In 1911 he suffered from bronchial laryngitis (Kehlkopfkatarrh) which later became chronic and forced him to temporarily give up teaching. In order to obtain a cure, he resettled his family of six in Petersburg where he was active in the book firm "Raduga." In the meantime, he completed his secondary education, and in 1915 returned south to become the director of the Gnadenfeld School of Commerce. Now he had the opportunity to dedicate himself to the welfare of the German population and especially the Mennonites. Then came the October revolution. I still remember the evening when father read about the uprisings in St. Petersburg and thanked God that we had left there and did not have to suffer hunger and cold. During the winter evenings father played with us children and told us the old sagas of our [German] peoplehood. In the spring and summer, he walked through the woods and fields with us to observe nature and to gaze at the stars.

Now the revolution with its destructive aftermath also enveloped us. A difficult period began during which the authorities oppressed us day after day. Village government passed from one hand to the other. One day, another group came, surrounded our school, and arrested my father and the teacher Rempel, because they had supported their [female] colleague, the daughter of Dietrich Rempel. They were to be shot on the yard where everyone had assembled. The cleaning lady was pleading for mercy, we children were crying, and father, with bound hands was bidding adieu to mother. Teacher Rempel was already standing against the fence awaiting execution when they unexpectedly began to negotiate with him. In exchange for warm underwear and a promise not to mix in other affairs, their lives were spared and they were released.

During the summer, my father worked in the district office. One day, he was taken to Tchernigowka as a hostage ostensibly for failing to deliver weapons. I can still remember the parting hour. My father stood before my mother who, sobbing, had sank upon the sofa. He asked her, "Shall I give up [working] for the good of the people? Then my family can have me completely." "No," Mother replied between sobs, "I can't keep you from what God has called you to do. The Lord will not leave our family in the lurch!" I cannot remember any other details. I only know that father returned after several weeks and gave himself to faithful service to his Lord. Every Saturday, he prepared himself for the Sunday sermon in Sparrau or Grossweide, where he went to preach every Sunday.

In 1922 my father was dismissed from his teaching position because of his religious convictions. On January 6, 1922, we left Gnadenfeld and moved to Grossweide. Undaunted he continued to work for his people, especially now that he had more time and opportunity.

In springtime, he participated in the division of the land. As a land surveyor, he was in demand everywhere in order to clarify the thorny issues connected with this process. When young Mennnite men were called into military service, he often defended their interests before the courts. As an official of the General Conference in Melitopol, he, together with elder Abram Klassen of Halbstadt, Aron Dyck of Marganau, Alexander Ediger, and many others, struggled for the welfare of the Mennonite people. At that time, the Commission for Ecclesiastical Affairs was also founded, which he and the three previously mentioned men headed. My father was treasurer for its publication, the Mennonite periodical *Unser Blatt.*

Often when we worked in the fields, we could see my father on his horse on the hillside. He was riding in the direction of Sparrau in order to attend a conference or the meeting of the Commission for Ecclesiastical Affairs in Margenau. A difficult period began for my father when he was taken as a hostage by the GPU in connection with an affair related to the commission. Since they could not find him guilty of any crime, he was released. He was repeatedly called in and asked to become an agent for the GPU. As a reward, he was promised a position as a "Red Professor." When he declined, he was dismissed with the remark that he would pay dearly for his refusal.

Then came the time of emigration. We, too, wanted to leave in order to avoid the steadily increasing pressure, but we were not granted an exit permit. "It is the Lord's way, he still needs me here," father declared. . . . Since my mother had a heart condition (Herzasthma), as a result of a typhus illness in 1921, and her condition became worse year by year, my father thought it best to remain. On a sultry summer's day on July 27, 1928, my parents celebrated their silver wedding in the Grossweide Church. The speakers, Alexander Ediger and Aron Dyck, expressed the best wishes of the congregation.

The introduction of collectivization brought a new wave of sorrow and unrest. We children were allowed to join while our parents were not. Over a period of time, our land quota had been reduced to sixteen *dessiatines*. In 1929 many large landowners were declared *kulaks*. We, on the other hand, were forbidden to sell our land and in the fall special taxes in the form of grain requisitions were levied upon us. We paid the levy within a week. Fourteen days later, we were given a double assessment. Father sold two cows, and during the night drove to the adjoining villages in order to buy the required grain. Consequently, this levy could also be paid. A week had barely passed when, in order to ruin us, they demanded a threefold levy. When my father realized this, he did not try to pay the assessment. Hence, our entire possessions were to be auctioned on November 27. Everything had already been placed on the yard when the order came that no auction was to be held. Everything was returned to its place and father said, "Thank God for one more Sunday under our own roof." Sunday morning passed quietly. We went to church. Just before the end of father's sermon, an official car drove up, which always meant trouble. We were barely home when father was called to the soviet. There he was informed that within twenty-four hours he and his family were to leave the district without taking any possessions with them. A guard was immediately placed at the house.

The next morning, while mother brought the youngest

three children to relatives, a wagon carrying no possessions left Grossweide. There were no tears in accordance with father's wishes. After my father had taken a last walk through the house and barn, I noticed a few tears in his eyes as he lovingly stroked his faithful horse. Father travelled to the Don Basin in order to search for work. There were often house searches for father during the night. In a roundabout way, we learned that we were to be sent north in fourteen days and that we should disappear from our sanctuary at our Uncle Abram's residence. One morning, we left unnoticed for the Don Basin where father was working as a bookkeeper. He was soon transferred to Stalino, while we continued to live in the Russian village.

In the spring of 1931, father obtained a position at the medical institute in Stalino as a teacher of Latin and German. In addition he was the bookkeeper for the district medical library. Here, father soon found a circle of Mennonite, Russian and German believers. Thereupon, he was called to the GPU who were precisely informed of his activities and forbade him any further contact. In the meantime, we had settled in the region of Stalino but had separated for reasons pertaining to accommodation and food availability. Mother and father and my youngest brother, Heine, had only one room in which stood one bed, one table, and two chairs. We four girls were housed some eight kilometers away. There, my oldest sister was a teacher and I worked as a nurse. My oldest brother worked in a steel factory in Makijewka, some fifteen kilometers distant. Though my father worked from seven in the morning to midnight, he could not earn enough money to pay for the high priced food. My brother was swollen from hunger and my mother was terribly emaciated and almost constantly confined to her bed. Mother died of a weak heart on February 28, 1934 after a five month illness.

In August father married Anna D. Klassen. Both worked at the institute, both had a faith in God. The food crisis gradually passed.

In the spring of 1937, father was again called to the GPU for reasons which were never clear to me. After a house search, he was arrested the night of August 4-5. For six months, he was in an overfilled prison in Stalino where one could sleep, while the others stood in the hall. My stepmother saw and spoke with him once. He was very emaciated and said to her, "I have passed very near death." They could accuse him of no crime even though the interrogators were changed twice. He was then sent to Moscow. My stepmother was informed that he had been exiled to the north for eight years without the privilege of letter writing. Three weeks after father's arrest, my stepmother had to vacate her housing and was dismissed from her post. She was even forbidden to give private lessons to small children. Later, with GPU permission, she became a teacher for the German language at the institute in Ruberschnoje. She moved there with her sister and with my two youngest sisters, Elfriede and Anneliese. During the war, Elfriede came to live with us in Stalino while training for her profession. Acquaintances later informed us that with the advance of the German army, my stepmother and Anneliese, together with a few German families, were transported to an unknown destination. Since then, we have had no word from them.

Finally, a law was passed that the dependents should not share in the guilt of their parents. That was after my eldest sister had lost her position because of father's arrest and after I had lost my scholarship for my further studies. Sara was reinstated and worked until the retreat of the Germans. Her husband, who had been drafted into the Russian army, was an early casualty, at least according to later reports. Sara came to Germany with both children and obtained a position as a teacher. She avoided the danger of repatriation after the Russian occupation by fleeing to the US sector of Berlin. She left Germany on the way to Paraguay on February 1, 1947.

My sister, Elfriede was a Red Cross nurse and she, too, managed to flee to her sister Sara.

My brother, Kornelius was settled in Warthegau. Towards the end of the war, he was drafted into the army while his family awaited transportation [to Germany]. It seems doubtful that the flight was successful, and they probably shared the same fate as many. My brother visited me in Bayreuth several times. Since the end of the war, however, there has been no word from him.

My brother, Heinz worked in a German army office during the war which was relocated from the Oder to the Elbe. There is also no word from him.

My sister, Lena Pauls, whose husband has vanished since 1937, has been in Siberia since the German advance.

I, myself, obtained a doctor's diploma in 1938 and worked at various places as a doctor. Later, because of my German background, I was dismissed from my post. After the outbreak of the war, I was arrested and was to have been sent to Kasakstan. I escaped during transport and managed to reach the German lines. During the German occupation, I was deployed as a doctor and came to Germany with the German retreat. Here I worked in the hospital as an intern. In Berlin at the end of the war, I separated myself from my sister Sara and fled northward from the Russians. I had married in the meantime and waited for the return of my husband. After lengthy efforts, we found emergency shelter in Haddessen.

Tusnelda Volkmann (nee Martens)
Germany, 1947

Heinrich D. Neufeld
Teacher and Minister
Ohrloff, Sagradowka, South Russia

November 29, 1919 will remain unforgettable for the Sagradowka settlement. It will be forever memorable as one of the bloodiest and most gruesome days of the revolution. An impenetrable fog covered everything like a thick blanket and haunted one like a nightmare. Rumors had circulated for several days that the Makhno bands were carrying on their gruesome activities in the region. Anxiously, one awaited nightfall: anxiously one awaited the dawn of a new day.

Around two o'clock in the afternoon, several groups of armed riders galloped into the village of Ohrloff. Without a word being spoken, everyone knew it: now they are here! Shots were soon fired and cries of pain could be heard. The fog turned reddish as it reflected the burning houses and straw piles. Mercifully, the fog hid the bestiality of men who had become raging animals, and one could only see what was happening nearby.

When the fiends left after two hours, some forty-eight dead, mostly men, were found lying in their own blood. There were also a number of more or less seriously wounded. We will only touch upon the experiences of a few of these.

There was Heinrich D. Neufeld, founder-teacher of the high school in Ohrloff, Sagradowka. He was in the school at the time of the attack. The students and teachers were ordered to go home. Followed by his children who attended the school, he walked from the end of the village, where the school was, to the center where the village school was located. Here, he was stopped and sent into the school while the children continued on their way.

In the teachers' room of the school were the two village school teachers, Abram P. Wiebe and Abram Toews. When Neufeld entered, he was followed by a number of the fiends. The teachers had to line up against the wall. There was a shot and Toews, shot through the head, collapsed and gave up his spirit. Next in line was the teacher, H. Neufeld. He had enough time and courage to ask the murderers, "Why?" Then he collapsed from a shot through the heart. Wiebe saw the gun pointed at him and collapsed when it was fired. This time the bullet missed its mark and when Wiebe later regained consciousness everything around him was quiet. He got up to investigate what had happened. The bandit had apparently assumed that he had shot him and did not think it worth his while to investigate further.

When the writer of this report took the place of the murdered Toews in the following year, the bullet marks were still clearly visible on the stone wall of the teacher's room. Neufeld was only thirty-six years old when he was prematurely taken from his work.

After Neufeld had completed his teacher training and taken Maria Walde as his bride, he first became a teacher in Reinfeld, Sagradowka. He faithfully carried on as the village school teacher for some years.

His active and striving spirit, nevertheless, struggled to leave [the confines of] this narrow environment. When time and circumstances allowed, he went to Switzerland to study in the Basel seminary for two years. He returned with new courage and creativity, driven by a desire to serve his dear people. He was elected as a minister and later ordained by the Mennonite church of his home village, which he served energetically and faithfully.

After several years of activity in the school of commerce in Alexanderkrone, Molotschna he accepted a call to the newly founded high school in Lugowsk, Neu-Samara. He worked here for several years. From Lugowsk, Neufeld went to the city of Alexandrowsk, south Russia where he was active in the city school. From here, he also served as a minister in the churches at Schoenwiese and Chortitza as well as others.

In 1917 he returned to his home in Sagradowka and founded a high school in the place of his birth, Ohrloff. It was of great blessing to the settlement. A murderer's hand suddenly called him away from this work.

The above came from the mouth of A.H. Wiebe, the survivor of that bloody scene in the schoolhouse and from the widow of the murdered man who later became my mother-in-law when I married her eldest daughter.

Jakob Janzen
Mt. Lehman, British Columbia

Peter J. Neufeld

Peter J. Neufeld was born in 1892 on the Ebenfeld estate near Guljapole in the province of Jekaterinoslaw. He had a lovely, carefree youth in the circle of his parents and brothers and sisters. In 1904, when he was still very young, he entered the school founded in Berdyansk by the well-known Mennonite pedagogue, A.A. Neufeld. I entered the same school two years later. We both lived on Lasarewskaja Street, he with the bank director H.A. Ediger, the father of the elder Alexander Ediger, and I lived across the street at H.P. Ediger's. We often met and became friends. P. Neufeld was of a friendly, gentle disposition which made him popular with his teachers as well as his fellow students. No one, least of all he, had any foreboding that this young man, so privileged by fate, would someday be so hard pressed by life, that he, like many others, was destined to walk through the deep waters of sorrow.

Soon after the outbreak of the revolution, the family Neufeld had to leave their estate, which lay near Guljapole, the headquarters of the bandit leader Makhno. They settled in the village of Blumenort, Molotschna where Peter married Anna Dick in 1922. In time they were granted two children, a son Peter, and a daughter Angelika. During the first year of his stay in Blumenort, P. Neufeld had an encounter with Batjko Makhno, the feared bandit leader. He was arrested together with other estate owners' sons and transported to Guljapole. Two were shot enroute. After he had spent several days in prison here, he appeared before Makhno who declared that he was free and could return to his loved ones. The clothes and shoes which had been taken from him enroute were returned to him. A Russian, a former coach driver on the Neufeld estate, brought him back to Blumenort. The Neufeld family was known in the entire region for its humane treatment of its Russian workers. Thanks to this, no member of the family was killed.

P. Neufeld lived in Blumenort with his young family until his exile in 1931. He made himself useful in various capacities. For a time, he taught in an evening school for illiterates and did secretarial work in the local soviet. For several years running, he was secretary for the Union of Citizens of Dutch Lineage, usually simply called the Union, for several years running. Because he was popular with the proletarian elements of the village,he escaped the first exile in 1930 which targeted former estate owners.

And yet Damocles' sword already hung over his head. One year later, in June 1931, he had already been arrested. His wife and children followed him to the Stalnewo station a few days later. The family was now sent beyond the Ural Mountains to Tscheljabinsk, on the border between Europe and Asia. Here, it was very difficult for them. A great number of exiles from various nationalities were cramped together in small barracks. Among others, there was also the family of the well-known teacher and minister, Aron Dueck of Margenau, former member of the Commission for Ecclesiastical Affairs. Because circumstances here were almost unbearable, they wrote to the Molotschna requesting someone to come take the children home. Two men, Harder and Regehr, the latter the brother-in-law of A. Dueck, came and took home twelve children including those of P. Neufeld and A. Dueck. The parents, the Peter Neufelds, were sent further north after a one-year stay in Tscheljabinsk. They came first to Solikamsk on the Kama, a large tributary of the Volga, then on to Krasnaja Wischera, a newly found industrial site. It was a very difficult journey in freight wagons and lasted thirty days. The beginnings at this new place of exile were very difficult, but in time things got better. P. Neufeld worked in the office of a large factory and because of his ability and reliability became the head bookkeeper and even received a reasonable wage. The parents missed their children and decided to get them from the south, if this was possible. Mrs. Neufeld obtained permission to do this and amid many difficulties journeyed to the distant home and got the children. Now several easy years followed. P. Neufeld, whose health had been severely affected, suffered under the burdens of his job and the heavy responsibilities associated with it. In a letter from that time, he states that he has turned white and that he would much rather do insignificant work which carried less responsibility. But this comparatively calm and happy time did not last long. The great purge of 1937-38 claimed many, many innocent victims throughout the Russian empire. P. Neufeld was taken from his family and sent to another location. Here he spent about a year in prison, from which he was transferred to a hospital, seriously ill. He died soon after. The wife was soon taken from the children, but was freed after a year and allowed to take the children (who meanwhile had gone to relatives in Turkestan) back north. Several more letters came from her in which she wrote that she had survived a serious operation and that things were very difficult for them.

H. Goerz

Abram K. Neustaedter
Minister
Friedensfeld, Nikopol District, South Russia

My father was born on December 12, 1864 in the Jasykowo settlement in village No. 3. It was called Dolinowka or Adelsheim. On May 24, 1887 he married Maria Schellenberg. Of his youth I know little, only that he had to work very hard. Shortly, before his conversion, he is to have jokingly said, "Many a good-for-nothing has later become a decent chap."

As a young married couple, my parents lived in Einlage for fifteen years where father was first accountant, then foreman in the factory of Johann Friesen. They manufactured agricultural machinery. In Einlage my father was also the choir conductor in the local Mennonite Brethren church.

My parents left Einlage in 1898 and then lived in various places, where my father was the business manager in a number of steam mills. He had some difficult experiences in this line of work. At that time, he was already a minister of the Word.

On March 1, 1915 my parents moved to Friedensfeld, Nikopol district. Here, they lived for fourteen years. The parents bought a farm here. Not long after, father became the leading minister of the local Mennonite Brethren church. He discharged his office faithfully. The years 1918-19 were very difficult ones for the parents. The roving robber bands which were everywhere robbed my parents of all they had. At times, my father did not even have proper clothes for his church duties.

A typhus epidemic struck in the year 1920, and our entire family succumbed to this dangerous illness. The daughter, Aganetha lay helpless for several months, then died in August. The son, Hans, was crippled and lived another ten years. When his parents were sent into exile, he, in his helpless condition was left behind. The Lord had finally released him and took him unto Himself. His sister Lena, Mrs. Jantz, cared for him until the end. His funeral was a sad one, for under the circumstances of the time, no services were allowed.

In 1923, when so many from Friedensfeld left for Canada, my parents found it difficult to make a decision. They still hoped for better times, but things turned out differently. The oppression in Soviet Russia grew steadily worse. When the Germans in Russia were overwhelmed by the great desire to emigrate in 1929, our family also journeyed to Moscow. But what happened? We, with thousands of other refugees, were forcibly loaded into cattle wagons, the doors were sealed, and we were returned to our old homes. When we arrived there, we found our homes completely plundered by the neighboring Russians. We had a difficult time getting back on our feet.

Furthermore, our father was constantly being harassed by the GPU. He was to go into the villages and persuade the people to give up all thought of emigration and to enjoy the privileges of their land. He was also pressured to become a secret agent for the GPU. When father steadfastly resisted such a traitorous action against his people, he was arrested and taken to a Nikopol prison where he spent five days. There, he was constantly interrogated and pressured but he gave only one answer: "No, I will not give up my faith." They, nevertheless, persisted and promised him a fine life if he would consent. When they got nowhere they let him go for a time.

He was able to serve his congregation for several months in the homes of his members, but not in the beautiful church.

It was the time when collective farms were being organized everywhere. All the farmers had to contribute their machinery and their cattle. Whoever resisted was expropriated by force, arrested, and exiled to the north or to Siberia.

"There is plenty of room there for you all," scoffed the Red agents. Our church was transformed into an entertainment club. In his last sermon, our father told his listeners, "If our path should lead to Siberia, we will still remain true."

His foreboding was soon realized. On February 25, 1930, my dear parents and two siblings were exiled to Siberia for five years.

There my parents experienced many hardships. They had to live in cold barracks packed together with people from all nations. The beds were two, three and even five-story bunks. The stuffy air was enough to make one sick. Mother writes,

It is so crowded that we do not even have a corner to pray.

The food from the common kitchen is completely insufficient. The inmates seek to supplement this by cooking a soup from horse bones which they can buy at the market, or they gather mushrooms in the woods and prepare them.

The parents bore the separation and deprivation in quietude and resignation. Their deepest sorrow related to the fact that they had left a crippled and helpless son behind who, as mentioned earlier, died soon thereafter.

Initially, the parents and children came to the city of Archangelsk in the north; later, they were sent to the White Sea. The son, Abraham, got work in a sawmill and father, for whom such work was too difficult, worked at a lathe as a woodworker. It was easier for those who had a trade to secure a livelihood.

During this time, they received many a package from their friends in America. This kept them alive while many others who did not receive anything died of hunger. The parents had to overcome many a severe test, but later they also reported many an answer to prayer. They did not despair of their faith and trust in God.

After their five years of exile was finally up, they were allowed to return home. In their passes, officials had noted, "unlawfully deported." They had nevertheless served their sentence. Our parents returned to the Ukraine on April 20. Because they could not go back to their home village of Friedensfeld, they moved to where their children were, the Franz Neustaedters, at Station Seljonaja. Here father and son earned their bread through carpentry. It was not easy for father who was old, and the five years of exile had weakened him considerably. Yet he was courageous and happy to be free again.

Our parents experienced another deep tragedy in 1938 when so many of our loved ones were dragged off to Siberia. Three sons-in-law, a daughter, and two sons, including Abram, were taken from them and sent away, never to be seen again. Father could truly say, "You have robbed me of my children." The sorrow was too much for mother. She became ill not long after and died in 1940.

In the same year, father moved to the village of Adelsheim in Jasjkowo. He fellowshiped for several years with the believers there. Here, he also married a second time.

When the withdrawal of German troops began in 1943, the great flight began and father with all the other Germans also joined the trek. They came to Warthegau and were settled there. The respite was a brief one. Soon the stream of refugees moved westward. Father was eighty-one and decided against further flight. He stayed behind and also died there. He was now free of all suffering. His wife and many others, including his niece Helene Jantz, were sent back to Siberia by the Russians and all trace of them has been lost. One of father's favorite hymns was:

Forever with the Lord
Amen, so let it be
Life from the dead is in that word
'Tis immortality.

This portrait comes from the time of exile: there are the parents, the son Abram, and the adopted daughter Maria Letkemann. She later married Isaak Bergmann. He alone came to Rosemary, Alberta, and she was sent to Siberia with three children.

Abraham D. Nickel
Elder,
Rudnerweide Church, Molotschna

Abraham D. Nickel is the son of elder David Nickel of Grossweide, and the younger brother of Peter D. Nickel, elder of the Lichtenau Mennonite Church. Like his brother, Peter, he was born in Steinfeld and spent his youth in Grossweide where he also received his early education. He attended high school in Gnadenfeld and then the pedagogical classes in Halbstadt. He prepared himself for the teacher's exam, and after he successfully passed it, he accepted his first teaching position in the village of Kleefeld. He became the author's successor in the large, two-roomed school.

He was baptized upon confession of faith by his father D. Nickel in 1906. He was only eighteen years of age when he became a teacher, yet his youthful enthusiasm made up for what he lacked in experience. He did not stay long in one place.

After two years, he relocated to Friedensruh. The following year, he took a teaching position in Alexanderkrone. From here, he went to Johannesheim near the station Gaitschur. In 1912 he was joined in matrimony with Katherina Kaethler, daughter of Peter Kaethler of Ebenfeld. Seven children were born to them, of which two died in infancy.

When WWI broke out and the reserves were called up, Abraham D. Nickel had to leave his teaching position and enter state service. Initially, he served in the forest near Tosno in the vicinity of Petrograd, as St. Petersburg was already called at that time. After a short period of time, he and others were transferred to the All-Russian Zemstvo Union in Moscow which, together with other organizations in the land, took over the care of the wounded from the government. He served on medical train No. 190. He was the bookkeeper on this train until the end of his service time. These trains had to take the wounded and sick soldiers from the front to hospitals inland. Each train also had doctors and nurses.

After the end of the war, he took a teaching position in the village of Mariental, Gnadenfeld district. Here, his service as teacher and adult youth worker brought blessing.

In 1923 he contracted rheumatism in his joints and spent the entire winter of 1923-24 in bed. He never quite got rid of this illness. In spite of all the cures he tried, it got progressively worse. He had to give up his teaching profession, and in the summer of 1924 he moved to his parents' house in Grossweide. Two years earlier, his home church in Rudnerweide had called him as a minister. In 1927 when his father, elder D. Nickel, laid down his office, his son Abraham D. Nickel became his successor. On May 8 he was inaugurated into the office by his father. He served his church as a shepherd for seven years.

Now his suffering began. His physical ailment worsened so that he could only walk on crutches. Now the Red government not only robbed him of all his rights and all possibility of making a livelihood, but heaped all sorts of high assessments on him so that he was plunged into bitter poverty and need. Hunger and deprivation steadily weakened his body and made it less resistant to the malady. He had to refuse packages of foodstuffs sent to him from Canada to a government agency, while his wife and children at home had nothing to eat.

His church members, who themselves were in dire straits, saved him from starvation by providing him with beets, potatoes, a bit of sunflower oil and similar foodstuffs. He, nevertheless, stayed at his post and served his church according to his strength and ability. Often, he went from Grossweide to the church in Rudnerweide— some three verst— on crutches in order to serve there. During the last years, he was the only remaining minister since all the others had to leave. When he could no longer walk, they carried him into the church. Sitting in a chair he proclaimed the Word of God to those who had assembled.

In 1934 the church was closed by Soviet authorities. That filled the cup of his inner suffering. In a letter to his brother Jakob in Canada he wrote, "Brother, I stand on the broken ruins of my life and before me stands death." The last doors had been closed for him. He and his family were harassed, oppressed, and vexed from all sides. In bitter distress, sick in body and soul, he looked for help and for a way out. Good friends advised him to go to the Caucasus. But where would he get the means? Good friends collected the monies. When he was ready to leave, men from the soviet levied a high monetary fine, because he had not registered the receipt of the travel money with them. Furthermore, his oldest daughter, aged twenty, was arrested because she together with other girls had sung spiritual songs at the bedsides of the sick. She could only follow her parents one year later. The cup of suffering was still not full.

Thanks to the sacrificial generosity of his church members, it was, after some delay, finally possible to leave for the Caucasus in January 1935. He and his family found a warm welcome among dear friends in the village of Ssablyi. Here, he also found a relatively tranquil life free from constant external pressures. But the measure of his suffering was still not full. Already weak from hunger and deprivations, crippled in both legs and feet as well as one hand, he now contracted bowel cancer. This agonizing illness caused him so much pain at times that he screamed day and night, until he could scream no more from hoarseness and exhaustion. He and his loved ones cried to God for a [quick] death.

Then on the last day of his life, the gracious Lord removed

all pain from this severely tested individual. Peaceful, calm, and with a smile on his face he, who had steadfastly clung to his Lord and Savior, slipped into that brighter world on June 3, 1935, truly redeemed in body and soul.

Though often troubled and driven to despair, the Lord carried him through this period of suffering to eternal heavenly bliss. There were many people present when he was buried in the cemetery in Dolinowka, Caucasus on June 5, 1935. His coffin was lowered into the grave as the sun set. Elder Aron Regehr, formerly of Pordenau and the minister Heinrich Friesen, formerly of Schoenau, served at the cemetery with song and prayer. His wife died three years later. In all the troubles and difficulties, she contracted tuberculosis. She died in Dolinowka on May 26, 1938 and like her husband, was buried there.

"These are the ones that have come out of great tribulation and they have washed their robes and have made them white in the blood of the Lamb" (Revelation 7:14).

This data is mainly derived from the family chronicle and the letters of his father, elder David Nickel, who remained in Russia and died there.

David Nickel
Elder
Grossweide, Gnadenfeld District,
Province of Taurida

David D. Nickel was born on August 30, 1853 (N.S.) in the village of Rudnerweide in the Molotschna. His father, David Nickel, came from west Prussia to Russia with his parents in 1819, and in that year settled near the school in Rudnerweide. His parents were David A. and Helena (nee Janzen) Nickel. David was the second youngest of nine children born to his parents. He spent his childhood in Rudnerweide and also received his elementary education there. He prepared for the teaching profession in a private school in Steinbach. He accepted his first teaching position at the age of twenty and worked in this profession for eighteen years: two years in the city of Orechov, two years in Neu-Halbstadt and fifteen years in the village of Steinfeld in the Molotschna. In 1872 he was baptized upon confession of faith in his Lord and Savior and accepted into the Mennonite church in Rudnerweide.

In 1875 he married Margaretha Dick from Pordenau. Three of thirteen children born to them died in infancy. When his parents and siblings migrated to America in 1878 and settled in Minnesota he, by God's leading, remained behind. The Lord had a great work for him among his own people in the old homeland.

In 1881 he was called by God and elected to the ministerial position by the Rudnerweide Mennonite Church. He pursued this calling in subsequent years and allowed himself to be ordained as a minister. Ten years later, when elder Franz Goerz resigned in 1891, this church called him to be their elder. Goerz inaugurated him in January 1892. Selflessly and faithfully, he served the church for another thirty-five years. On January 1, 1917, he and the church celebrated his twenty-five year jubilee. During this period, he also served and worked outside of his church. He was prepared to serve whenever a call came to him, whether from an individual, a church or a people. At the request of the conference, he undertook lengthy mission journeys to the new Mennonite settlements and served them with counsel, preaching and ministerial functions.

On December 3, 1896, he journeyed to St. Petersburg with elder Heinrich Unruh of Muntau as a representative of the Mennonite churches of Russia in order to present the newly crowned tsar, Nikolas Alexanderovich II, with bread and salt, a symbol of the fealty of his Mennonite subjects in the empire.

In the years 1898, 1899 and 1900, he visited the settlements in Samara and Orenburg. In 1902 he visited the churches in Terek and those near Suworowka in the Caucasus. In 1909 and 1911, he travelled to Siberia and served the churches near Omsk, Pawlodar, and Barnaul. In 1913 he made another trip to the Caucasus in the region of Stawropol and visited the settlers near Kalantarowka.

He also participated actively in the Molotschna education system. As a member of the Molotschna Mennonite School Council, he annually visited a number of our village schools in order to test the morale and the progress of these schools and to encourage and stimulate the teachers in their work. He loved his church, was wholeheartedly united with her, and always had her spiritual well-being in mind.

On November 30, 1915, death claimed his beloved wife Margaretha (nee Dick) who had stood faithfully beside him in his work. Though his children surrounded him with love, he felt lonely and forsaken. They had walked together for forty years in this life and had already celebrated their silver wedding anniversary in 1900.

In 1918 he entered a second marriage with the widowed Mrs. Elisabeth Bartel (nee Kaethler) from Gnadental. This second wife staunchly stood beside him in the difficult times which now descended upon our people. In 1927, at seventy-four years of age, he resigned the office of elder. His son Abraham became his successor. His quiet unobtrusive manner, his calmness and imperturbability won him the love and respect of his constituency. When the turmoil of revolution, anarchy, civil war, and the Soviet regime erupted and raged, he was not touched personally. The protective hand of God was upon him, his servants and his family. He was certainly robbed of his earthly possessions and deprived of his civil rights. He also had to leave his home in Grossweide, but he was not exiled and sent away. God did not let it come to that.

It happened on January 21, 1931. Forced by circumstances, the impossibly high assessments, the taxes, and the threats of northern exile, he with his loved ones secretly left home and the village by wagon under cover of night. This journey from Grossweide to Gnadental was something of a flight. Both of the old parents stayed with the children of the second wife, the Kornelius Heidebrechts. But they could not stay. Since the food question became critical and the external pressures steadily increased, these two homeless old people decided to move to the Old Colony, where they were not so well-known.

His youngest daughter, Anna, lived there. She was married to Heinrich Loewen, Chortitza, who had a good position in a hospital. Here in May 1932, they found accommodation and care with their children. On June 16, 1933, his second wife died after a brief illness. They had shared joy and sorrow for fifteen years. Now he was again alone in old age. How he lamented the general decline which spread among our people and all the churches. The shepherds were beaten and the herds scattered. He was deeply wounded in 1934 when his beloved church in Rudnerweide was closed and turned into a club. He had preached and served in this church for forty-five years and saw [in its closure] the horror of the desolation of a holy place.

How he agonized when he saw the severe fate which struck believers and messengers of the Gospel and even his own children: imprisonment, exile, death through starvation, cold and deprivations of every kind. How he agonized when he saw the suffering and fate of his son, Abraham D. Nickel, his successor in office.

In 1937 his son-in-law, Heinrich Loewen, with whom he lived, was arrested, taken from wife and child, and exiled. In one of his letters he writes, "As an old man I can only lift up my hands in prayer for all my children and for all the oppressed, persecuted, despairing and sorrowing." He remained in regular correspondence with all his loved ones as much as it was allowed, comforting, encouraging and admonishing them to remain true to the faith. All this suffering, his own and others, drove him ever closer to the father heart of God. Longingly, he looked towards the hour of his final salvation. The hour for him came on August 31, 1940, the day after his eighty-seventh birthday. Ten days earlier, he experienced a stroke which kept him bedridden. Though he was helpless, his mind remained clear until the very end. He recognized all his visitors and spoke with them, though speaking became difficult. Often he spoke the words, "Why does it take so long before I can go home?" On his last birthday, the day before he died, some dear friends dropped in and sang the songs which had become dear to him in life. He died at twelve noon on August 31, 1940 and was buried at the Chortitza cemetery on September 2. "Someone came and read the Word of God—John 5:24, 25—and spoke," so read the verbatim report of his death. We do not know who this "someone" was. Caution dictated that his name not be mentioned. "Blessed are the dead who die in the Lord from now on. 'Yes,' says the Spirit, 'that they may rest from their labors; for the results of their labors follow them'" (Revelation 14:13).

J.D. Nickel
Rosemary, Alberta

Johann Nickel
Elder
Sagradowka, South Russia

My father, Johann Nickel, was born in Muensterberg, Molotschna in 1863. He was elder of the Tiege Mennonite Brethren Church in Sagradowka for thirty years. My mother died on December 1, 1920. She was a Warkentin born in Spat, Crimea in 1867. In 1928 our father entered a second marriage with Luise Frisch. He lived together with his second wife for just over three years. After his arrest, mother had to leave her home. All the possessions were taken away. The arrest followed on September 6, 1933. In prison, he lived for only five months. He died on January 6, 1934. The heavenly Father brought his sufferings to an end. He is now with the Lord and is seeing what he believed. His great [bodily] weakness was the probable cause of his death. Because he was in the second story of the prison, he could not quickly walk down the steps like the other prisoners when all were let out to the prison courtyard in the morning. In addition, he was stout and could not carry his body weight very well. He was given a push by the guard so that he fell head over heels down the steps and lay as if dead at the bottom.

He had had a stroke. He was taken back in an unconscious state and lived for a day and a night. He suffered severely during this period. A Russian fellow prisoner who was later released related how they had always placed elder Nickel into the cell with the worst criminals. He was to preach God's Word to them. Naturally, there was only scorn and ridicule on the part of his tormentors. The criminals mistreated him terribly. In this sense, father died a true martyr's death.

My husband, Isaak Hiebner, was working in the city of Cherson, where father died in prison. Otherwise, we would probably not have learned that he died. My husband bought a coffin, placed him in it, and nailed it shut. He was then placed in the bottom of the grave and eight naked bodies were piled on top. Then the grave was closed. A crude wooden cross adorns his resting place. He is waiting until the resurrection morning. We were able to visit the grave once more.

Anna Hiebner

That was the report of the daughter. After a lifetime of faithfully serving the Lord, our elders, our fathers in Christ, left this world devoid of human praise.

His wife and eight children preceded him in death. Out of a large family, only two daughters are still alive: the reporter Anna Hiebner and Anna Regehr, nee Nickel. The husband of the aforementioned daughter, Isaak Hiebner, is still somewhere in exile in Russia.

Peter D. Nickel
Last Elder of the Lichtenau Mennonite Church, Molotschna, south Russia

Peter David Nickel was born in the village of Steinfeld, Molotschna, South Russia on January 29, 1884. His parents were David D. and Margaretha (nee Dick) Nickel. His father, later elder of the Rudnerweide Mennonite Church, was at that time a teacher in the Steinfeld village school. In 1891 his parents moved to Grossweide, where Peter Nickel spent his younger years. After completing the village school in Grossweide, he attended the high school in Gnadenfeld and then the pedagogical classes in Halbstadt. Thus, he prepared himself for the teaching profession. For two years, he served as a teacher on the estate Jeletzki in Cherson province. The well-to-do estate owner made it possible for him to attend the St. Petersburg Teacher Institute following the political unrest of the years 1905-06. Here, together with other Mennonite young men, he studied for three years. During the time of his study at the Teacher Institute, he clung to his faith while several of his fellow students lost theirs and embraced atheism.

In 1903 he was baptized by his father upon confession of his faith and accepted into the Mennonite church in Rudner-weide. Following his second year of study in St. Petersburg, he was united in holy matrimony on June 26, 1908 with Anna Fast, daughter of Jakob Fast of Muntau, Molotschna, and formerly of Chortitza.

After completing the Teacher Institute in St. Petersburg, he accepted a teaching position at the high school in Spat in the Crimea. Two children were born here: Margaretha and Victor.

With the outbreak of WWI, Nickel was drafted into state service and served at the [so-called] "Black River" until the end of the war. Many of our Mennonite reservists served here; they had to construct roads or make wood in the forest.

After the war, Nickel accepted a teaching position at the high school in Ohrloff, Molotschna.

Now came the years of unrest, civil war, anarchy, and the soviets (workers' councils). It was probably in 1917 when he was called to the ministry. This was a difficult struggle for him, for teachers were not allowed to preach. Yet he strongly felt the inner call of God, which he followed, and preached God's Word in defiance of the law. When the Union of the Citizens of Dutch Lineage was founded, he received temporary employment in the office as a technical worker. Benjamin B. Janz of Tiege was chairman and Philipp D. Cornies, his associate. This union led the exodus of the Mennonites from the Ukraine to Canada.

In 1926 he was elected as elder by the Lichtenau Mennonite Church and ordained on May 9 of the same year by his father, elder David D. Nickel of Grossweide. He served the congregation in Lichtenau for five years. In February 1928, he had to flee with his family to Memrik where he lived in Waldeck and Kalinowo. Later, he had to leave here and moved to Stalino. In this region of coal mines and industry, he found a position as an office worker. Here, he met elder Alexander Ediger from Schoensee, who had also fled.

After only one year, on April 14, 1932, he and Alexander Ediger were arrested and imprisoned. The reason for their imprisonment: Peter Nickel's work with the union and elder Ediger's activity in the Commission for Ecclesiastical Affairs. Another reason was because both had leading positions in the churches as elders. For a time these two, Nickel and Ediger, were fellow sufferers and together bore their afflictions. They had to spend five months in prison, at first in Stalino, but most of the time in the capital city of the Ukraine, Kharkov. At the beginning of August both were exiled to the north for three years. Initially they were to be sent to Archangelsk or Kem, but eventually they were sent to the Murmansk Canal. This was a very cold swampy region in the far north on the Polar Sea. At first their condition was tolerable, for both worked in an office: Nickel during the day and Ediger at night. Later, their situation worsened. Nickel soon became ill with nerve inflammation and scurvy and spent considerable time in a temporary hospital. Nutrition was meager. He attributed his survival to God and the foodstuffs sent by his family. After almost two years of exile, Nickel and Ediger were separated. The latter was sent to the Moscow Canal, while Nickel remained where he was and received a position as a teacher. Their paths of suffering separated forever. When the Murmansk Canal was completed after two years, Nickel's sentence was reduced by a year and on April 19, 1934 he could return to his loved ones who had remained in Stalino. That will have been a happy reunion!

Here, he lived very quietly and withdrew as much as possible, for he felt or sensed that he was being carefully observed by the GPU. He was able to stay with his loved ones in Stalino for exactly four years. Then, unexpectedly in April 1938, together with his son, Victor, he was again arrested, taken away and—though no one knows where— exiled. Since that time, his wife and daughter have received no news, no sign of life, no trace of father and son. Gone, unknown, vanished. Forever? God alone knows.

In short terse sentences, a human life has been portrayed. Yet what testing and suffering, struggle and striving, prayer and sighing, tears and pain, but also what faith, trust, submission to God's will and overcoming is included. It is known only to God.

This data has been partially reconstructed from memory, but in the main from the family chronicle and the letters of the father, elder D.D. Nickel.

Only two relatives of the D. Nickel family have come to Canada: a daughter, Mrs. Peter Wall of Tofield, Alberta, and elder Jakob D. Nickel of Rosemary, Alberta. The latter placed the data at my disposal. These are the next of kin of the exiled Peter D. Nickel.

The latest information comes from Russian Mennonite

refugees in Germany. It reads:

> The Reds took Peter D. Nickel's daughter Gredel to Stalino as well. There she worked in an office. When the Germans advanced in 1941, the Reds killed many of the young people who worked as slaves in Stalino and threw them in a deep pit. Then, even though they were not quite dead, poured lime over them. (For the uninitiated we will explain what this means. This lime is activated when it comes into contact with water and becomes seething hot. Many a person has seriously scalded himself in this way.) Thus, the innocent victims were tortured to death. Gredel Nickel was apparently among these. Her mother, who had also moved to Stalino, became mentally ill through this experience. There were many such unfortunates among the exiled, the tortured, and the refugees. Their nerves shattered amidst all the terror which they witnessed, heard of, and experienced. The great suffering of these victims cry to heaven. When will the Lord hear the cry of those who call upon Him day and night?

Elder Peter D. Nickel was my class colleague in the pedagogical classes in Neu-Halbstadt. How different were our later ways!

The Author.

David D. Paetkau
Minister and Leader
of the Mennonite Brethren Church
in Kamenka, Orenburg, Northeast Russia

He was the son of David Paetkau, who came from Einlage in the Old Colony. The parents later lived in the Kuban, where David was born in the village of Alexandrodar in July 1882. Here, he completed the two-level school. He did not have high school training, but devoted much time to self-study, and in the process acquired a good understanding of theology and other subjects.

He later moved to Orenburg with his family and was elected as a minister in the Mennonite Brethren Church in Kamenka. Following the death of elder Cornelius Fehr, the church elected him as leader, and he faithfully served it for many years until his arrest.

In the year 1926, he was taken from his family and imprisoned in the city of Orenburg. His wife and their nine children had to remain on the farm, which had been severely decimated by the Reds. He was interrogated on various subjects by the GPU while undergoing various tortures. I want to mention only one which was reported by one of his cousins. She writes:

> I was able to visit the dear brother David Paetkau in prison. In the short time which was granted me, I was able to hear and see terrible things. During various interrogations, he was at times so badly beaten that his flesh on his legs below the hips sagged to his knees.

After half a year of suffering in this prison, he was exiled for five years to the high north. He finally came to Kornilowka close to the right shore of the northern Dvina [river]. He was exactly at the place where brother J.J. Toews from Ignatjewka was an exile.

In exile, he had his quarters in the very small home of an old widow amidst very impoverished circumstances. His meals there were very meager. In a very short time, he suffered from malnutrition and began to swell from prolonged starvation. We got his address here in Canada and sent him several packages of food. Through these, he somewhat recovered and became stronger. Since he himself could not work because of a stiff arm, he became the overseer of a group of exiles. He spent several years here during which he read and studied the Bible a great deal. In the loneliness of the wilderness, he experienced profound blessings and profound fellowship with God.

God in His love manifested Himself to him in a special way. On a beautiful day as he went to the post office to pick up his food package which we sent him, he saw another package addressed to the dear brother J.J. Toews. To his joy, he discovered that he was in the same village as he. He made further inquiries of the postal official. Deep in his heart, he formulated a plan: somehow they must try to get together. This plan was brought before the heavenly Father who understood it well. Paetkau made arrangements to present his petition to the authorities. Thanks to his good behavior, he had credibility with them and had been privileged, in some respects, which was not the case for many in his circumstances. After he had discussed the matter with his good landlady, he requested that brother J.J. Toews be allowed to share his quarters. His petition, bolstered by God's grace, was soon granted. Brother Toews came to him in his house.

Later, he wrote us that this was the most blessed time of his whole life. Here was a Bible school which for him would never be equalled. We received many letters from him with many hundreds of Scripture passages which he had seen in a new light and which had become important to him. He had always been a great reader and researched in various books. He was especially partial to theological writings.

But this blessing was not of long duration. The dear brother Toews, who had been so weakened by the many earlier torments, could not regain his strength. He became seriously ill and, after a short time, went to his Lord, to his heavenly home, for which he had so often longed.

David Paetkau described his funeral. He, himself, made the coffin for the dear brother. The old widow, who had been so good to them, sewed the death shroud. Decrepit though he was, David Paetkau dug the grave. Though Paetkau was weak and the widow old, the two managed to carry the coffin to the cemetery. The dear brother Toews was so emaciated that his weight did not make the burden too heavy. At the grave site he preached with the widow as his only listener. She wept with him and thanked God with him. After the sermon, they knelt at the grave site and poured out their hearts before God. Together they covered him with the cool earth and so protected him from further torment. The brother wrote that never in his life had he felt a loss as keenly as this one, but that he gladly granted the weary pilgrim his rest.

Soon after this, his five-year exile came to an end. Because he had always been so faithful in his service while in exile, he was allowed to return home. During his absence, his family had been deported to a desolate mountainous region some fifty verst from the Orenburg settlement. Here his wife, who had only taken along a spade and an axe, had dug a cave into the mountainside and made it into her home. This primitive residence could not accommodate the entire family and the mother was obliged to give up several of her children. Her oldest son, who had to live in constant hiding from the Reds, took over their care. Here, D.D. Paetkau found his wife and several of his dear children, all whom he had so longed to see. From here, he walked to the villages every week in order to obtain some bread for their sustenance. This modest joy only lasted nine months. One day, when he was walking to get bread, he was arrested by the Chekists and sent into exile without cause or reason. He ended up in a factory near Leningrad. Here, he served his sentence in a clothing factory.

We received a letter from him there in which he wrote that his treatment was not intolerable but that he only received one cup of tea and a small piece of bread per day. In a short period of time, this would mean death by starvation for him. After that, we received no further word from him.

No one knows what happened to that poor family in the cave of those desolate mountains. Oh, that help would come out of Zion for all these unfortunate victims at these so-called "world benefactors." Is God's arm shortened that He cannot help?

Report by his brother, Peter D. Paetkau
St. Catharines, Ontario

Jakob H. Paetkau
Teacher, Minister, Elder
Kalinowo (Marienort), Memrik
Settlement, Bachmut District, Jekaterinoslaw,
South Russia

He was the son of the mill owner and minister Heinrich Paetkau from Karpowka, Memrik. He was born on April 1, 1895 in Nikolaipol in the Donetz region in the Borissow settlement. There, he also attended the village school. In 1907 he entered the Chortitza High School and then continued in the teachers' college located there. He had scarcely completed the first year when he was called into state service in which he remained during WWI until 1917. He became a medical orderly in Moscow and received a position in the office of the

All-Russian Zemstvo Union. After the first upheaval during the February revolution of 1917, he was dismissed and could return home. In the meantime, his mother had become a widow and rejoiced at the return of her eldest son.

In the same year, he accepted a teaching position in the village of Karpowka in the Memrik settlement. Here, he worked until 1922. He worked enthusiastically among his colleagues, attended teacher conferences, introduced new directions, new instructional methods, etc. For example, he introduced the Hey-Pfeiffer eidetic images which were rapidly accepted in all schools, did pioneer work in the area of local geography, elevated composition to a new level, and was responsible for the introduction of a new math book, etc. Especially successful was his religious instruction in the schools.

In the spring of 1921, he was elected as a minister in the Memrik Mennonite Church but remained in his teaching position. Already in the fall of that year, the congregation in Kalinowo elected him as elder. He was only twenty-seven years old at the time and had barely preached half a year.

Kalinowo Mennonite Church had had Peter Janzen as elder for over twenty-five years. He had died somewhat earlier and elder Franz Enns, who was in Memrik as a refugee from the Terek at the time, temporarily filled his position. Elder Franz Enns convinced the congregation to elect an elder from their own midst, and the choice went to the young minister and school teacher, Jakob H. Paetkau. After some hesitation and objection, he finally accepted the position and was ordained as elder of the Kalinowo Mennonite Church in 1922. Elder Enns later emigrated to Canada and lived here in Lena, Manitoba, where he also died and was buried. His son, Gerhard Enns, was a doctor in Rosemary, Alberta for many years and later [moved] to Chilliwack, British Columbia.

Elder Jakob H. Paetkau now gave up the teaching profession and moved to the village of Kalinowo where the church had been built and where the congregation had erected a house for its pastor. Here, he wholeheartedly worked for his Lord and Master as long as he could; though at times, because of the Bolsheviks, his freedom and his life were in danger.

He dedicated his entire energy and time to his people. At first, he stood at the head of the church in ten villages but then gradually expanded his sphere of activity. When he and his family had the chance to emigrate to Canada in 1926 he, at the request of his congregation, declined in order to further serve his people. When the All-Mennonite General Conference met in Moscow in 1925, he was present as a delegate and actively participated in all the proceedings and discussions.

J. Paetkau also became a member of the Commission for Ecclesiastical Affairs and worked on *Unser Blatt*, the only periodical which the Mennonite churches of that day still possessed. [One of the editors] Jakob A. Rempel, Gruenfeld, wrote of this periodical:

> *Unser Blatt* is always in danger of demise—in the October issue of 1927 the censor crossed out twenty-two of the thirty-two pages—all religious themes. It is really rather difficult.

Thus, our brethren steadily struggled for their religious freedom. They managed to postpone the end, but at last they succumbed totally to the fate of extinction, as did all their other endeavors.

In 1927 elder Jakob H. Paetkau undertook a lengthy journey to Siberia in order to strengthen the many coreligionists in those congregations.

In the fall of 1929, he also went to Moscow in order to assist the refugees. His relatives cannot determine whether or not he also planned to escape the Soviet hell. But he, like so many other leading brethren, fell into the hands of the GPU and was deported. Soon after, he and his family fled to the Caucasus, a place of refuge for many of our ministers during that time. He now lived like a hunted deer, unsettled and fleeing, once together with the family, then in hiding. Yet he still continued to work for the Lord. During the terror years of 1937-38, however, he was found and exiled. Since then there are no further words as to his whereabouts.

In 1945 word came from Mrs. Abram Paetkau, his sister-in-law in Siberia, "Jasch (as he was known in the family circle) is silent." In February 1947 there was again a report from the same source: "Jasch is no longer . . . ."

When, how and where has this hero of faith fallen? God knows. His mother, now the widow of the deceased elder C.D. Harder, Rosemary, Alberta, writes:

As with all the others we do not know what happened to him. The most difficult thing for me is that I do not know what happened to my loved ones. He will certainly have suffered severely. One of my sons, Abram Paetkau, was sentenced to ten years in exile. These ten years expired in May 1946, but it cannot be assumed that he was released. A son-in-law has vanished since 1937; the daughter has never received any word from him.

The last letter from Siberia from Mrs. Abram Paetkau contains the following information:

Mrs. Jakob H. Paetkau, Baerbel, lives with her daughter Hilda. They both work in an orphanage. Baerbel looks after the sick and her daughter, Hilda, is governess. They buried her [Mrs. Paetkau] youngest daughter, Hermina ,in November, after she had suffered for several months. She had overworked herself in service during the war and could not recover. She also mentions that her daughter, Hilda, will have already written you that Jasch (elder Jakob H. Paetkau) and his son, Jascha, are no more.

These sketches are collected from information provided by his mother, the widow of C.D. Harder, from his brother D.H. Paetkau, Rosthern, Saskatchewan, and from Heinrich Wiens, one-time member of the Kalinowo Mennonite Church and currently a resident in Alberta.

Gerhard Plett
Elder
Hierschau, Molotschna

He was born on June 30, 1860, baptized May 21, 1879, and died in the village of Friedensdorf, Molotschna on April 1, 1933.

First marriage: on June 3, 1882, married Elizabeth Klassen in Hierschau, who was born on June 4, 1862, died June 2, 1890 in Hierschau.

Second marriage: on September 22, 1890, he married Katharina Willms in Nikolaidorf, who was born on January 15, 1869 in Nikolaidorf.

Shortly before his death, my dear grandfather expressed the wish that the [records] in "the golden classical Bible" (family Bible) be continued under all circumstances. In fulfillment of his wishes, I now feel compelled to write his life story. Today, May 1, 1946, I find myself in Muendersheim, Germany, where I have been employed as a public school teacher since October 25, 1945.

[I] do not only want to preserve the eventful story within the framework of family happenings. Even more than this, I want to portray my grandfather's unshakeable faith, which became a kind of refreshing oasis during the Red reign of terror, and his conviction that not a hair on our heads would be singed without God's will. [I] want to portray his strength to patiently bear the hardship visited upon the Mennonites, without murmuring, and in the fear of God, [a strength] which stemmed from this conviction. I want to honestly depict his upright desire to serve the Mennonite people with his life and work, his actions and activities.

Another one of his last wishes must also be carefully taken into consideration, namely that no words of praise about his life work be mentioned in his funeral sermon. Therefore, it is my humble wish that my attempt to show dear grandfather as he was in everyday life will not be construed as a form of praise. His God-fearing lifestyle is to be the ongoing example for all his descendants.

From the very onset, I have to regretfully note that the portrait will not be without its gaps. During the retreat from Russia to Germany, valuable pages containing grandfather's handwritten memoirs were lost in flight. Many important incidents in his life which find a welcome place [in these jottings] came from the recollections of his daughters Maria, Katharina, Nelly, and Aganetha, who were on the Ringelsbruch estate in Westphalia while these lines were being written. Time references cannot always be given exactly but, in general, are correct. The loss of the said papers was especially regrettable, because the fate of a considerable section of the Molotschna settlement was intimately associated with grandfather's activities.

After completing village school, grandfather received his further education in an evening school run by the teacher Johann Doerksen. It cannot be argued that this was more of an inspiration rather than an education for grandfather, since this style [of education] suited him admirably. His knowledge, which was rather impressive and diverse, was largely acquired by self-study.

For some years, he was a teacher in the village of Sparrau, Gnadenfeld district. After his first wife died, he moved to Hierschau. Here, he purchased a small farm and also acquired the clay pit near the village. At the same time, he built a small store. Here, grandmother sold bread, meat, rope, nails, etc. to the Russian travelers who came from far and near to buy the much soughtafter clay. Grandfather had married again; and so they worked together. At that time, the clay pit brought a rather good income. The clay was also called "white earth" or lime. Russian clay huts were plastered with this inside and out. Even Mennonite housewives bought this from Russian peddlers who went down the street shouting, "Bella Glina," and used it to paint the brick walls in their rooms so that they appeared snow-white. The brick fences in front of them were also painted once a year, usually for Easter or Pentecost. This gave a festive appearance to the entire farm.

Through this business, my grandfather was soon able to accumulate capital, and when his father, our great-grandfather, died, he bought a fine, full-sized farm in the village.

For a lengthy period, he was the district judge in the Gnadenfeld district. Unfortunately, I cannot give the exact time when he held this position. In 1904 he gave up this post in order to devote his full time to the ministry. He had already been elected as a minister by the Margenau Mennonite Church in 1899. When elder Peter Friesen died in 1907, he was ordained as elder of this church the following year by elder Heinrich Koop of Alexanderkrone. One or two years later, he also took charge of the Landskrone Church where a fine meeting house was being constructed: this was in 1910. Following the death of elder Johann Schartner, Gerhard Plett also took over the congregation in Alexanderwohl. He baptized some 2,000 people. It is evident from statistics, which he carefully kept, that in one year he made 400 trips on behalf of the Molotschna churches. This naturally included all the travel required of him as elder of the three churches, especially at funerals, weddings, worship services, etc.

Though he spent almost all of his time in the service of the churches, his farm was in model order.

In 1919 he was arrested by the Reds and imprisoned in a very unhealthy cellar for fourteen days. Why so many Mennonites were locked up never became clear; they were mistreated for no real reasons. Sixty-four men were crowded together in a room of fifty-six cubic meters. The wet and cold floor was of stone. After several days, grandfather could no longer stand on his feet. With great difficulty, enough room was found for him to lie down, but he had no protection from the [cold] floor. When his son Gerhard visited him several days later, he did not recognize him. With the help of the Mennonite doctor, Franz Dueck, grandfather was transferred to the hospital after fourteen days. After one month, he was allowed to go home, without ever learning why he was imprisoned in the first place.

Grandfather even spoke of this period as the leading of God. He was able to comfort and pray with many men in prison, and for some of them these were the last minutes of their life. Men had not only prayed but cried to God. Many a man was taken at night and, not long after, one heard shots. Why the prisoner had been shot, no one knew.

The health of our grandfather Plett had deteriorated severely while he was in prison. After that time, he never fully recovered. He obviously contracted rheumatism there, which later, virtually crippled his legs. By 1928 he could hardly move without the help of his cane. Because of his poor health, he felt compelled to resign his office as elder and placed it in the hands of his younger colleague, the minister Heinrich T. Janz of Landskrone. This happened in the year 1928.

In 1928 Russia initiated equalization, in simple words the liquidation of classes. This generally referred to those who had more possessions than the average person. The procedures were rather harsh. First, a money levy, the so-called "extraordinary tax," had to be paid. Then came the second levy which also had to be paid to the state within a very short period of time. This went on until the last resources were exhausted. This, of course, was the purpose of the whole operation. All the possessions were then confiscated by the state and sold at a ridiculous price in order to pay the debt to the state. In this fashion, three-quarters of all the farmers had to part with their belongings accumulated over many years of work. They were only allowed to take what they carried with them on their own person.

In this manner, grandfather saw his earthly possessions vanish in December 1930. On February 17, he had to bid his home adieu. When they came to take his furniture, grandfather commented, "For his livelihood a blacksmith needs a smithy and a bed. The one is as important as the other. My chair and my bed mean the same to me as a shop and a bed to the craftsman. I go from the bed to the armchair and the armchair to the bed." Amazingly, they left him these two items but no more. His farewell to the men who forced him out of his own house was characteristic of his whole lifestyle. In a warm, forthright manner, he shook each hand and wished them all the best for their later life. The men, normally not given to sentimentality, were dumbfounded by such behavior.

Grandfather found a secret refuge with Heinrich Sawatzky of Landskrone. In the summer of the same year, Sawatzky suffered a similar fate: he had to leave as well, and grandfather went to Kornelius Toews, also of Landskrone. By April 1932, the difficulties generated by the local political administration made a further stay in Landskrone impossible.

On a pitch dark April evening, my father, Hildebrand, secretly obtained horses (which did not belong to him) in order to get grandfather. Though the wagon was almost empty—what did the grandparents still possess?— and the four strong horses did their best, the journey made slow progress because of the deep mud. I, as a thirteen year old, was along at the time.

Grandfather's stay at our house had to be kept secret so that he would not be found by his pursuers. Meanwhile, his health deteriorated, and, after several months, he was confined to bed where he remained until the end of his life. His daughters Aganetha and Maria were with him. Katharina and Nelly were in Kharkov. The political situation steadily worsened and so, one hot June day, grandfather, with no regard for his condition, had to be loaded onto a wagon and taken to Friedensdorf.

During the last days of his stay in Hierschau, his

daughters Maria and Aganetha had to hide in the gardens and hedges in order to avoid arrest. This time it was Jakob Voth in Friedensdorf who placed his home at the disposal of the grandparents. Here, grandfather was privileged to spend the last months of his strenuous life. If he was confined to his bed before the move, the move itself certainly did not improve his condition. Instead, the pain intensified month by month, and later, week by week. His bodily weakness steadily increased. His body became sore from lying in bed. Sitting brought some relief, but soon his weakened condition did not allow this. He could not even turn in bed.

He consistently viewed the political chaos as God's leading, as he did the arrest of ministers, the prohibition of public worship, the closing of churches, the deportation of Mennonites to Siberia, etc. During his entire period of suffering, no one ever heard him make a complaint. He was as calm in death as he had been in his pain and suffering. On April 1, 1933, he died quietly in the Lord.

The funeral service was held on April 5, 1933 at the home of Jakob Voth in Friedensdorf. Elder Heinrich T. Janz from Landskrone, his successor in the office, preached the funeral sermon. All the children, except Gertrude were at the funeral. The small room could not hold all the visitors. Even men like Heinrich Kliewer, director of the high school in Gnadenheim and a communist, as well as several of his colleagues were present.

In a quiet spot in the Friedensdorf cemetery, grandfather Gerhard Plett gently sleeps until the great resurrection morning.

The Family of Elder Plett

Mrs. Plett and her four daughters, Maria, Katharina, Nelly, and Aganetha (with her three children) fled before the Russians to Germany where they work on the estate Ringelsbruch. Aganetha's husband, Heinrich Kaethler, vanished during the war as a member of the German army. Mrs. Plett is very weak and confined to bed. She only wishes to die and go home. (The latest word from Germany which just arrived, states that Mrs. Plett has died and was buried on January 29, 1947.)

His son, Johann Plett, was exiled to Siberia before the Germans occupied the Ukraine. His wife and daughter also came to Germany but were forcibly deported back to Russia by the Russians.

His son, Gerhard, was murdered in Saporoshje. He was found dead, his clothing covered with blood. His wife and children were sent back to Russia from Germany.

His daughter, Liese, and her husband, David Hildebrand, together with several children, were also sent back to Russia. Two children remained in Germany, among them the writer of this report.

The son, Heinrich, was arrested by the Russians in 1938. His wife and their child were deported before the occupation. She is to have been in a train on which the Russians poured oil and set on fire. There is no word as to her fate.

Daughter Gertrude and her husband remained in Russia, and no one knows whether they are still alive.

Note by the Author

For a time, elder Gerhard Plett was a member of the Molotschna School Council. As such, he had to visit the schools and evaluate and supervise the instruction of religion and German language. School council members also had to be present at the final exam of the village school pupils in order to test the verbal and written skills of the graduates and provide them with an appropriate certificate.

They were also the examiners in religion and German for the final exam in high school and for the candidates in the pedagogical classes. They also represented the interests of the school to the community and the government. They were elected by the Molotschna Ecclesiastical Council for a specified term. The Ecclesiastical Council was comprised of all the ministers of all the churches of the three [Mennonite] groups in the Molotschna.

Elder Gerhard was a man possessed of a calm objectivity and presence of mind. His verdict meant something in the churches. He had respect among the congregations, in the community, among his colleagues and the teachers.

I was able to visit him on his sickbed in Hierschau in the last years before my emigration. At that time, he was still vitally interested in the affairs of our churches. May the Lord reward His servant according to his work. I Corinthians 3:8: ". . . each one will receive his own reward in agreement with his particular labor."

Postscript from his Diary

Most of my childhood and youth was preoccupied with learning. On May 21, 1879, I was baptized in the Margenau Church by elder Bernhard Peters. In the fall of 1881, I was called into state service, but was released because of family obligations, served as a teacher in the Crimea at the Spat station in a tenant village called Schamk. From there, I was transferred to Sparrau in the Molotschna Colony where I served for six years as a teacher in the village school.

Isaak Poettker
Evangelist Among the Russians and Mennonites
Wernersdorf, Molotschna, South Russia

He came from Wernersdorf where he lived until his expulsion. He was converted at a young age and felt the call to work in the Lord's vineyard. He founded a choir of young believers in his home village and tried to exalt the name of the Lord in song.

He also went abroad in order to broaden his theological knowledge. If my information is correct, he first attended Bible school in Berlin and then went to England where he took a medical course. Later, he worked as a homeopathic doctor on the side.

He selected his life's partner, Luise Wolf, from among his choir members. She was the only daughter in the family but had three brothers. All three were later exiled. The Lord blessed the marriage with three children. The oldest two were daughters: Magdalena and Paula.

Brother Poettker did much evangelizing among the Russians and Germans. His sphere of action was mainly among the Mennonite villages of the Molotschna and the surrounding

Russian villages. He was once severely beaten on the street by young men with sticks following an evangelistic meeting in one of the Mennonite villages where people, including a number of young ladies, turned to God. That was truly suffering for Jesus' sake.

In a letter written to friends in Canada by his wife in May, 1928, she states that brother Isaak Poettker spent the entire winter in Leningrad (formerly Petersburg) studying in the Russian Bible school. It is not clear from the letter whether he was a teacher or a student. Like all other ministers, he was harassed and finally forced to leave his native village and move to the Caucasus. Here, together with his family, he lived in the Mennonite village of Kalantarowka. It was difficult making a livelihood. Sister Poettker worked on the side as a midwife.

Here, a fate suffered by so many of God's messengers also overwhelmed him. One day, he was arrested with many other ministers who had fled there, imprisoned and together with three others was sentenced to death by a People's Court after a long period of interrogation.

He and the three others were now incarcerated in the death cell for three months awaiting the implementation of the sentence. His wife visited him now and then and found that her young, energetic husband had completely white hair. She presented a petition for clemency and the sentence was commuted to ten years exile in Siberia. Elder Heinrich T. Janz from Landskrone, Molotschna was also among those who were condemned and eventually exiled. This was in 1936.

While in exile, brother Poettker had the opportunity to work as a dentist. There is no further word about his fate since all correspondence was forbidden. His family remained in the Caucasus. As of 1937 Mrs. Poettker had her mother with her. With the advance of the German army in 1941, all Germans in the Caucasus were either deported to northern or Asiatic [Russia]. The sister-in-law of Mrs. Poettker, Gretta Wolf, came to Germany and is in correspondence with the bosom friend of Mrs. Poettker, Mrs. Heinrich Doerksen (nee Siemens) from Wernersdorf. They live near Pigeon Lake, Manitoba. I thank them for providing the information about the Isaak Poettkers. Brother Heinrich Doerksen is the second eldest son of the teacher and minister Gerhard Doerksen who, in his day, was teacher at the model school in Halbstadt. His older brother, Gerhard, and his two uncles, Peter and Herman Peters, were hacked to pieces by the Reds in Schoenfeld in 1919.

Benjamin Ratzlaff
Teacher and Minister
Gnadenfeld, Molotschna

His father, B.B. Ratzlaff, returned to his home in Gnadenfeld in 1896 after studying in Switzerland. He had studied for two years at the St. Chrischona school. He was the only surviving son of his parents; the rest had all died young. His father, Benjamin Ratzlaff, was a minister and farmer in Gnadenfeld. On the side he also had a small shop where grain cleaning machines were manufactured.

Our father married Susanna Voth from Gnadenfeld. Like his father, he was also a minister of the Alexanderwohl church which still belonged to the Old Flemish group, as did the churches in Gnadenheim and Waldheim. Every Sunday father and son drove the long way to the church in Alexanderwohl where they preached alternately. At times, they preached in other churches as well.

For some years, the son worked together with his father on the family farm, but his heart was not in the matter. Consequently, he took a position in the Gnadenfeld High School as a teacher of German and religion. He could not remain a teacher for long because he contracted laryngitis (Kehlkopf-Katarrh). The illness was a very serious one. He sought healing everywhere but could not find it. Finally, the Lord granted him help through homeopathy. The medicine soon worked and he overcame his illness. His voice, however, remained weak. He did not take up teaching again but was soon elected to the Molotschna Mennonite School Council with the obligation of supervising the instruction in German and religion.

His father died from dropsy in 1912, and father had to carry on the family farm alone. He soon became a member of the Gnadenfeld Mennonite Church. Missionary H. Dirks and my father were good friends.

Until the communists took power in Russia, we lived joyfully and contented in the Lord. Our family consisted of ten children. During Makhno's reign of terror and the civil war, our family was hard hit, but no lives were lost. However, tragedy was not long in coming. The Lord soon visited us in a grievous fashion. Willms, a son-in-law and my husband of one month, was taken from our midst and executed by the *troika* (a three-man tribunal) in Waldheim. This was very difficult, especially for me. Later our child was born. During the same winter, all the grain was taken out of the attic. Then came many heavy assessments. Even the cracks in the attic had to be cleaned of grain. The Reds wanted to punish us even if they found a kernel of wheat. We starved a great deal during these years. When the land was divided, we were not severely affected. Since we were a large family, we still retained thirty-two hectares. The most difficult aspect of this period was the high product assessments and other obligations which we could not fulfill.

In spite of all the difficulties, our father did not neglect the Word of God. He attended church services whenever he could and often drove great distances in order to participate in the Bible studies held in the various churches. He introduced Bible studies and prayer meetings to the village of Gnadenfeld. If rain was lacking for a long period in spring or summer, special prayer meetings were held in church. These were well attended, though some ridiculed them.

My father did not fear the communists, even though they observed him through the window and reported him to the village office. Then the Lord placed a heavy cross upon our family. At eighteen, my second sister attended baptismal instruction in the church. My father urged her to take this seriously and only be baptized on faith. We soon noticed that she spent much time alone and did not open her heart. When Pentecost arrived and it was time for baptism, she stood up in church and walked out. The parents, sensing trouble, immediately stood up and followed her. She could not be found at home. We searched everywhere and finally found her in the forest, leaning against a tree and crying. When mother came closer, she only said, "Mother, what have I done?" They came home and when the parents asked whether she still desired to be baptized, she gave no answer. After that, she remained mentally ill. This caused great consternation in the church. There was even more [consternation] when, soon after, the parents left the Gnadenfeld Mennonite Church and, out of inner conviction, joined the Molotschna Evangelical Mennonite Brethren Church whose headquarters was in Lichtfelde.

Because father was a minister, both he and his sons were disenfranchised and deprived of their civil rights. Soon his son was conscripted into forced labor reserved for the disenfranchised. The young people had to haul earth with a wheelbarrow and build up the earth along the railway track. If they could not fulfill their prescribed norms, they received less bread and cucumber soup. When the son returned home, he had developed an enlarged heart due to excessive strain in the service.

In 1929 my oldest sister became ill. She was prayed over at father's request, but the Lord had determined otherwise. She died during Christmas, 1930. The parents submitted themselves to God, and the family became even closer to the Lord. On August 25, 1931, two men came from the village soviet and assessed father with a very high tax of grain or money. Father immediately declared that he could not pay such a huge sum. They then listed all our inventory: house, barn, and everything else in order to confiscate it.

The following night the parents and their eldest son disappeared from Gnadenfeld. They sensed what was coming. The fourth son brought them, together with the bare necessities and foodstuffs, to Berdyansk by wagon. When they arrived there late at night on the next day, they could find no accommodation because they were disenfranchised. After much pleading, they were allowed to stay on the yard overnight.

Early the next day, they had to leave the city. They returned to the Molotschna Colony. For several days, they received secret accommodation in the village of Mariental. My brother and mother walked to Gnadenfeld at night in order to visit those who had remained behind. They left Gnadenfeld the next night. As they walked through the lovely garden and past the blooming asters along the garden path, they tearfully said goodbye to their home. After three weeks, they left Mariental, spent several days in Rudnerweide and from there journeyed to the Caucasus where many ministers and other refugees found sanctuary. They found a welcome in the Mennonite settlement near Kalantarowka.

Here, our father soon found friends through his amiable disposition and the preaching of the Gospel. Mother was so homesick that my brother secretly brought her to her other children in Gnadenfeld. Mother's presence had to be kept secret which was not possible for long. The brother went to Stalino and received work there driving a tractor.

Mother spent three months with us. One day, I received an order to come to the village office immediately. I anticipated nothing pleasant. I was accused of harboring my disenfranchised mother. My defense of mother was to no avail. During the next night, there was a knock on the door and on the windows. I took mother into hiding, then finally opened the door. Among the visitors was a couple for whom my parents had done much good. The entire house was thoroughly searched. They left the house after two hours.

My mother had to return to the Caucasus. She took two of the children with her. After several days, the officials came to me and levied a high fine. When I said I could not pay it, all my possessions were listed and, after several days, taken away.

Our parents were very concerned about us and in letters warned us that we could be sent north at any time. We now decided to go to the Caucasus as well. This was already very difficult at that time. When we finally arrived there, it was a sad meeting with our parents. We had taken our mentally ill sister with us.

Our father did not despair and complain. He said, "The Lord has given us a heavy burden. He will also help to carry it. We want to trust Him further." As a large family, we were to live in one small room. At father's request, the [local] executive committee placed a larger house at our disposal. We got an earth hut with two rooms, a kitchen, cellar and barn.

Father and his three sons made clay bricks for the village inhabitants. One sister earned money with spinning, the other worked in a household and I sewed. When the harvest came we were all busy gleaning. There were very few wheat ears, so we gathered barley ears. We threshed these ears, brought the seeds to the mill, sifted the flour, and baked bread. Our father called it Mara bread.

179

At the end of August 1932, our mother suddenly became ill. The doctor diagnosed malaria and typhus. A few days later, our father also became sick with malaria. Many other refugees became ill as well. After one week, the entire family was ill. Only one brother remained well and made us coffee. All the medicine was of no avail. Father also contracted diarrhea. Everyday the residents of the village brought us food. May God reward them!

During his illness, our dear father often expressed the wish to be buried in the Gnadenfeld cemetery. He hoped that mother and the [mentally] ill, Eliese, could die with him. The Lord granted this last wish. Shortly before he died father said, "My, how bitter death is." His eyes closed and he rested in the Lord. After three days, our severely tested father was laid to his last rest. The minister Isaak Poettker, also a refugee from the Molotschna, held the funeral sermon. His text was Isaiah 57:1. "The righteous man perishes and nobody cares; godly men are snatched away, while no one lays it to heart, that the righteous man is taken away before calamity comes; he enters peace."

Our father faithfully clung to God's Word. During the last years, he memorized a great deal from the Bible, the hymnal and *Heimatklänge*. "There will come a time," he said, "when they will take the Bible and good books from us. The things we have in our memory no one can take from us."

The inhabitants of Kalantarowka made our father a lovely coffin.

After three weeks, my mentally ill sister died of the same illness. Shortly, before her death her spirit regained its clarity, and she made preparations for death. She sang two songs all by herself, "Nimm, Jesu meine Hände" and "Einst war ich gar weit von dem Heiland." Thus she died.

Our father died on October 28, 1932 at the age of fifty-nine years. The doctor advised us to change climates; and so, we survivors returned home to Gnadenfeld. This journey was much more difficult than the first. We were all sick. Mother was bent and stooped. On the trip, linen and clothes were stolen from us. Amid great difficulties, we reached home. We moved into my house. Almost immediately, my mother had a stroke and died after three days. During this time, she could not speak. She only lifted her finger and pointed upwards. She died on March 11, 1933.

The five sons were exiled to the north. My oldest brother was arrested in 1936. Three were taken in 1937. The last one was taken in 1941 together with my son. The two youngest sisters were captured during the flight from Poland and sent to Kazakhstan.

I, alone, have come to Canada. I'm trusting God that I will find a home here. I long for my son and siblings in the distant land.

Susanna Willms

Isaak H. Regehr
Caucasus, South Russia

His parents originally settled on the Terek lands. His father, Heinrich P. Regehr was a minister of the Mennonite church there. His son, Isaak Regehr, was a cripple and was so handicapped that he could only walk with the help of a cane. Since he could not help his parents on the farm, he studied to become a teacher.

He was a teacher for many years, first in the Terek, then in Suworowka and Kalantarowka, and later in the new settlement of Ebental, also in the Caucasus. As the prohibition against all religious instruction intensified, Isaak H. Regehr gave up his beloved teaching profession. He then worked in the collective farm, first as accountant, then as secretary, and finally as treasurer.

The jealousy of his fellow workers soon made further work on the collective farm impossible. Afterall he had his own house, a cow, a pig and chickens. In addition, he had a sizable rabbit business. That was great wealth in those times. The people could not accept the fact that he was better off than they and tried to get rid of him.

When Regehr noticed that he was being slandered, he sold his house and cattle and moved his family to the new settlement Konosawod, a state farm where purebred horses were raised for the government. Here, he and his wife worked diligently on the collective farm. Only Mennonites had been hired here. The majority were refugees from the Molotschna.

Even here, they were after him. One evening in July 1938, the police arrived on his yard with the order to arrest him. The police were baffled when they found an invalid. They believed it was a misunderstanding. They asked his name and compared it to their papers. Perhaps there was another man in the village with the same name? When Regehr denied this they commented somewhat sympathetically, "Well then, we'll have to take you with us." They ordered him to pack his things: linens, a blanket, and pillows. When Regehr noted that he could not carry anything because of his lameness, the police carried his things to the waiting truck, and they were off. The family did not hear from him for a long time.

After three years, a returning Russian came to the house and told Mrs. Regehr that her husband was on an island in the sea where he worked as a shoemaker, because this is what he previously did on the collective. He had been sentenced to ten years and was not allowed to write or receive letters. The Russian related that he had been exiled to the same island but that he had been freed. He had promised Regehr to find his wife and give her news of his whereabouts and his well-being. He did not give his name nor his residence nor the name of the island for fear of the GPU.

The Russian further said that a Mennonite in the settlement had betrayed Isaak Regehr to the GPU as he had secretly been holding services in neighbors' homes. Regehr, however, had only ordered Bibles from Germany by request and then delivered them to the people. When the Bibles arrived, this false Mennonite casually came to the house under the pretense of buying a Bible. When he learned that Regehr no longer had any, he walked away angrily and slammed the door. Since that time, he was his enemy and did not rest until his neighbor was exiled.

Isaak H. Regehr remained in exile—whether he's alive or dead no one knows. In his home [village], he was a minister of the Word in the Mennonite Brethren church. These people were the special targets for the enemies of religion.

Adolf A. Reimer and Family
Alexandertal, Molotschna

He was born on October 1, 1881 in the little village of Wiesenfeld, province of Jekaterinoslaw, south Russia. His father was Abraham Reimer. His grandfather on his mother's side was a Kalweit, who was one of the founders of the Russian Baptist Church in south Russia. In many of the homes of Russian believers in the Ukraine, Kalweit's picture hung next to those of Pawlow, Dyatschkow, and others.

He was converted to the Lord at an early age; he had already preached his first sermon at fifteen years of age.

Since the home he came from was poor, he had a difficult struggle obtaining his higher education. He, nevertheless, completed the pedagogical classes in the Halbstadt High School. He was often teased and ridiculed when, as a student, he picked up match boxes from the street and sold them at one Kopeck each in order to earn some pocket money. And yet, as a "poor one", he knew how to do personal work with his fellow students and bring them to their knees [before God]. He later became a teacher—first in a little school in the country and then in the village school in Tiege, Molotschna.

In 1902 he began to proclaim the Gospel among the Russian workers' servants and maids in the villages. It was a difficult task, yet he had success.

In 1905 the founding of the first small Russian congregation took place. Several converted Russians had decided to be baptized. In the countryside, the government still punished such acts, while in the larger cities, the law allowed such congregations to exist. It was during one night in May of 1905 in the Ohrloff school that local young believers from the Mennonite Brethren church heard the testimony of the new believers, four Russian hired men and one maid. They were then baptized in the river some two miles from the village. They returned, were accepted into the congregation, communion was celebrated, and at five a.m., everyone returned home.

In the fall of the same year, he (Adolf) resigned his teaching position and devoted himself fully to mission work among the Russians.

He crisscrossed Russia from the south to the north and

not only preached in the churches, but also in the theatres of cities where there were no churches. When the training school for ministers was founded in St. Petersburg by J.S. Prochanow, the head of the Evangelical Russian Christians, he became a teacher at this school.

On January 1, 1905, he married sister Sara Goossen from Alexandertal, Molotschna. The Lord blessed this union with five sons and a daughter, who died at age two. When the hatred against old Germans intensified during WWI, his wife was arrested and imprisoned in St. Petersburg. He was serving as a medical orderly at the time. The reasons [for her arrest]: she had written to her parents and commented on how sad things were in this world. When the "great King" would some-day rule, she continued, hate would cease and the swords would be turned to ploughshares and the wolf and lamb would graze together. The police thought the expression "great King" referred to Kaiser Wilhelm and she was sentenced to one month in prison.

After Adolf Reimer's return from state service, the family lived in the village of Alexandertal.

When the revolution of 1917 erupted and the Reds seized power there was much destitution and misery, especially in the Molotschna. The fronts moved back and forth through the Mennonite villages. During this time, Adolf Reimer diligently proclaimed the Gospel to the soldiers. The yards of the villages were filled with soldiers. On Sundays, he held from one to four services in these yards. In the neighboring village of Mariental, the general assembled the entire commando and brother Reimer had a crowd of 1000 before him. He preached the simple Gospel of Jesus the Crucified, conscious that some of his listeners would no longer be alive in a few hours. In the volost village of Gnadenfeld, the colonel of the regiment gave brother Reimer fifteen minutes to preach to mounted caval-rymen. They then were off to bloody battle. Under such circumstances, each moment is so precious. This was during the time when the White Guards were in the villages and con-stituted the front.

Then came the Reds and with them the punitive expedi-tions with their terror. There were many murders. People feared for their lives. One person remained courageous. He had no fear of men. He had only one mission: to save souls from eternal damnation. When the Mennonite Brethren Church council met in Alexandertal during this time, he pleaded from the innermost depths of his soul: "Brethren, the Reds, too, have souls which want to be saved and we must preach the Gospel to them." The brethren warned him, but his only response was, "I must." Brother Heinrich Goossen, his brother-in-law, offered to lead the choir and a service was organized for seven p.m. to which all were invited, including the leader of the punitive expedition with his heavily armed men. Evening came and 300 listeners appeared. The leader stood before the audience with his riding whip, threatening a bloodbath. The situation was very tense. With a silent prayer in their hearts, the singers entered on their wooden shoes (leathers shoes were no longer available). They stood up in front and sang the beautiful Russian song, "O sinner come to Jesus" so pleadingly and invitingly that the feelings calmed down. The leader [of the punitive expedition] sat down in front. In a brief, earnest sermon brother Reimer was able to proclaim the Gospel. No one was hurt. The Lord shielded and protected all with His grace.

During the famine, brother Reimer again journeyed to visit the Russian churches. This was very difficult and associated with many dangers, but he could not be held back. Concerning his life one could write, "The love of Christ constraineth me."

He spent four months in the city of Kiev where there were several large Russian churches. He also served with the Gospel in the surrounding region. Here, he became ill with typhus which claimed many victims everywhere. He was brought home. After suffering four difficult days from the vicious, contagious disease, he went home to his Lord whom he had served. He was deeply mourned by his bereaved family, his church, and his many dear friends among the Russians who honored and loved him as a father. They had lost much. His last words on his deathbed, which he repeated three times, were, "Lord Jesus, your Gospel is so simple and your grace so great!"

His grandfather, Kalweit, was shot by the Reds while preaching the Gospel to them. He was over eighty years of age. His father, Abraham Reimer, was also shot. His brother, Jakob

Reimer, who lived in the Caucasus and worked for the Lord there, was likewise shot by bandits. He was making home visitations and had kneeled down to pray.

His family suffered severely after his death. Brother Reimer died in May 1921 and left a destitute family. They were impoverished and the children were all minors. The congregation and others helped, but they, too, had become poor through all the robbery by the Reds.

It was especially difficult for the widow, Sara Reimer, after 1929. All the ministers and their families were disenfranchised and also deprived of their civil rights. They had no employment opportunities and received no ration cards.

All churches were closed and all Sunday schools forbidden. Sister Reimer remained active and so was first fined 500 rubles, then later 1,000 rubles or alternatively a prison term. As young ministers her two oldest sons, Daniel and Heinrich, followed in the footsteps of their father, and both were arrested. After a six-month imprisonment, during which he was terribly tortured, Daniel was exiled for eight years. The younger son, Heinrich, was initially sentenced to one year in prison. After much mistreatment he was also sent away and they lost all track of him. After a night of torture Daniel, the eldest son, wrote, "Mama, this night was terrible. Pray to God that He will grant me the strength to be faithful." His mother sent this note to her brother in Canada, H. Goossen in Manitou, Manitoba .

Robbed of her two eldest sons, subject to imprisonment and fines, this sorely tried woman fled to a Russian town, Guljapole and found a warm reception among Russian Baptists. She was able to remain here for one year before she was expelled as a disenfranchised citizen. After wandering to and fro, she finally found refuge with her youngest sister in Waldheim, the Heinrich Driedigers. It was not long before the soviet ordered him to expel his sister-in-law. When he refused to do so, the entire family was disenfranchised and stripped of legal rights. When this proved fruitless the family, each and all, was banished from its ancestral home. They journeyed to the Caucasus where they temporarily found a home near Lawarow.

And what of sister Sara Reimer? She and her ten year old youngest son went to Elisabethal and found a room in the poor district. Expelled from here she purchased a small sod hut with two "food drafts" sent to her from Canada. Again, she was expelled by village authorities as a persona non grata and could only take as much as she and her son could carry.

At the same time, the widow of another minister, Heinrich Enns (the deceased brother had worked amid great blessing for many years as an evangelist), was also expelled with five small children. These two widows and their children, together with a few belongings, walked sixty-five verst to the city of Melitopol.

"I was hungry and you fed me"—that is what the poor Russian Baptist brothers and sisters did. They accepted them but had only two rooms. For one year, sister Sara Reimer slept in the kitchen. Boards were laid on the bathtub for night and there was a bed for mother and son.

"Each year I celebrate my birthday in a different location," she wrote to her brother in Canada. Soon she was forced to leave again. She journeyed to Ekaterinoslaw and then is to have gone to the Caucasus.

In November 1948, Mrs. Mariechen Regehr (nee Fast), the adopted daughter of the Adolf Reimers, sent the following information from Siberia: "Our stepmother, Mrs. A. Reimer—Sara—came to us in Lawarow, Suworowka in the Caucasus from St. Petersburg via Melitopol. Together with others, we were exiled to Siberia. She died here of typhus on May 5, 1946." She was also buried there.

Do we not think of the words in Hebrews 11:37,38: " . . . they roamed about, destitute, afflicted, ill-treated—the world was not worthy of them."

Supplement

The young hero of faith, Daniel A. Reimer of Alexandertal, was arrested together with the teacher and minister Johann Bekker of Prangenau early in 1935 and taken to the prison in Halbstadt. In May, both were sentenced to eight years in exile and were brought to the prison in the district capital of Melitopol.

When a large transport of exiles was sent north, a large crowd of relatives had gathered on the prison yard and the street. The young wife of brother Daniel Reimer was among them. When she saw her husband coming out of the prison gate, she shouted to attract his attention. He saw her and audibly called, "However we are not of those who shrink back so as to perish, but of those who have faith and save their souls" (Hebrews 10:39).

Mrs. Johann Friesen of Pordenau, Molotschna and currently in Paraguay writes to her friends in Canada:

> During the advance of the German army in the fall of 1941, the remaining women and children and a few old people in the villages from Mariental to Elisabethal were loaded into the freight cars of a train for transport to Siberia. As our train slowly travelled through the vast steppes of Russia, it was bombed by German aircraft. A few cars were completely blown apart; one was on fire. We all rushed into the open. When the aircraft noticed that there were only women and children aboard they stopped their attack. What a scene! Dismembered bodies—hands, feet and other body parts lay scattered about—others lay in death rattles. Among these was Tina Reimer (nee Pauls) of Alexandertal, the wife of the young minister Daniel Adolf Reimer, who was languishing in exile. A bomb fragment had blown a hole in her chest. One could still see her heart beating. It was not for long and life ceased. A grave was dug alongside the railway, the bodies and limbs were gathered together. A sister (it was apparently Mrs. Peter Reimer of Steinbach) led in a song and prayed. Then the grave was covered with earth.

> We survivors were again loaded on the train and transported further—homeless, frightened, facing exile to Siberia!

> During the night, I and another woman escaped from the train and after several days got behind the German front. Later, we came to Germany and from there to South America, our new home.

Adolf Reimer's grandfather Kalweit worked in Tiflis and the surrounding region of the Caucasus as an evangelist among the Armenians for many years. He also did mission work among the Russian workers on the large estates. Brother Kalweit was captured by the Reds on an estate and shot. He had chosen to stay, while others had fled. Before he was shot he testified of his Savior to the Red bands, and as an old man became a martyr for his Master.

His great-grandchild, Daniel Adolf Reimer, was beaten and hung from the ceiling by hooks attached to his nostrils. They wanted him to deny his faith in Christ, but God gave him the grace to remain faithful.

Abram Rempel
A Servant of Christ
in the Difficult Soviet Period 1936-37

Abram Rempel was born in Hochfeld, province of Ekaterinoslaw in 1903. He received a good Christian education: first the village school and then several years of high school. He was converted to the Lord in his youth and became a member of the Mennonite Brethren Church. The selection of his life's partner fell upon Anna Froese of Schoenberg, Old Colony, also a disciple of the Lord Jesus.

The beginning of home and family life was most auspicious. He obtained a good position in an office in Dneprostroj. It paid well and there were no difficulties related to their livelihood. Yet amid all the [prevailing] suffering and injustice, the young man was apprehensive as to their good fortune, for they had nothing to worry or complain about. The situation changed one day when he received a citation from the terrible NKVD. In one blow, his happiness ended. He was to appear before this dreaded organization, formerly called GPU at seven p.m. At first there was a reception and friendly conversation. Soon they got to the heart of the matter: Rempel was to become a spy or informant at his place of work. This caused a short, intense inner struggle, but he refused. There was a raving and threatening which lasted into the night, but without results. In order to make him willing, he was repeatedly cited and interrogated. For three days, he was imprisoned in the *Urka*, the prison in which the worst bandits, who often mistreated the new arrivals horribly,were kept. When the attendant placed him into the cell, he said, "Leave this man alone!" Rempel still had some money with him which he gave to the bandits for distribution. The official had hoped to wear him down, but Rempel remained steadfast. The official finally declared, "Go home and see that you are out of this entire region within two hours, then you can still preach elsewhere."

Rempel was a Sunday school teacher and an occasional preacher. In 1931, when in nuptial bliss he had married Anna, she left a home where, in 1918, the father had been shot while seeking to fend off bandits. Now the Rempels had a fine lodging which they simply left standing without even informing the landlord. Another Mennonite with a wagon was called to take them away. Only the bare essentials were taken. The train brought them among the mountain people of the Caucasus. At first there was mistrust and enmity, but that all changed once they learned to know the new people. Things went well for the next one and a half to two years. Meanwhile, from back home, people wrote that circumstances had changed and that it was safe to return; but things did not turn out that way. The Rempels went to Schoenberg where, for a time, he worked unnoticed in a business. Here, he served in a small church. Bernhard Dyck from Hochfeld had been the actual minister. He had been exiled for three years, then returned to Schoenberg. His service was soon interrupted, and he was sent away for another three years. The orphaned church requested Abram Rempel and Jacob Wiebe to serve them. He was, naturally, not ordained during that time.

October of 1936 again became a time of severe testing for Rempel. They had taken several men from the village who were to be declared injurious by the People's Court. False witnesses were now coerced who were to attest to the imagined wrongdoing. They had already rounded up four or five Mennonite men from the village. Now they wanted [to arrest] Rempel. He strenuously resisted. That added an inner agony to the existing fear that he would be taken from his family. When he did not return all night, his wife took counsel with neighbors and brought him his breakfast. Then she could learn whether he was still here or had left. The official was seated in a large room. Rempel sat on an oven bench. She was allowed to enter, but Rempel did not want to eat. The official came and urged him to eat and even made him go to the table. Then the wife was asked to leave, and she went to the back of the house to the people who owned this farm. There she could hear how severely her husband was being interrogated. It ended with the Soviet official promising to come and arrest him in three days. In the providence of God, he did not appear.

The young couple, nevertheless, felt uneasy. Would it not be better to leave the business? Even in the business, there were difficulties. The materials were increasingly rationed and there was not enough to go around. When an opening occurred on the pig farm, the businessman became a worker and even became a watchman when his turn came.

Then came that terrible October 29, 1937. The so-called big "machine," the truck which came to collect its human cargo, arrived just after dark. Behind it came a smaller machine to illuminate and guard the scene. The men were herded into the school building. The women slowly followed crouching to the ground, kneeling or otherwise remaining near the school in order to see what would happen to their men.

There was great tumult and scolding, yet silence on the part of the men. It ended with the repeated shouting in Russian, "You are enemies of the people! You are enemies of the people!" The men finally thought, "So let it be." Since Rempel had not returned, Mrs. Rempel and a neighbor and her children went to investigate how things stood. Just then, the loaded truck appeared followed by the second truck. The children shouted into the darkness, "Daddy, are you there?" "Yes!" Then one of the prisoners shouted, "We're going to Nikopol!" From others, Mrs. Rempel learned that her husband was among them. It soon became clear that most of the captives belonged to the Mennonite Brethren Church, except two who belonged to the other church. In all there were seventeen. The youngest child in the Rempel family was two months and four days old. Immediately afterward, the village administration tried to confiscate the wages of the men, since they were "wreckers." They petitioned officials in Saporoshje in this regard, but little came of it.

Since the majority were simply rounded up and taken away without food, not even having time to put on [appropriate] clothes or shoes for the journey, the women collected these things in order to meet their men in Nikopol. It was not possible, since they were under interrogation. The items were listed and delivered to the prison. The list was returned with the note, "Everything received."

Naturally, they were all exiled. A card came indicating they would be there (Nikopol) until a certain date. It was time to say goodbye, but the local soviet would not give a permit for the journey since the [anniversary of the] revolution was to be celebrated the next day. As always, the masses were rounded up. Woe to anyone who stayed away without a good reason. Great speeches were held and as always the purification of the village from undesirable elements was advocated. The people had to applaud and agree. Woe to those who refused. With tears in their eyes and with wounded hearts, the women had to join in. It was, after all, a question of bread. Next day, they received their papers.

In Nikopol, they could visit for fifteen minutes, three at a time. The men and women were to speak in Russian. Mrs. Rempel spoke Low German. That was the last glance, the last word until today. No letter. No report as to whether he was alive or dead.

Without work, there was no bread. Three children remained at home alone, while mother worked all day. In the morning, it was naturally decided how they should behave and what they should eat. Even then, a passing woman had to drop by from time to time to calm the children who were crying for their mother.

Another episode. After some seven months the news came that someone had met Rempel beyond Moscow. It seemed that uncle Cornelius Rempel was on a journey to Wyasma to take consignment of some purchases. He had been standing near the railway when 300 prisoners marched by. All of a sudden someone in the crowd yelled "Uncle Corny! Uncle Corny!"

Jakob A. Rempel
Elder

Elder Jakob A. Rempel was probably one of the most prominent personalities among the Mennonites in Russia during the last decade, not only in terms of his theological training, but also in terms of his outstanding character and public service. What elder J.J. Toews accomplished and endured as a worker and martyr in the Mennonite Brethren Church, elder J.A. Rempel accomplished in the Mennonite Church. When one studies their experiences and inner struggles, one finds two warriors, combatants and sufferers who are temperamentally related. The word of James 1:12 can rightful-

192

ly be applied to them: "Blessed is the man who stands up under trial; for when he has stood the test, he will receive the crown of life."

The author only met the dear professor twice in his life. The first time was in the Alexanderkrone Church in the Molotschna where, at the end of 1925, he gave a report on the Mennonite World Conference in Switzerland to which he and professor B.H. Unruh were sent as representatives of the Mennonite churches in Russia. To this day, I see that stately person in my mind's eye. I also remember the song which he recited and which was still new to me: "Es schaut bei Nacht und Tage Dein holdes Bild mich an; Und legt mir vor die Frage: Ob ich dich lassen kann." And then the mighty refrain: "Mein Gott, ich bin entschieden, Auf ewig bin ich Dein; Ich kann ja ohne Frieden und ohne Dich nicht sein."

He had to experience the truths of this song to the full and prove them in his practical life. But which of us at the time would have thought this or held it to be possible?

On another occasion, we were together in Neu-Halbstadt for a general consultation of the representatives of all three Mennonite groups for the purpose of founding a common seminary either in Odessa or in Ohrloff, Molotschna. At the time, he was already thought of as a teaching candidate for the seminary. Nothing came of the project thanks to the intervention of the Soviet government which, through cunning or force, sought to suppress all religious endeavors.

His youngest son, Paul, who came to Italy as a prisoner of war, writes to Canada from his English prison camp:

Since March 5, 1945 I am in English captivity in Italy. (He had been taken by the Germans from Russia to Germany and inducted into the German army.) My father, Jakob Rempel, professor of theology, was elder of the Mennonite church in Gruenfeld, south Russia prior to 1929. In 1929 we possessed a visa for entry to Canada and wanted to leave Russia. My father was arrested in Moscow, and we were not allowed out of Russia. In 1936, after he had previously escaped captivity, he was again arrested.

My mother, Sophie Rempel nee Sudermann, was and presumably still is with the family Landes, Lauterbacher Hof near Heilbronn-Wuerttemberg in Germany.

The MCC representative in Germany, provided further details about the suffering of the dear elder J.A. Rempel.

He had to spend some time in prison in a room filled with human excretion and a dreadful smell. Then his eyes were subjected to such strong electric lights that he almost went blind. On the way to exile near Issilj-Kulj, he jumped from the train into the deep snow. For three days, he ate only snow. He contracted typhus and his cousin was able to nurse him. He and his friend, Dyck, then tried to flee to Persia but were caught by the border guards. He was sentenced to one year in prison. The other refugees were treated worse because they carried valuables.

Thereafter he went to work and became acquainted with a Jew. Together they fled towards the border and hid in the tall grass. Sheep dogs began to bark and they were discovered. The shepherds captured Rempel, who had suffered a heart attack and could go no further. The others apparently escaped, but Rempel was sentenced to another year in prison.

When his son, Alexander, once found him almost unconscious under a tree, it turned out that he had no fingernails. Needles had been placed under his nails so that they eventually dropped off. What pain that must have caused. Even a small sliver under the nail is so painful! Together they travelled to Chiva and both stayed with Mennonites at Ak-Metschetj where they found a warm welcome. There they met seven ministers and three deacons, mostly refugees. One day all the Mennonites of this settlement were loaded on trucks by the GPU, taken 150 miles into the desert, and unloaded. Father Rempel and his Sascha, however, were sent to European Russia: father to Oryol, the son to Solowoki.

When the front passed over the region near Orjol in 1941, the bodies of five executed men were found. It is believed that elder Rempel was among them. The bodies were badly decomposed so that exact identification was not possible.

The author

Excerpts from the Life of Elder J.A. Rempel

Jakob Aron Rempel was born on April 9, 1883 in Heuboden, some twenty-five verst north of Nikopol. He was the oldest in a family of thirteen children His father was Aron A. Rempel from Schoenhorst, district of Chortitza; his mother was

Justina Peters. The parents were farmers. Father, however, wanted to go into business. He built a mill, but was forced into bankruptcy and later had to support his huge family as a tradesman.

Amid these circumstances, the future elder did not experience many happy days at home. He was a great help to his mother, who had much work with the children. He loved children and therefore was an outstanding care giver.

His parents repeatedly changed residence during the period when Jakob was of school age. The circumstance and the fact that he had poor eyes made study difficult. He was, nevertheless, very gifted and made good progress in his studies. He was a logical thinker and mathematics suited him well. He was generally a "bookworm." Unfortunately, he could not satisfy his thirst for knowledge until several years after the completion of elementary school. For a time, he served as a stable hand. This certainly did not satisfy his ambitious spirit.

God had a way out for him. In each village of the Jewish Colony, Mennonites had been settled as well. These were to be model farmers for the Jewish settlers. These Mennonites were entitled to their private school in each village. They often appointed teachers who weren't fully qualified. For two years, this brother was able to teach to his heart's content in one of these villages.

He, then, had the prospect of obtaining a teaching position in a village in the Orenburg settlement, but this required a teaching certificate. Instead of teaching, he went to the city of Orenburg and took private tutoring with a college teacher. After this instruction, he took his teaching exam and returned to the mother colony. Here in Neuhorst, district of Chortitza, he taught enthusiastically for one year. He derived great satisfaction from this. He was a teacher by the grace of God.

Since Jakob was on his own at such an early age and was far from home, he was obviously subject to the sins of youth. He, nevertheless, possessed a wonderful heritage from his pious mother, namely a deeply religious temperament. Our mother had influenced us religiously through the many Christian songs which she sang, through the telling of Bible stories, and by her lifestyle. The bonds between mother and her firstborn son were especially strong and tender. Jakob converted to the Lord early, perhaps at age seventeen.

At first, he felt a strong urge to become a missionary in the heathen world. He even had a conversation with elder Isaak Dyck on the matter, yet he never became one. In my estimation our churches lacked a sense of missions. Instead of a missionary, he became a teacher.

2.

After he had taught for one year in Neuhorst, the owner of the large mill in Jekaterinoslaw, Johann J. Thiessen, wanted to send a young Mennonite teacher to Basel in order to attend seminary. Many of our teachers had already done this and with good results. They served in our congregations as religious teachers and church workers. My brother applied for this grant and also received it.

During the course of six years in Basel (1906-12), my brother was very much in his element. In addition to his seminary studies, he also caught up on his general education. After three years, he took his degree. He studied at the seminary for another year and a half and was simultaneously a student of philosophy and theology at the University of Basel. Following this, he only attended the university. He was also a teacher at the seminary which he had earlier attended, where he taught Greek and church history.

After four years, he came to his old homeland for a summer visit. His mother, whose darling he was, was still alive at the time. When he returned home two years later, he arrived just in time for her funeral.

My brother did not quite finish his studies. In order to complete his doctorate, he should have remained abroad another year, yet Chortitza needed a teacher for its high school and its teacher's college and so he was offered this position. This was not the only reason for interrupting his studies. The other related to the suffering and death of his mother and the fact that he wished to help his family. Thanks to him, the younger siblings were all able to obtain their education. While he was still in Switzerland, he had already sent hundreds of rubles for the support of his loved ones at home. He could have easily spent the energy and money to complete his own education. The needs of his parents and family were more important, and he was prepared to sacrifice and be without for their sake.

The six years abroad meant strenuous work for Jakob yet, without doubt, they were among the best of his tumultuous life.

3.

When he accepted the teaching position in Chortitza, he wrote:

January 30, 1912—I have been dealt a lovely fate. Now I have the hope of once more participating in public life. That in itself would not make me so happy. The fact is that I can devote my energies to the Chortitza High School.

To be there; to live there; to have young people about; to portray with love and compassion the story of our forebearers' life struggle; to introduce them to the life of today; to focus their minds on God; to take them to the people who, exhausted after the day's labors, cultivate the muse; to join with them in song until their breasts fill with the joy of life and with courage—all this will be such a joy!

In Chortitza, Jakob was only a teacher for three years, the period 1912-15. So far as I know, he loved his work. His colleagues and former students would know more about the matter.

Two very important events took place at this time: the call to the ministry and to marriage. While still a student, my brother expressed his desire for a life's partner on March 16, 1911 as follows:

First I want to be stirred by and learn to know nature, through which I have known and experienced God. God, whose love envelops me like a breath of spring, in whose presence I stand, from whom strength upon strength descends upon me, who has taken me out of the depths and lifted me to the realms of light. First I want to be ready to enjoy the pleasures of life, to be happy in order to make happy. Then I want to appeal to the heart of some young lady: 'Let me offer you bliss and happiness. With you I want to conquer heaven, which has saved me from destruction. [Let me offer you] a noble aspiration

197

which will carry us upwards to the Excellent, the Perfect, to the One who blotted out my transgressions, [an aspiration] which shall sanctify us, that will strengthen the good in us.'

The young lady which my brother saw standing before him in 1913 was Mariechen Sudermann, daughter of Johann Sudermann who lived fifteen verst east of Milloradowka. The wedding was held in the spring (or summer) of 1914 on the Sudermann estate. D.H. Epp, later elder in Chortitza, officiated at the ceremony. We still have fond memories of the wedding celebration. Things were still so quiet and peaceable and people seemed happy. It was the quiet before a terrible storm which has not subsided until the present day.

Two children, Alexander and Leonora, were born of this marriage. In 1918 influenza struck thousands, yes millions. My brother's wife was also a victim. The pain of this blow was so severe that we best pass over it in silence.

The work in the school and the ministry became a balm for the brother's wounded heart. His steadfast trust in God also sustained him.

Then came the dance of death: the collapse of the Russian Empire, revolution, and civil war. At the time, my brother was teaching at the college in Nikopol and finally came to Jekaterinoslaw. Here, he was minister in the Mennonite church in that city and a teacher at the local university. I do not know for how long. Within the city, banditry and war swept to and fro. God protected the brother and his loved ones. One brother-in-law, nevertheless, became a victim of the murderers.

Around 1919, the Lord led the Neu-Chortitza congregation to invite the brother to lead or participate in a Bible conference. When an elder election was held in the church one year later, two-thirds of the vote went to my brother. This initiated a great turning point in his life.

He wrote about this from Jekaterinoslaw on April 24, 1920:

> I will not write much about the momentous event which has so suddenly overwhelmed me. I do not possess the inward calm to talk about it. For me, this is contrary to all expectations. It is so incomprehensible and unfathomable that I completely submit myself and allow the Will of the Most High to

prevail. He had called me and I will follow His word.

On May 2, 1920 the elder of the Alt-Chortitza Mennonite Church, Isaak Gerhard Dyck, ordained the brother as elder in the Neu-Chortitza Church. If it had been a turbulent time for the brother earlier, it was even more so now.

The Neu-Chortitza Church and its affiliates had lost a number of ministers during the war. A number of new ministers had to be elected. With the Lord's help and under the leadership of the Holy Spirit, he worked with great enthusiasm during the next three years. Ministerial courses and Bible conferences were organized. The ministers met regularly, working and planning. The Lord gave His blessing to the efforts. The famine was a difficult visitation which also affected the brother's family. There were two [significant] events in the brother's family during these three years. On March 10, 1921, he married Sophie Sudermann, the sister of his first wife. Then on October 14, 1921, Jakob's mother-in-law was buried. The most significant event for the congregation was the emigration to America in 1923. The Neu-Chortitza Church was deeply affected by it. Over 500 persons from our church left with the third train. Later, more and more emigrated. This departure and the pressure from the Red government made congregational nurture very difficult, yes, almost impossible.

My brother remained behind. He believed that he had to serve the Mennonite community. From 1923 to his exile in 1929, he tried to serve the churches willingly and conscientiously and to the best of his abilities. Many of his letters testify to this. On May 31, 1924, he wrote from Moscow,

Persistence and great self-control are needed to stay on top of difficult circumstances. The struggle at home is two-sided: the congregation (that is the main thing), and the outside opponents. It is difficult to assess which is the more dangerous front. For me the community is the most important.

We have had two audiences with the Central Executive Committee: one hour and fifteen minutes and one hour and forty minutes in length. Many issues were discussed. I could relate many things, but where is the time for it? Some things have been promised us.

On November 10, 1924, he again wrote from Moscow,

So much work awaits me at home that I almost trip over myself. This is the fourth week that I have been away from home.

The work was not only time-consuming and nerve-racking, but also dangerous. On July 22, 1924 he wrote from Gruenfeld,

Thank God that I have been able to testify before the anti-Christs this last time. That was very satisfying to me, a small thank-you for the unending love of God for me, that He saved me, a sinner, from eternal death. Our discussions were permeated with martyr thoughts. Each time we went for an audience there was a hallowed surrender to God. We never knew if the return way would lead to freedom or imprisonment. Many are suffering in exile.

Some will ask, "Why didn't he leave Russia when it was still possible?" Others might go so far as to say that he himself was responsible for his fate. I would like to respond by saying that he did not seek his own advantage by staying. He wanted to serve God and our people.

In 1925, when the 400th anniversary of the Mennonites was celebrated in Switzerland, my brother was sent as the representative of the Russian Mennonites. From Germany, he wrote,

It is quite something to be outside of Russia. I think one could forget everything and begin life anew. But what of those suffering at home, what of the many large congregations! I'm drawn back there. Wife and children can be taken along, but not the congregation.

October 2, 1925:

It would be easier and more advantageous for me to teach in a high school. Many in the congregation thought that after I returned from Germany, I would prepare to emigrate. One thing is certain: if it were not for the church, I and my family would have been in the USA long ago. But we have an obligation here.

If, through practical Christianity, we today want to uphold

the Kingdom of God as a light in heathen darkness, then it must begin with us. Here is the opportunity.

Because the ministers were steadily emigrating the congregations were frequently obligated to hold ministerial elections. This resulted in two difficulties:

a) It became more and more difficult to find suitable candidates.

b) The candidates, because of the generally unpleasant circumstances (suppression) ministers found themselves in, refused to accept the nomination.

If the religious life in the churches was not to be extinguished, intensive work had to be done. In a letter of November 4, 1926, we get an insight into the efforts which were made.

> God still gave me the courage and strength to continue the work, though at times I almost succumbed. On November 1-2, we had a Bible conference in Jekaterinoslaw: theme - the Prophet Amos. We ministers meet on the first and fifteenth of every month for mutual Bible study. On November 22-27, we're having a ministerial week where we want to cover the following themes:
>
> 1. The Concept, Nature, Function and Purpose of the Sermon - one day.
>
> 2. The Content of the Sermon - two days
>
> 3. The Structure of the Sermon - one day
>
> 4. The Personality of the Preacher - one day
>
> Two sermons are held in the evening which are critiqued the next morning. I have a similar program for Sagradowka early in December and in the Crimea after Christmas.

The Mennonite Bible School and *Unser Blatt* were two issues which generated much worry and work for the brother.

March 20, 1926:

> We are leaving Gruenfeld. We are leaving the congregations here and going to another place, a location which is unfamiliar to us. God willed it and we want to be quiet and listen. It was a difficult struggle. Now the worst is over, the decision has been made. As you may have heard, we Men-

nonites want to establish a Bible school. The government has granted us the permission, but the location has not been finalized. We think it should be Ohrloff, and if a school can be opened there, that's where we will go. Leaving here will be very difficult. I do not even want to think of it. The congregation is suffering, because I am working for the school. Yet the school will not be established if further strenuous efforts are not made. If God wills, we leave here in the fall. I firmly believe I will someday conclude my life here. I once came here with that idea in mind. God's ways are different from ours, however. I still want to be obedient, even when I cannot understand. Currently, I am working on the curriculum of the school. This is fairly complicated. The school is not only to train ministers, but is to be a cultural center for the overall cultivation of the mind.

February 11, 1927:

The rough blows which are coming from the outside . . . raise various questions in our mind. Emigration is out of the question. We do not want to do anything without God's will, yet we have made some small preparations. I have always said that if the Bible school cannot be opened, we must leave. If it is not possible to open it, we are forced to pack our bags. The Lord's will be done.

October 17, 1927:

The Bible school has been unequivocally rejected. I do not know whether we will try again. *Unser Blatt* is also threatened. In the October issue the censor crossed out twenty-two of the thirty-two pages—all religious articles. It is very difficult. The young men have returned from the service. It was very difficult for them. Soon we have to go to court again because of our non-resistance.

July 16, 1928:

Our passes have been categorically refused. For the present we are stuck. Is this God's will or human action? We certainly want to submit to the will of the Lord. It is so very difficult to remain here, however, especially after I quietly said goodbye to the congregation and they to us. Support is so difficult that I have decided not to be a burden to the congregation any longer. The Commission for Ecclesiastical Affairs has proposed that I travel to Simferopol and open the school in my name, that is, if it is allowed. The Commission thought it was possible since the churches, they felt, would support me.

April 12, 1927:

Everything which shows any vitality is being suppressed.

The extensive work which the brother was able to do is illustrated by a northern journey. He speaks of it in two letters.

March 27, 1929:

I am again at home with wife and children. I was gone for forty-three days . . . three days in Arkadak; sixteen days in the Orenburg region; six days in Neu-Samara; a day in Moscow. I was invited to Orenburg for Bible conferences. A number of other visits automatically followed.

April 8, 1929:

I worked in the twenty-four villages of Orenburg for two weeks. There were five uninterrupted days in the church at Deyevka. There were two hours of Bible discussion in both the morning and afternoon. In the evening there was a service. God gave me joy and strength to testify to His grace. From Orenburg I travelled to Neu-Samara, where there are fourteen Mennonite villages. I served there for a week. God be praised that we have such freedom. It does not come often.

5.

As a motto for this chapter let us use the words of Jesus from Luke 14:26. "Whoever comes to Me without hating his father and mother and wife and children and brothers and sister, yes, even his own life, cannot be My disciple."

On September 8, 1929 it pleased the Lord to give the brother a far more difficult task than ever before. As of this day, he had to leave Gruenfeld. He was found worthy to endure a long chain of heartrending afflictions because of his faith.

On October 6, 1929 he wrote,

I have been in exile for four weeks. I will tell you what happened on another occasion.

September 7 was a crucial day in our life. There was a hearing resulting in the expulsion and then the night departure from Gruenfeld. It would have been easy for me to stay there. For Christ's sake, I selected the most difficult way, the way of exile. Without saying goodbye to my congregation or my neighbors, I left the same night, never to return. My wife and children remained behind. After that they seized all our goods, confiscated our money, and drove the family out of house and home so that, in the night and in the rain, they had to find shelter in the neighboring village. Merciful people took pity on them and gave them accommodation. I wandered far and wide during this time and searched for refuge. I have not found it until this day. Tomorrow, if God wills, I am meeting with my family. I do not know where we will go. When Sophie comes we will be able to decide. Perhaps we'll go to our relatives. The way is deep and rugged. We are travelling to the far north homeless and destitute, but the Lord is with us. He has marvelously helped us and will not leave us in the future. I left home with thirteen rubles. When my means were exhausted enroute I received a gift from a [fellow] countryman in such a wondrous fashion as can only happen in such times as these. That encouraged me. The name of the Lord be praised. Even Sophie accepts our lot like a true heroine. She had to witness the loss of everything. She prepared for the journey without anger or hatred. God willing we will meet tomorrow morning at a prearranged location. Together we want to suffer and die. We no longer have a home on this earth. Driven from house and home, my wife does not even possess papers. Anyone can abuse us, expel us or force us to move on. Then, too, winter is approaching. These are all temporal thoughts and concerns. Please know dear family that we are going with joy. At first, I felt sorry for Sophie. Now she has given me proof that she is as stalwart and strong as I am. "Now we are free of everything," that was her response to the situation. No earthly possessions tie us down, nothing binds us to any one place. Heaven is our home! God is our father! Dear family, it is something very special to fully trust Him. Everything within me struggles against the notion that I am a martyr. O wretched man that I am, [am privileged] to suffer for His namesake. I am a sinner and am atoning for my past actions. If God desires that we and the children perish as blood witnesses to our faith in Christ, we will gladly give our bodies as we have already given our possessions. But pray for us that we do not falter in the darkest hours. The spirit is willing but the flesh has also not lost its instincts. Greet all the brothers and sisters in Christ! Also greet elder T. in R. and elder B. in Gr. I greet you with Colossians 4:8.

This letter of October 11 has a short note attached to it: "In three hours we are all in the city of our brothers and sisters."

When thousands of Mennonites gathered in Moscow in the fall of 1929 in order to go abroad Jakob at first came alone, then brought his family. There he was arrested with many others and spent eight months in the fearsome Batyrka. He was tried and sentenced to ten years on the Solowoki Island in the White Sea. As far as I can determine from the letters, his arrest occurred during the second half of November 1929. A fellow sufferer in prison who was later released wrote as follows:

When there were about one hundred families in Moscow, I saw your brother one day. He stayed out of the public eye. He had come alone since he was forced to disappear from Gruenfeld.

He (Jakob) was very concerned about his family. In the last day or two he had helped his wife do the laundry. Anticipating arrest, he had dressed himself in clean clothes. He did not feel right about the fact that so many of our brethren were suffering and he was standing aside. He often said, "Our people are experiencing something great which they have not experienced before, but very few are really aware of what we are experiencing." It was very important for him to suffer with his people.

Before us we saw the Lubyanka building but from a different angle. Inside I met forty-five refugees, young men, older men, and stooped men grey-haired with age. Here, I saw Professor J. Rempel again. They had all experienced what we had. We felt pleased that there were so many fellow sufferers.

After several calm days, there came a difficult night. "For interrogation," the guards announced and read several names. There were prayers: "Lord help!" Here and there one sees small groups in prayer. The lock jangles, the door opens. Who will be called? N.N. for questioning. This went on all night long. Your brother J. Rempel was also taken. They kept him for a long time. While others were questioned by one person, he was questioned by several.

There was pressure to sign that one would return home of one's own free will. Very few did so and certainly not Rempel. The food was poor. There was extremely sour bread which churned in the stomach, for lunch a thin soup without meat and a kind of Russian porridge. In the morning and evening, there was tea and one and a half sugar lumps per day. Under duress, one could survive on it. After several days fifty persons, including Professor J. Rempel, were called out and sent away. I do not know where, but in any case not to better circumstances.

After this my brother stayed in Moscow prisons where the food, as Jakob told his wife via someone, was very bad. His greatest concern was the whereabouts and condition of his family.

On March 11, 1930 Sophie, J. Rempel's wife, wrote,

Things are getting steadily darker. Someone was together with Jakob a month ago. He (Jakob) requested that I send him trousers for his were completely torn. He had regularly encouraged that person, but he could not remain constant and signed that he would no longer preach. Now that other man is home. A minister Rosenfeld (from the Molotschna) was no longer normal when he returned home; apparently they use steam [in their torture]. As far as I know they have been questioned several times. Jakob was apparently questioned seven hours in succession. I can imagine what effect it must have had on him. If only this time of testing would soon end. I had sent him cookies and buns, but he does not get them. They can only get things from the store. They can write letters twice a month but strangely enough I have not received any nor has he. What happens to them?

The reader may ask, "What happened to the Rempel family after his arrest?" They were sent to [central camp?], where there were other families. On November 23, 1929, Jakob's family also came to the [central camp?] The good Lord aided the family through good people there and compassionate people here, so that they did not have to despair.

The help was so necessary. There were six children who had to be looked after in a strange land by an exhausted mother without a husband. Furthermore, the seventh child was on the way. This child was born during its father's absence. It died after some five weeks and so was saved from this evil world. It is difficult to clothe in words the deep trauma which was associated with these experiences.

On July 6, 1930 Jakob's eldest son wrote,

A card from papa! I will copy it. It was written on June 29, 1930 at the station Bagoslaw, Tversk.

"Dear Sophie. God greet you! All that is human must keep silent. We are walking a rugged road of suffering for the sake of our faith. For seven months there were the pangs of hell, now a ten-year sentence. God help us. Greet the congregation in Neu-Chortitza. Move there for the winter, for they must support you. Send me my winter clothes, my coat, etc. I am on the way to Solowoki. We cannot see each other before the summer of 1931. There are four of us brethren. When we get there, I will write immediately. God be with you. Do not despair, my beloved wife. Kiss the children. Your beloved, suffering witness for Christ."

His son wrote on November 5, 1930,

There is a special delivery letter from papa. He writes that Mama and I should come as quickly as possible. He is very sick and believes he will die.

Then his eldest son Alexander writes on January 19, 1931,

Now I will write as much as I can about papa. You will know that mother was there. He is now well again. When they saw he was too weak for physical work, for he had collapsed on the job site, he got a position working in the pharmacy. Then he was made bookkeeper, then teacher. He still has that position. He only has to instruct four children.

Then the brother may have attempted a flight from exile, possibly abroad. We have no firm information. On January 17, 1932 his wife writes,

We have no letter from Jakob since the beginning of December. He was about to make a journey. I am waiting for a letter.

On May 5, 1932 his wife again writes,

Sophie Sudermann has word from her husband. He had typhus and lay unconscious and was thinking of jumping over the moat . . . . Greetings with Genesis 31:20. From this I assume that Jakob attempted to escape in 1932 but was again tried and condemned.

As I understand it, the brother again made a futile attempt

to escape on May 1, 1934. After he had been recaptured, he escaped once more to the Mennonites in central Asia who lived in Chiva. He almost died enroute. For a time, he lived under a tree where his son found him, incoherent, despairing and near insanity. Together they travelled to the Mennonites in central Asia. This was something of an oasis for the severely tried family. During this time, his friends in Canada cared for him and made considerable sacrifices on his behalf. He even managed to travel home for several days. I want to (heartily) thank the generous benefactors on behalf of this family.

On October 7, 1934 Jakob wrote to his wife as follows:

> Yes, Sascha is here by me. When we met and during our first days together, I was virtually impassive. I simply did not have the strength to express my strong inner feelings, which naturally affected Sascha. I am so thankful for the grace to speak to at least one [family member] after all these years. We have done the best we can for ourselves.

> We travelled over 1,000 kilometers into the sand desert where we want to spend the winter in a small locality (Ak-Metschet). I am currently staying with Mennonites and seeking to recover. The Lord is with me and I am getting stronger. I have been warmly received. Perhaps I will get a little aid. If I could only sleep on a pillow and have a blanket to cover myself in winter. I hope to God that my life will again have meaning. Let us be glad and wish for all the best.

My brother was able to spend the winter of 1934-35 in peace and tranquility among the Mennonites in Asia. During this winter there was a pause in his many sufferings and he had time to reflect upon these events. In a letter of January 1, 1935 he described this process:

> I rarely experience severe worries or troublesome thoughts. When I was taken out of my work in the past, separated from life, led into solitude, into suffering after suffering, when sicknesses alternated and the end of one marked the beginning of another, then I asked myself what Jesus would say about this. When I was inwardly sure that Jesus would have kept silent as He kept silent in His suffering, then I not only became silent but loved silence above all else. In deep seclusion I endured the hard struggle without human help. God led me into suffering, men executed it. God, however, protected and led me out. The deeper the suffering, the quieter the surroundings. I learned

silence and suffering. Only when I was free from suffering did I call for help—sometimes more loudly than was necessary. Later, I often regretted that I disturbed people or interrupted their tranquility. Yet on the cross Jesus called, "I'm thirsty." That gave me courage to cry for reassurance in my distress. I write as if all went according to plan. My dear ones, in such great affliction there is no [set] plan. No guidelines, whatever sort they might be, decide things, but the power of the Gospel. If there seems to be a plan in such circumstances, it is not the plan of the person who is suffering.

The old year has passed. In the new year I anticipate a reunion with my loved ones. Sascha is with me. That is the beginning and I am very thankful for it.

Here (in Ak-Metschet), I have come to understand brother D. Toews' reflections on his childhood. Greet him warmly from me. Greet all who ask about me, especially D.H. Epp. There are so many of whom I have fond memories.

The plan to visit his family was successfully executed by my brother in the spring.

After this, the reports of the condition and whereabouts of the brother [J.A. Rempel] are sparse. His wife writes on October 9, 1936,

I would tell you more about Jakob but I have heard nothing for a long time. I received a card from Sascha that he was sentenced to three years. He is on the journey to Achta, Petschorskj Kraj. I am waiting for a letter. God be merciful to us.

I surmise the following: father and son have been rearrested and sentenced. I have never learned the sentence of the father.

An excerpt from a letter of December 2, 1937:

Since the time, when I again began to correspond with you, I can imagine your [daily] lifestyle, something I could not do for a while. The thoughts of you have almost driven me insane. Yes, in April and May of 1936, I actually lost my mind, yet that had passed and completely vanished by April 1937 when I was sentenced. Now I am completely at rest. I know that God has willed this for me and, therefore, I want to carry this burden worthily. It would certainly be easier for you and me if I could die. I am, however, thankful to God that He has found me worthy to experience all of this. I trust Him and await the

209

resolution and conclusion of my case. God protect you against despair, my beloved ones. A heartfelt greeting to all.

From the letters which we possess the last report of the brother's fate comes from January 27, 1939.

The elder has been mentally ill for eight months. He rarely receives letters from his wife though she and the children write [frequently]. When he receives one he is much encouraged.

His further fate is unknown. In 1945 brother C.F. Klassen spoke with the brother's son and made some notes. Unfortunately, Klassen is so busy that I have not been able to learn what the notes contain. In his report in Altona, he did provide some information, however. According to this, the last letter of my brother to his family was in 1940. This was a bequest of the father to his family. When the German front was pushing into Russia during the winter of 1941, some five men were shot near Oryol. It is presumed that elder J.A. Rempel was among these. The bodies were badly decomposed.

Alexander, the brother's oldest son, writes as follows on May 26, 1946:

I am not lying when I assert that aside from those who were in prison or exile, no family (except for perhaps one percent) starved and suffered as much as ours. Now the entire family is collapsing. Mother began to spit blood in winter. Today she is flat in bed. Paul collapsed at work. Peter looks like a consumption patient, the rheumatism in his knees is so bad. Ernst is always tired, thin and hungry. Only Martha is somewhat better.

The brother has now left the stage of life. In eternity God will again place him on stage and we hope that the verse in Revelation 2:10 will apply, where we read: "Be thou faithful unto death and I will give you the crown of life."

P.A.Rempel
Gretna, Manitoba

Johann D. Rempel
Minister from Nodnitschnoje, No. 10, Orenburg

"The task generates the strength and in suffering and sorrow man matures to quiet greatness." This can also be said of the life of the minister Johann D. Rempel. He was born on November 2, 1874 as the son of the farmer and carpenter, David Peter Rempel, and his wife Anna, nee Thiessen. Both parents came from farming stock who migrated to the Ukraine early in the nineteenth century from the Danzig-Elbing region.

The parental home was not blessed with great earthly riches. Diligence and hard work, nevertheless, ensured daily bread for the many children. The parents possessed one thing above all else: fear of God, which kept all sordid things far from the souls of the children. The early severe discipline of the home exhorted the seven boys to diligence and work. After completing public school, one held one's own, either on father's land or in his shop.

At that time, because of the large families, the Mennonite settlements already possessed too little land in order to supply the upcoming generation with their own farms. For this reason, new settlement lands were bought near the Ural [Mountains], in Siberia and in other localities. Johann D. Rempel, who had married Katharina Krahn on January 6, 1898, moved to the Orenburg settlement together with his three brothers in 1906. Here, he also found his work in the Kingdom of his Lord and Master. Here, too, he found himself standing side by side with all the other settlers who, as pioneers, had to erect their first home in the expansive, wild steppe. With the energy and pioneering spirit unique to our Mennonitism, the work was begun and [soon] mastered. Within a few years twenty-five fine villages, characterized by neatness and an exacting layout, were erected in the midst of the Russian world. In spite of a difficult beginning, a considerable prosperity was achieved within a short time.

In addition to his many farming obligations, J. Rempel also had the work in the church. In 1910 he was called to be a minister in the Klubnikowo Mennonite Brethren Church. In all this activity his wife, who bore him twelve children, stood by his side as an indefatigable helper, prudent housekeeper, and

211

faithful intercessor.

During the long Russian winters, Rempel immersed himself in the Holy Scripture. It was the norm and guideline for his life. His multiplicity of gifts was reflected in the multiplicity of his interests. His main interest, however, remained the Holy Scripture. Through Bible courses and self-study, he attained a broad and deep knowledge of the Word of God. His ministerial duties carried him far beyond the borders of his own congregation. In some winters, he travelled to Siberia and preached the Gospel to Germans and Russians. Besides his German countrymen, the Russians lay close to his heart. He recognized the great longing for light from above in a people held captive by darkness. Even his Russian servants and their families honored and loved their Ivan Davidovich as a fatherly helper and friend. During the World War, he cared for the wives and children of his servants who had been drafted. The doors of his home stood open for all who suffered want, all homeless, all wanderers and all disconsolate who needed night accommodation. When the revolution of 1917 began, dark storm clouds threatened the peaceable Mennonite colonies. When the ministers also were in danger, the servants who had returned from the front came to the aid of their former master:

We will intercede on your behalf before the Soviets so that no hair of your head will be touched, for you have always been a friend of the oppressed. Should you ever need a place of refuge our homes are open to you and we will share our last crust with you.

The political situation turned out quite differently than expected. The Soviet government allowed the Mennonite-German congregations to carry out their ecclesiastical functions for some years. As before, J. Rempel continued in his ministerial position with great enthusiasm. Yet to the days of domestic peace and bliss were added days of difficult inner struggle: four children were snatched away by death and in 1920 the Lord God took his dear wife from his side.

When in 1929 the Soviet government clearly indicated its intention to end the independence of the peasants in favor of collectivization and to end religious freedom, the familiar farmer's flight to Moscow occurred. J. Rempel also travelled to that destination with the object of emigrating to Canada. But God in His counsel had determined otherwise: he was to stay in Russia as a witness. He was forcibly transported back to Orenburg together with his entire family. Soon, thereafter, he was ordered to appear before the GPU. Rempel knew what that meant. He supplied himself with the basic necessities— he rejected the idea of flight— and made his way to the GPU building, erect and with a determined stride, trusting his God. Here, he was arrested and put in prison. GPU officials were astounded that the arrest did not cause him the least consternation. Questioned about this he answered, " I knew it would come to this and know that I must now suffer for the sake of my service for Christ." This stance was characteristic of his future pathway. His son, Dr. Hans Rempel, who had been arrested several weeks earlier and found himself in the same prison, reports of his father:

Deep sorrow filled my breast when one day I saw my dear father coming across the prison yard. I had hoped he would be spared this sorrow. No one knew that we were father and son. After the few words which we exchanged during this first meeting, I was encouraged and strengthened by his trust in God and the manliness of his bearing. Later, when we lived in the same cell and together journeyed into exile I was again and again encouraged and at the same time shamed by the quiet, trusting, courageous, hopeful sufferance of my father, who was always looking towards eternity. When we once spoke of flight he rejected the idea with the words, "I am here because of my service in the church of Christ: I cannot and must not flee." Thus he bore his imprisonment as a service for the sake of Christ.

And God gave him the strength to endure, yes manifold and great strength. God bore him in His hands through the days, through the nights, through the months, through the years, through the heat of summer and through the cold of the polar winter. In the cells of the GPU, in the prisons of Solj-Jletzk, of Moscow, of Archangelsk, and later of Saporoshje and in the northern forests— there, God spoke with him and he became quiet and inwardly great.

During his interrogation in the Orenburg prison, he was accused of political, anti-Soviet activity with [specific] reference to his sermons. Undeterred he declared that he preached

Christ and not politics. When he was accused of not affirming Soviet politics, he declared with equal decisiveness that he could not affirm politics which were directed against God's commandments.

As a prisoner under investigation, he was transferred from Orenburg to Solj-Jletzk where he, as well as his son, received sentence after six month's imprisonment. The verdict read, "He is sentenced to three years in exile in the Archangelsk region." After an arduous journey, Archangelsk was reached in April 1930. Broken down by frost, hunger, and illness, father Rempel was near death. Russian believers in Archangelsk took him in and cared for him. Later, his path led to the Petschora [river] where he worked in a cabinet shop under GPU supervision. He soon won the respect of the GPU through the quality of his work. He was soon allowed to accept twenty workers in the shop from the ranks of the exiled. He, himself, was freed of all difficult work and only given supervisory tasks. In addition, he received adequate maintenance and enjoyed other special privileges. He found special comfort in the fact that among the prisoners there was a certain minister Schirling who became his deputy in the shop and with whom he shared the exile and loneliness for four long years. God had given him a father, placed a friend beside him, given him a fellow sufferer—what a great gift in misery and loneliness.

How much could be said about the years near the Petschora River! Only the forests know of the prayers of thousands upon thousands of prisoners which ascended to God's throne and perhaps are still ascending. Without any due process of law, Rempel was held for four years instead of three. The hour to return home finally came. But how different he found it all. His second wife—prior to his arrest he had married the widow Katharina Huebert—was overwhelmed with anxiety and grief. He could no longer work in his congregation, which had no shepherd. His oldest son-in-law, the minister Abram Petkau, was exiled. He [Rempel] was despised in his community, for no one dared to associate with someone who came out of exile. Under these circumstances, it was necessary to change residence, and so father Rempel with his wife and several daughters moved to the Ukraine in order to disappear as a day laborer in a workers' settlement. The wish to return to the place of childhood may have strengthened the decision to settle in the Ukraine. His spiritual and physical powers still intact, he worked here as a day laborer and on some evenings and Sundays held secret services here and there in the homes.

But the GPU even found the day laborer. He was again arrested on account of his correspondence with his children abroad and this time charged with treason. Once again, his journey led to the depths. One of the daughters daily wandered to the prison and stood at the gate for hours, knocking and waiting—perhaps she could leave the bread or hear if a verdict had been passed. At "home" mother Rempel sat on a hard bench, her eyes blinded by tears, bowed down by affliction and grief—enveloped in prayer. One day when the daughter returned from prison, mother Rempel sat on the old bench slightly more bowed down and slightly quieter—quiet for eternity. God had taken her prayerful soul from a sorrow which she could no longer bear.

After seven months, J. Rempel was acquitted by the court. Undeterred and unfaltering, he again took up his work as a day laborer in the world and a day laborer in the Lord's vineyard. Once more, the sun shone in his life. The widow Maria Klassen gave her hand in marriage to the lonely one and provided him with a modest home filled with peace. Father Rempel did not complain about the injustices he suffered, he did not fear an uncertain future. He had become quiet and secure in his God. He was thankful for the rest which God granted him in his suffering. This made his eyes sparkle and his days happy. Mother, Maria Rempel, with a faint smile on her face, often tells how father Rempel was so happy and cheerful. How can we hope to understand the joy of heaven which inhabits a human soul that has been so severely tested and chastened, that is so near eternity?

During the night of July 20, 1938, the GPU appeared at father Rempel's door. It seemed as if his tranquility passed over to the GPU men. They allowed him time to collect all the essentials. Then he went. The rest which God had granted him was at an end. He went trusting that God would give him the strength to walk this last pathway as a witness for Christ. He never returned. He never wrote. He never sent a greeting. There was never a word from him.

We do not know the duration of his suffering. God knows. But we believe with unshakeable conviction that God bore him in His hands through the Jordan of death. And we believe that when the great day shall come he, according to Revelation 7:14, will join the crowd of those who came out of great tribulation and washed their robes and made them white in the blood of the Lamb.

> For this reason they are before God's throne, and day and night they serve Him in His temple, while He who sits on the throne spreads His tent over them. They will nevermore either hunger or thirst, nor will the sun or any scorching heat whatever beat upon them; for the Lamb who is in the center of the throne, will shepherd them and will lead them to springs of living water. And God will wipe away all tears from their eyes (Revelation 7:15-17).

Report by his son, Dr. Hans Rempel, Germany

Heinrich P. Sukkau
Evangelist

We know little of his origins, only that he was born in southern Russia and that he then moved to the village of Kuterla, Neu-Samara with his parents. I will allow several brethren from Neu-Samara to describe his life and work in a free, narrative form.

The dear brother H. Sukkau was really an extraordinary man who the Lord was able to fill with His love in a special way. He was also an upright Christian. He did not possess a good education as he only attended village school for seven years. He was a simple farmer and lived on the land of Franz Regehr, an estate owner. Each year, he gave one-third of his harvest back to his landlord. Such farmers were simply designated *Garbensaer* or renters. Up to that time, there was nothing particularly unique about him.

Then it was suddenly said, "Brother H. Sukkau is having an auction sale and henceforth wants to work as an evangelist among the Russians." After the auction, he moved to his parents and with his family lived in the so-called auxiliary house on the yard.   Here in America we would call it a "bunkhouse." For the winter he travelled to the city of Samara (though some say Busuluk) in order to study the Russian language, especially its biblical usage.   In Samara, there were a considerable number of Russian believers and they had a church in the city. In the spring, he began to work among the Russians.   He had great success wherever he preached the Gospel, and many people were converted to God.   He didn't have a missions committee or conference to support him but was entirely dependent on faith.   When he became better known among the Russians through his work, he received invitations from everywhere: Orenburg, Samara, Taschkent, Ufa, even Siberia. On one occasion, he told a brother that it was rather difficult to work among the Russians because they were so desirous of salvation. That was good on the one hand but caused difficulties on the other.

In the beginning, he often preached in small, low huts packed with people and filled with stuffy air. When he wanted to stop at nine or ten in the evening, his listeners begged him to tell them more about Jesus. Then he continued with his preaching until two a.m. Now," he thought, "they will be tired and want to go home." Nothing of the sort! They wished to hear more. Finally dawn broke and the people went home. That did not only happen once but again and again.

When he returned tired and exhausted from such a mission journey, the people at home wanted to hear him as well. He preached in the forenoon and was invited to a youth meeting in the afternoon. Then late in the evening after he had gone to bed, exhausted from the day's activities, there was a knock on the window. Someone wanted to talk with him about the welfare of his soul. Cheerfully he got up, lit the lamp and showed the anxious soul the way to the Lord and to peace. It was not unlike the way Jesus dealt with Nicodemus.

Brother Sukkau carried on an intimate life of prayer and fellowship with his God.   He experienced many wonderful answers to prayer which he shared with the brethren for the [greater] glory of God.

Here is one of them. It was winter. The temperature stood at minus 30° Reaumur. He received a telegram from a Russian church requesting him to come immediately, since a great split had developed in the congregation. This was rather common in the Russian churches: each new convert immediately wanted to be a missionary, teacher or even a leader. What now? Brother Sukkau stood in constant fellowship with his Lord. He immediately entered his prayer room and brought the situation before his God. "I am your servant," he said among other things, "and if you wish me to go there and preach then give your servant a pair of felt boots, for without them he cannot travel." Then he went about his work. The next day in the morning he went into the village on business. A sleigh approached him on the street and the man on it stopped and asked him, "Where does Andrei Petrovich live?"

"What do you want from him?" Sukkau responded.

"Oh I'm bringing him some warm felt boots!" the Russian replied.

How quickly the Lord had heard his prayer and in what a wonderful fashion. Perhaps the Russian brother had already been on his way while brother Sukkau was still in the prayer room. The brother knew nothing about his personal needs. This [experience] strengthened the brother's faith and prepared him for the difficult work ahead.

He left immediately. When he arrived, they held prayer meetings for two or three days. Then he said, "Now three brothers from each group will come with me into a room." How long they remained there is not known. When they came out and reported their discussions to the assembled congregation, the members became as one heart and one soul.

His friend, brother Jakob N. Thiessen, tells of another answer to prayer. He was in the village of Lugowsk where the H. Sukkaus lived, at the time, and where the large church of the Mennonite Brethren was located. Brother H. Sukkau sat at the very back of the church with a number of Russian believers and in a whispering tone translated from German into Russian. When the service was over he said to the Russian brethren, "Come with me for lunch." It was the year of the famine (1922) and many people died of starvation. In some of the Russian villages, entire households perished. Bread was a rarity. Many only ate flour soup or bread made from weeds. When he came home with his many dinner guests, his wife said to him, "My dear man, what's the matter with you? We have absolutely nothing to eat for dinner."

Then the brother replied, "That's not our worry. Set the table and God will supply the rest." When the table was set, he said to his guests, "Come to dinner!" They stood around the table and said grace. When brother Sukkau said "Amen" the door opened and a girl walked in with a large basket of food.

Sometime later, they learned how the Lord had worked. When a sister who was better off saw the large group of Russians walking down the street with brother Sukkau she said, "There he goes again with a large number of people and yet he had nothing to eat." Then she said to her daughters, "Quickly pack a basket and bring it there!" How simplistic and childlike!

He told of many similar experiences with the Lord. The word which the Lord addressed to His disciples surely applied to this brother: "Whoever loves his life will lose it, but whosoever loses it for My sake shall gain it."

An example follows of how he lived and labored according to this precept. Brother Sukkau often made house visitations among the Russian believers. On one occasion during the year of famine, he visited a poor old sister. When the visitation ended he stood up to leave. The old sister begged him to stay for tea. As is well-known the Russians, and especially the believers, were very hospitable and could be very compelling. Hospitality naturally included drinking tea. The Russian tea machine, the "Samovar," usually stood on the table and the water was kept boiling with charcoal so that tea could be had at any time of the day. The teakettle often stood on the Samovar. A piece of sugar was added and a piece of bread, usually dry, was eaten alongside. A true Russian could drink or better sip eight to ten glasses of tea. This, naturally, took a long time, which he had.

When brother Sukkau accepted the persistent invitation and came to the table, the poor widow could only offer him a piece of moldy bread to eat with his tea. Naturally, he was in a dilemma as to what he should do. He soon decided that he could not offend her under any circumstances and ate the bread as if nothing was wrong. As a result, he became very ill on the long journey home and was brought home unconscious by his friends. Later he recovered.

Once, he told the people that he was ashamed of the fact

that he had not fully trusted the Lord. During the famine, the people sold many cattle because they did not have enough feed. For this reason, he also sold his cow. Later, when the Russian brethren brought him enough hay, he saw that he had acted hastily. He was ashamed that he had not completely trusted the Lord. His words were, "A Christian must have an unshakeable faith in God."

On another occasion, a brother asked him if he had enough flour. He replied that he did not want to bring dishonor to his God by disclosing to men whether or not he had enough flour. The brother involved guessed rightly, and the next day brother Sukkau found a sack of flour in his larder.

The reporter continues:

> When we wanted to emigrate to America we urged him to join us. He expressed some interest in doing so but when the Russian believers heard of this they asserted, "This is our brother, we will not let him go." He then decided that he had to stay. Before we left Russia, we heard that the Russian churches in northern Russia had elected brother H. Sukkau as the elder over all their congregations. He was both shepherd and bishop to ninety congregations. Isn't it amazing what the Lord can do with a simple brother if he is totally committed to His service?

> Later, we heard that he was also transported into exile. One thing is certain: wherever he was sent to he would have testified of his Lord. When for example he travelled on the train, it was not long before he had a group of people around him and was telling them of the love of God.

> He completely adapted to the Russian mode: shirt and belt without a collar or a necktie; in the food he ate - and if necessity demanded he could give an old man with a scruffy beard a hearty, brotherly kiss.

> We believe that this courageous and fearless witness of Jesus Christ has long gone to be with the Lord and can see face to face the One whom he served so faithfully.

We know little of his family life or of the material circumstances in which he found himself. He had the misfortune of losing both his first and second wife through death. Yet the Lord provided him and his family with a faithful life's partner who was prepared to share all the difficulties with him. He was very thankful for this.

As we already reported, he lived on his father's yard for a time. When his father died and the farm changed hands, he had to leave his residence. He then rented a house from a farmer in the village of Lugowsk, but was so poor that he could not pay his rent in cash. Instead, he repaired the straw roofs which often had many holes for the farmer. When the mud walls began to crumble, he had to repair them with his own hands using clay. He was always happy and content with such humble work. Then he would soon leave for another mission journey among the Russians.

When he had struggled with poverty for some twelve years and the wealthy farmers whose houses he repaired did nothing to better his lot, two brothers in the congregation decided to take action. They went ahead and bought a house and some land in the village and gave it to the poor minister's family. Some nine acres belonged to the property.

Brother Sukkau was so unassuming that he did not wish to accept the gift. Then his wife stepped in and said, "If you're not taking it, I am. We need it for our family." The matter was closed, and henceforth they lived in their own home. What happened to the family after his exile no one knows. His first wife bore him seven children, all girls.

He was between thirty and thirty-five years of age when he began to preach among the Russians. When he was brought to trial from time to time, his tormenters finally concluded that "Heinrich Sukkau knows nothing but the Bible" and let him go.

Since we are already talking about the work among the Russians, we want to mention one event from the life of the Russian congregations which brother H. Sukkau also related to the brethren.

In one of the churches, there were three young Russian brothers who were to be drafted into the army but who were nonresistant and did not wish to shed any blood. On account of this, they were put in prison where they were severely mistreated. When they continued to resist, they were placed before a court martial and sentenced to death by a firing squad. The three youths were taken out and each had to dig his own grave. Then they were returned to the prison. They took one, led him to the grave, and forced him to make a decision: "Will you now take a weapon or not?" He remained steadfast and answered, "I am ready to die for Christ." They did not execute him but closed the grave and led him away to another location.

Then they got the second young man and put him through a similar process. They showed him the new grave and said to him, "Look, your comrade is buried here. If you want to live, promise that you will take a weapon." He, too, remained steadfast and answered with shining eyes, "I am ready to die for my Lord." Then this grave was filled and he was led to the same house as the first one. They now showed the two graves to the third youth and threatened him, "If you do not take the weapon we will shoot you like we have your two comrades. You have a choice."

The young man was overwhelmed with such a fear of death that he promised to bear arms. "You are a hypocrite and have lied to us," the executioners replied, "your comrades have not been shot, but you will be." He had to remain standing at his grave until his two companions were brought. When he saw them, he wept bitterly and cried to God for mercy. He was, nevertheless, shot and the other two were freed. So there were not only pacifists among the Mennonites but among the Russian believers as well. To God be the glory!

When the wife of a Russian alcoholic was converted to God and wanted to be baptized, her godless husband threatened to throw her into the heated oven after her return. This was the so-called "Pietsch," a large brick oven in the middle of the house on which the Russians slept during cold weather.

The woman would not be deterred. The minister had chosen the text of the three men in the fiery furnace and she derived comfort from it. The brother knew nothing of the situation. After the sermon the woman explained her dilemma. She was baptized and received communion. The congregation was about to leave when the woman requested they remain in order to pray for her and her husband. She refused to allow anyone to accompany her home. When she entered the house, she found her husband heating the stove. He was so astounded to see her return home without fear or accompaniment that he fell on his knees and began to call on God. Both returned to the congregation which was still at prayer. Her husband was converted and became a changed individual.

This was another incident which brother Sukkau related to his congregation.

Compiled according to information
supplied by Jakob Loewen, Gem, Alberta
Jakob N. Thiessen, Coaldale, Alberta

Additional Comments

The Russians simply called him Andrei Petrovich. Usually he only wore the Russian "Tushurka," a jacket with an upright collar, buttoned to the top and without a necktie.

In his giving, he was overgenerous. Often he gave all he had, once he even gave his last "Threesome" (a three rubel note) when he was on his way to market to buy bread for the family. He came home without it. The experience of his wife was similar to that of Mrs. Bernhard Harder of Halbstadt who, amid similar circumstances, once said, "He is always doing that."

His lifestyle was impeccable, his morals exemplary. He was highly respected by all the brethren who knew him. On occasion he is to have said, "When I see how the brethren suffer for Christ's sake and I remain exempt, I tell myself I am not worthy [to do so]."

During WWI, brother Sukkau was drafted and served in Moscow as a medical orderly. He became an active member of the Christian Soldiers Union founded by Mennonite medics right after the revolution. He preached, distributed tracts, and was active in other areas.

In the final period of his stay in Moscow, he worked at an evacuation center among soldiers suffering from venereal disease. He also tried to show these patients the way of salvation in Christ.

In exile, brother H.P. Sukkau spent some time with J.J. Toews of Ignatjewka, and brother David Paetkau from Orenburg.

When the term of his exile ended he came home once more but then went to Turkestan in order to cover his tracks. Further information is lacking.

Peter Goerz
Lindbrook, Alberta

Julius Jakob Thiessen
Teacher and Minister,
Paulsheim, Gnadenfeld District, Molotschna Colony

He was born on January 1, 1872 (O.S.) in the village of Muensterberg, Molotschna. His parents were Jakob and Katharina Thiessen (nee Friesen). He grew up amidst impoverished circumstances. He lost his father when he was only thirteen years of age. In the village school, he distinguished himself through diligence and unusual ability. Because he lived near the school, he often helped the teacher correct the pupils' books during his last school year. Since his teacher (a certain J. Janzen) and the local school board recognized his gifts and abilities as a [future] teacher, they made provisions for further study. He first attended the Ohrloff High School. His mother died during this time, and so he was completely orphaned at age seventeen. After completing his studies in Ohrloff, he spent two years in the teacher training school in Neu-Halbstadt. After graduating from the pedagogical program, he accepted his first teaching position in the village of Paulsheim near Gnadenfeld. Here, he served as teacher for an uninterrupted thirty-one years, from the fall of 1891 until Christmas, 1922. Then the Red government forbade him to teach any longer, because he was also a minister.

He loved the teaching profession and participated in it wholeheartedly. As the school term approached in the following fall, he compared his feelings with that of a migratory bird locked in a cage, who could not follow his comrades in the flight south.

What he accomplished as a teacher and what he meant to his colleagues, I don't know, for I was too young to rightly assess that. (His son, Dietrich, writes this.) While he was a teacher, he received two commemorative medals from the tsarist government: the first when two of his students, Gerhard Dirks, later teacher in Fuerstenwerder, and Jakob Rempel, later teacher in the Gnadenfeld High School brilliantly passed their final exams in the village school. He received the second commemorative medal during WWI, around 1915, for long term service as a teacher.

On January 1, 1917 (O.S.), his birthday, the village of Paulsheim together with many of his colleagues and past students celebrated his teaching jubilee. The teacher, who had turned grey in the course of his service, was honored with speeches and gifts. Poems and songs were presented by young and old students.

Besides his teaching profession, he was also the minister of the Margenau-Landskrone Mennonite Church. I (his son) have no data as to when he was ordained as minister. I only know that he was often misunderstood. He was a serious Christian, exacting about his lifestyle, and wished to apply the biblical principles to the life of the church in his district. At that time, many ministers in the Molotschna were seeking to implement radical reforms in the spiritual life of their churches. There was a demand for baptism on faith alone, communion with believers only, the exercise of severe church discipline, etc. Bible conferences, Bible studies, ministerial courses, etc. were held in the [various] congregations in which members of all three groups worked together in one spirit. There was a spiritual spring in the Molotschna and, to a degree, in other Mennonite colonies during those decades. Many were converted, at that time, and a lively spiritual life developed. An energetic mission work began, especially among the Russians. We had a number of fruitful evangelists who were supported by congregations and mission societies.

The teacher, Julius Thiessen, actively participated in all of this. In 1923-25 a great revival occurred in other villages as well as in Paulsheim and many turned to God, in fact almost all the youth of the village. This could be largely credited to the quiet untiring spiritual ministry of the dear teacher and minister J. Thiessen.

In the fall of 1902, he married Susanna Baerg of Tiegerweide. For thirty-six years, he shared joy and sorrow with her. She was a great support to him in his vocation. The Lord granted them seven children, four daughters and three sons, of which two daughters died in infancy.

His son, Johann, died in 1940 as a result of maltreatment in the service of the Red government, because he refused to do military service. But he remained true to his Lord and his conscience and died as a martyr.

In 1925 his twin sons, Jakob and Dietrich, emigrated to Canada. The sorrow of parting was great, but at that time the parents and children still nurtured the quiet hope that sooner or later they would be able to follow them.

The Lord led very differently. The exit visa, which he requested from the government on several occasions, was refused.

In November 1929, he travelled to Moscow with his family where, like many others, he hoped to obtain his exit visa. Though he and his family had the entry visa to Canada and prepaid tickets in hand, the Reds sent him and his family back to their old home. Once they arrived there, they had to begin all over. After several months had passed he, as a minister, was assessed a very high tax which he couldn't possibly pay. As a result, the government confiscated all his belongings, arrested him personally, and wanted to exile him to the far north. He escaped from their custody and fled by night to the Old Colony where he got a position as carpenter with the large power generating station on the Dnieper. His family soon followed. Here, they lived in peace for several years until, on the invitation of their next of kin, they moved to Issilj-Kulj near Omsk in Siberia. Here, they had peace and tranquility until August 1937. During that year, the Soviet government launched its last great dragnet. Almost all German men twenty years and over were arrested and sent into exile, never to return.

I quote from mother's letter: "Prior to this he was already very tired and very quiet. Often in prayer he spoke the words, 'Lord, if you will lead us in ways we don't understand, give us the strength to be quiet and trust you.'"

The great fear became reality. One day, in spite of his advanced years, he was sent into exile. Like Job he did not deny his faith and did not reject God in all his suffering, but took leave of his family with Psalm 91 and Psalm 121.

After three months of suffering, he apparently died in a hospital while still in exile. None of his relatives were with him. His dear mother and sisters only learned of his death five months later. His memory remains dear to us.

Thus far the report comes from his son, Dietrich J. Thiessen, Vauxhall, Alberta.

The author knew the dear, departed teacher and minister well. He was a pious, quiet man loved by everyone. He was not a man of many words, but a man of the secret, unobtrusive deed.

Mother Thiessen was still alive in Siberia in 1946 and was in regular correspondence with both of her sons in Canada, a situation which was certainly exceptional. Most are strictly forbidden to have contact with the outside world.

Aron P. Toews
Chortitza, Old Colony

He was born on January 28, 1887 in Fuerstenau, Halbstadt Volost in the Molotschna, province of Taurida. His father, Peter Aron Toews, was the minister of the Schoensee Mennonite Church. After completion of the village school, he first graduated from high school and then finished the pedagogical classes in Neu-Halbstadt. Then he became a teacher in the Nikopol district, province of Jekaterinoslaw until the outbreak of WWI in the fall of 1914.

He served as a medical orderly on train No. 194 which brought wounded and sick soldiers from the front into the interior of the Russian empire. He participated wholeheartedly in the "creation and organization of a better world" after the outbreak of the February revolution of 1917.

During this time, he also found his Savior, whom he grasped in faith and never let go. As a staunch Mennonite, he had great interest in the affairs of his people. His lively character and jovial temperament ensured that he was never found in the back rows. He had many friends and a large circle of acquaintances. In school, his pupils clung to him.

He married Maria Sudermann, daughter of David Sudermann. The Lord gave them three daughters and a son. During the famine in Russia, he held a position in the AMRA (American Mennonite Relief Association) which had its headquarters in the city of Alexandrowsk.

His youngest daughter, Maria, who has come to Germany as a refugee, describes the subsequent fate of her father as follows.

When the help from Holland and America arrived during our great crisis in 1923, my father worked in the AMRA. He became a good friend of the brethren who had come from overseas: Messrs. Yoder, Schlegel and Krehbiel. He travelled in the colonies and among other things inspected the feeding kitchens which had been set up everywhere. After AMRA was dissolved, he became a bookkeeper in an office.

In 1925 he had to make a difficult decision: the Chortitza Mennonite Church elected him as a minister. Many of the ministers of the church had already emigrated to Canada.

In the evening of the same day, a representative of the Bolshevik government came and informed him that he had been elected as the chairman of the district executive committee. Would he accept the position? Father faced a decision. On the one hand, a carefree future for his family with splendid prospects on all sides; on the other, the call of the congregation to a pathway which would become steadily more difficult. He had to choose. He decided for the pastoral position. Doesn't that remind us of Moses' decision as found in Hebrews 11:24-27?

He was ordained as a minister in January 1925. The scripture for his ordination was Revelation 2:10: "Be thou faithful until death and I will give you the crown of life." Trusting God he took up his office. Father soon became the beloved Aron Petrovich and during the last years the supporter and co-worker of elder David Epp.

For the church, the times became more dangerous and threatening. It took a great deal of strength and fortitude to withstand all the evil attacks of the anti-religious government. Father knew the law and on the basis of existing laws defended these rights as best he could. As each group of Mennonite young men was called up for military service according to their year of birth, he defended them before the courts. All of them voluntarily joined the government work brigades (a type of alternative service allowed until the 1930s) and remained nonresistant. These young men were close to father's heart. He even sent them words of consolation and encouragement when [they worked] in Siberia. As the years passed, the struggle steadily became more difficult. Father was attacked from all sides, yet he walked his way erect and straightaway.

As a minister, he had no vote. In 1925 his taxes were already so high that he had to sell his farm and his cattle in order to pay them. Those were difficult years for him and his family. We rented accommodation from strangers.

In 1932 some good friends gave him a pig barn which was torn down in order to build a "new" house for us. It was a very difficult time for him: hard work, poor food, and then also the many duties of office. He was almost the only one of the many ministers who was left. He had to serve several congregations at once and had to perform all the functions of an elder, since there was no one left. The farmers had lost their horses through collectivization. Father had to visit the surrounding villages on foot, sometimes eighteen kilometers distant.

In 1932 they wanted to close our church. A commission cited structural defects as an excuse. Father travelled from Pilate to Herodes and once more saved our church. Materially, those years were very difficult for father. (Without your help from America we would have starved at that time.) What depressed father more than anything else was the wave of destruction which broke over the congregation. How many had already travelled the distant way of martyrdom into the "white death?" This of course refers to frigid, northern Russia and Siberia, where many froze to death or starved.

Yet the Lord still needed father in the congregation. During this time of dissolution and growing opposition, father had already begun his path of suffering. Later when the hour of parting came, he had experienced this bitterness of suffering a hundredfold. Yet submission to God's will filled his soul with peace and calm.

Because of the pressures of his office, father was always tired and tense. The internal and external crises in the congregation demanded comfort and help. Father heard this call day and night. No way was too far for him, no weather too severe. He was always there when called. In November 1934, he had a bad ulceration of the jaw and was operated on in the city. He had barely returned home when he took up the duties of office. He was very weak and had to rest often. At that time, father's vision was turned inward. His glances often indicated that he was not in our midst.

Then came November 28, 1934. Two men came for him.

After an hour long house search, he was taken away. He had a word of love for each of us. The parting was forever. For the last time, he walked over the doorstep of his poor little house. We all stood at the window and looked after him. Slightly bent, his hands slipped into his coat sleeves behind his back; he walked through the gate in the snow. He did not look back.

He was brought to the prison in Saporoshje, where the terrible interrogations began. They could accuse him of nothing. They tortured him so that he might confess to crimes he had not committed. On November 30, they returned his papers and said he was free to go.

Free! How must this word have sounded to father and what joy he felt. He said goodbye and went to the door— it was only a trick. The ordeal begins anew. The terror of solitary confinement and death cells bring him close to insanity. Wherever his hands reach out in the darkness only stone, cold stone. But even in this dark room, there is God's comfort and light.

The first time I saw father was in prison before he was hospitalized. I was allowed through a gate and came into a large room which was separated in the middle by two wood barriers. The prisoners stood on that side of the barrier, the visitors on this side. In the middle, the guards walked back and forth. When I walked in, father signalled with his cap from afar. He looked wretched and grey! Yet he tried to comfort and encourage us. The visit lasted ten minutes. On May 16, our parents stood across from each other in this same room on the occasion of their twenty-fifth wedding anniversary. Father stretched over the barrier in order to caress mother's outstretched hands once more. Brutally, the guard pushed him back. "Excuse me, but today is our silver anniversary," said father quietly. The guard turned away and once more they stretched out their hands to each other and looked into one another's eyes. The ten minute anniversary celebration was over all too quickly!

In order to torment father, they had placed him in the same cell with bandits. These took everything from him: his coat and all other things, and, for added mockery, his dentures. He preached the Gospel to these people and had sympathy for them. Gradually, all in this cell learned to love father. In the absence of his dentures, father contracted a serious stomach and intestinal illness. Near death, he was taken to the hospital.

Here, I saw him for the last time. Two men brought him into the waiting room. When I saw him my heart almost stopped. What a sight! His hair was white as snow. When the men left us alone, he took my head in his hands and cried! It was an incredible sight: his hands, his lovely hands were still somewhat swollen and his fingernails were missing.

Then he asked about mother, Olga, and Natascha. He had been told his family had been eliminated. This was another means used to get something out of him. He had endured everything, and yet this was only the beginning of his long path of suffering, which would take him into the uninhabited steppes and the forests of the taiga (Siberian virgin forests and swamps).

On August 10, 1935 mother went to the prison to bring father food. Mother stood and waited for hours together with 500 people, all women, who wanted to bring their loved ones food. Finally, her turn came. Suddenly, the crowd presses forward to the large prison gate; a transport of prisoners is being sent to Siberia! Mother stood in the front row. The gate opens. Guards with guns and dogs stand on both sides. A troop of prisoners comes out from the gate. In the first row, supported by a young man, walks our father. He looks up, sees mother, lifts his hand and signals—five years. He is not permitted to speak. A long human chain follows enroute to the railway station. The prisoners are loaded onto freight cars with barred windows. Mother stands at the barbed wire which separates the platform from the crowd. Father comes to the small window and says three words in Russian, "Mariechen, I am calm." Then he left for the unknown.

After two months of waiting, there is finally a sign of life from him. He lay in the hospital in Novosibirsk. He had collapsed enroute. The strain of deprivations and torments had been too much. God sent him help in the person of a German doctor who nursed him back to health. Then he went on into exile.

He is dropped off in a small forgotten locale. Here he is a "free citizen" and must earn his own bread for five years. He walks from house to house, and no one will accept him. He is finally allowed to sleep on the floor in the last hut. He tries to make himself useful and helps with all work in order to get some food. He is allowed to stay in his corner. He manages to build a table and a chair and makes his corner livable. Letters of love, comfort and encouragement are directed to us and the congregation. Some time passes. One day, he is taken away and transferred to a dairy farm a kilometer away. Here, he is to work as a bookkeeper. Joyful letters, filled with thanks, arrive from him. Things are going well for him. He is loved and respected. But this lovely time does not last long. He is now taken to a small village at the edge of the taiga and has to forge a new existence for himself. There is the harsh Siberian winter, and he has to go from house to house and beg for handouts in order not to starve. He chops wood in the forest. The work is very difficult for him. The wood is then floated south on the river. Abandoned by men, he lives his life in a lonely, distant place. Yet his letters and writings which he sends us and the congregation, as well as others, are a blessing for all of us.

A harsh blow came in 1938. All our letters were returned marked "addressee unknown." What had happened to father? Long, anxious months passed in uncertainty. An inquiry at the headquarters of the concentration camp was only answered after a lengthy interval. I was called to the police [station] where they informed me that my father had committed new, serious crimes in exile (which were naturally lies) and had been sentenced to a further ten years in the remotest camps. He had lost all right to correspondence.

New arrest, new interrogations, a new sentence? His last letter was filled with thanksgiving to his Lord and Master for all the manifested grace. And now the Lord led His faithful servant into the dark, deep valley once again? Is he still alive? Or is his earthly body decaying with thousands of other martyrs in the vast steppes of Siberia? In his distant past, he remained faithful to his Lord and his church.

In 1941 his name came to our attention once more. A certain Neustaedter from Chortitza had written a note which he threw out of the window of a transport wagon: "The minister A. Toews from Chortitza is with us. We are all being sent further away. No one knows where." That was the last news.

Johann J. Toews
Minister and Teacher
Nikolajewka, South Russia

Johann J. Toews was the second eldest son of the minister Johann Toews, initially living in Fabrikerweise and later in Muntau near Halbstadt, Molotschna. He was born on June 25, 1878 (O.S.). After a thorough schooling, he taught in the Molotschna villages for thirteen years. When he was a teacher in Friedensdorf, he once wrote an article, "Ich und Abdera," in a major German newspaper, probably in the *Odessaer Zeitung*. He imitated the work of the German writer Wieland, "Die Abderiten", and with liberal doses of humor, portrayed the foibles of Mennonite society. This focused the attention of the community upon this remarkable young man for the first time. One of the leading members of the school council remarked, "We must take off our hats to this young man." The village, whom he served and whose shortcomings he had so masterfully portrayed, did not agree. When they learned who the author of the article was (he had used a pseudonym), he was dismissed from his post. That was his first martyrdom for truth. Later on, it would be much worse.

His spiritual qualities were soon recognized, and he was elected and ordained as a minister in the Petershagen Mennonite Church. His inner spirit, revitalized by God, could not be confined by narrow religious orthodoxy. He later became a member of the Mennonite Brethren Church where his spiritual talents could develop more freely. This move did not win him many laurels.

J.J. Toews worked to attain a higher level of education and as a result received several offers to become a high school teacher. In 1909 he decided to take a position in the high school at Nikolajewka (Kronstadt), where he became a teacher of religion and the German language. In the following year, he passed his examinations as a tutor in the city of Kharkov.

He especially loved to serve as minister and elder and later as the leader of Bible courses. When political circumstances demanded that he become either minister or teacher, he chose the work in the church. He loved to work among the youth, and the Lord blessed his efforts with many offspring for eternity.

When the persecution became so intense that many Mennonites and their leaders left Russia, he could not join them. He felt the responsibility to remain with the "flock." He soon became the object of severe persecution. His intensifying activity in the Lord's vineyard brought frequent interrogation by the Red rulers. In time, he would have difficult experiences. Threats and interrogations did not cause him to desert. He had to live with the fact that he was under constant observation by GPU agents. When the pressures threatened to destroy his spiritual labors, he tried to emigrate in 1927. His persecutors blocked his way, and he had to give up this plan. He did not, however, give up his struggle and wanted to remain true to this calling as a minister of the Word until the very end.

During the last two years of his ministry, the Lord blessed his extensive activity in a special way. Yet the days of tribulation intensified, and it became impossible to successfully continue the work.

When thousands of our people wanted to cross the borders via Moscow in 1929, J.J. Toews and his family joined them. In Moscow everything was in order, but his pursuers had not forgotten this fearless witness of the Gospel. He was forcibly taken from his family and for eight months endured grisly prison experiences.

His family got across the border but could not reach their intended destination— Canada— and with many others went to Brazil. The head of the family, Johann J. Toews, spent further time in prison and was finally sentenced to five years in exile. All petitions to authorities were in vain. The efforts of his family in Germany brought no success. They had to give up their hope for a speedy reunion. Their dear husband and father was sent to Russia's far north.

At first, he had to live in a barrack—with its dampness, swearing, lice and bedbugs, dirt and mud. He lived like this until October 1931. Then he received accommodation with a Russian couple. Here, circumstances were somewhat better. Then he was led to the deep forest some forty-five verst away where the sorely afflicted one was subjected to hard labor with axe and saw.

The doctor established that he suffered from cardiac dilation: he had experienced three severe fainting spells. He also had a severe case of neurasthenia. Protestations as well as the doctor's diagnosis were of little avail.

He could only eat in the morning and in the evening. Living and sleeping took place in a smelly barrack into which twenty-four men had been packed. The days and nights were terrible. In the forest, he had to stand up to his waist in the cold snow, so that even the best felt boots were inadequate and his hands froze in double mitts. From this place of torture, he wrote to us, "Be comforted my dear, dear brother. I want to be brave, even in the raging torrent of the flood of death, and submit to the will of the Father and in Christ accept all things."

Later, he had to give up the difficult forestry work and, because he was no longer working, he could not get food. As was once the case with Elijah, everything had to come to him in an extraordinary fashion. He noted in one of his letters, "The 'bread raven' and the 'raven's bread' is still available; the murmuring, crystal water still flows through all adversities; even the Zarephath flour and the Zarephath oil" (I Kings 17). His many friends sent him food and clothing in exile, so that he was wondrously preserved.

When he could no longer work, he was sent to Kornilowka on the right shore of the Dvina River in northern Russia. He called this place his "beautiful, quiet Zoar" (the city where Lot and his family took refuge during the destruction of Sodom and Gomorrah - Genesis 19:20-30); it was for the old who were incapable of work.

David D. Paetkau, the elder of the Mennonite Brethren Church in Orenburg, lived with him. The two enjoyed fine times of fellowship as they studied God's Word together. Daily they edified each other, and the Lord blessed them abundantly.

Yet for him, it was and remained an exile. He once wrote, "Exile—what a terrible word. You have become an accursed wood for me on which the best fruits of my mature years have been 'crucified.' Shoreless yet shore bound. Homeless yet homeward bound! Thus the ship of my life steers onward upon the dark sea."

They tried to persuade him to give up his faith and choose

freedom, but he remained stalwart to the end. Though his body collapsed from the weight of his sufferings, his spirit was renewed from day to day through his joyous communion with God, whose leading he did not understand but whom he reverently worshiped and loved, nonetheless.

He became seriously ill with a heart condition and died in exile on February 21, 1933. The following day his fellow prisoners, elder David D. Paetkau and a Mohammedan priest, carried him under the evergreen trees of the forest, where they dug his grave.

Much more could be said about his joys and sorrows, his observations and activities as a prisoner of the Lord, but enough has been said. Brother Johann J. Toews is not the only one who suffered. We have the confidence that our faithful Lord will still allow their testimonies to speak to the salvation of undying souls.

Wilhelm J. Toews
Mountain Lake, Minnesota

Reminiscences of One Sorely Tested

"Thou hast put me in the pit of the lowest, in dark places, in deep regions Psalm 88:6.

About one year before his death my brother, Johann J. Toews of Ignatjewka, wrote the following lines from exile.

My recent period of suffering is beautifully yet very realistically portrayed in the verse in Psalm 88:6. The three steps of the intensifying phenomena are typical and classic of my own accumulative experiences.

First came the pit - my Gethsemane: the prison with its interrogation and thousand fears, though I was always able to find tranquility. Two processes, becoming quiet and intense struggle, went hand in hand in this pit. When in desperate hours the flood tide of surging waters in the prison cell reached a breaking point, I was still able to speak of grace in that I called to others:

"Whoever can conquer himself is strongest among us,"

236

or

"Who can imprison himself fears no prison,"

or

"He who has become his own stinking prison is the most wretched,"

or

"Who himself brings a noble prisoner into prison, for him prison is no prison."

Then came the dark place, my Sabbatha in the life in the concentration camp: with all its mockery and scorn, with the indignity of being placed on exhibit, with its trial in Pilate's court where acknowledged innocence is cruelly misjudged. Established authority reconstituted submissive victims into dedicated "criminals."

Then came the deep, my Golgatha: the free exile with its rape of all innocence and all nobility of spirit, where broken strength was fastened upon martyr wood of hard labor with irons. Oh the hours of forsakeness by God and men; what deep furrows you have left in my heart. This was my highest schooling in the practice of my faith and suffering, a final exam upon the sacrificial altar of [my] love for Jesus. This was the supreme test. Here everything had to mature, everything had to come into the open; every mask, like any pious garb, gave way before the weighty hammerblows of spiteful, scornful laughter over weakness and illness, over age incapable of work and intelligent mental power.

My life ascended to such a fruitful "Sursum Corda." I cannot help it if others felt it less intensely. Overcoming my life was never as difficult or as clearly necessary, nor as precious. Here it was a question of becoming and becoming until one overcame.

Not a breeze, not anywhere
Deathly silence, fearfulness
And amid the endless vastness
Not a single wave bestirs.

That has become the deep experience of my soul. And the

beauty of it was: "It happened!"

When I was completely overcome, then I overcame, then the overcome became the overcomer.

A letter from the minister J.J. Toews in exile to F.F. Bargen, Carman, Manitoba.

May 30, 1932

Dearly beloved:

Oh how much you mean to me! May it please God, my eternal Benefactor, to cause you to rejoice, to give you good health, joy and happiness, but also to prepare you for all things. I am so deeply concerned that you, according to the measure of eternal grace, will have a good, a very good life here on earth. Regardless of how important our overall goals are, I know that your main interest is not focused upon the security of the intellect nor the criterion of reason. The thing that is most important is and will remain a conscience sharpened by the Holy Spirit. Romans 9:1-3 and Acts 24:16 and I Timothy 1:5.

Naturally, I don't love anyone more or more intimately than my dear family, especially my dear wife and faithful life's partner, who has had such difficult experiences in the recent past. How would I feel if people were to carry that person from my house to the cemetery— [that person] who knows all my struggles, my deepest experiences, the most important moments of my life— in a word if one were to take my wife from my side, then words, sufficiently profound and heartrending would fail me in portraying it with truth and love!

Several dear people are so exceptionally close to my heart and as comforting to my spirit as I could only wish. My dear wife is so far from me, so very far and yet, what benevolence of grace, so near to my heart. [She is] much nearer than formerly, deeper and more securely rooted and inwardly more united

My chief struggles here in exile lie on a completely different plane than that of the marriage relationship. Sodom was a temptation for Lot but not for Abraham. That is why God tempted Lot with a region rich in water and with Sodom's riches and glitter. For Abraham this was all of no consequence. His loftier spirit demands more rarefied dangerous temptations. But God only tempts for the good (James 1:12, Genesis 22:1). But when the proof of the most precious and exalted promises was to be taken from him— not only the child Isaak but the sum total of the divine and eternal "yea and amen"— when this [composite] "Isaak" was to be sacrificed, then the true level of the exercise of spirit and faith was reached for the believer, [was reached for] an overcomer like Abraham. In this Abraham was victorious. This naked faith, without visible or concrete proofs, that was what Abraham had to learn and so be an example for us. I have recited no verse as often in exile, with or without tears, as the profound words of the song:

> When I feel nothing of Your might
> You still bring me to my goal
> Even through the night.

I no longer knew anything, felt no help or strengthening. Again and again there was only one thing: God's word— [His] promise! How often I fell asleep completely exposed with only naked faith. Next day I awoke only to practice this anew. Not I, only the Lord, the Lord securely held me.

This I wish for you, you endurer of pain. What is the status of that dangerous illness, dear ones? Or, dear sister, have you already gone to join that triumphant Church? Brother and sister your compass must only be directed upon the will of Jesus. I purposely said "will," not upon Jesus' help. Under that we usually understood the taking away of illness, while He often wants to take the sick one away from the illness. That is why I'm glad I detect a deep submission in your letters. That is what I have done here for two and a half years. I manage best of all with this practice. When after all the prayers, petitions and all the waiting, the Lord in love answers with death, then this answer is a Hallelujah for us.

If we really believe in God we believe in a real God who has taken everything but everything into account. Oh how often this was my bath of faith. When I submerged myself in it, I always became well.

Thus all the leadings of our Father in Christ are only and definitely only love. My exile is love, only love. God's love removed my loved ones out of pure love for me. He fears nothing when He tests our love for He knows: pure love will only gain through such testing. He cannot use and does not want other love. Therefore He comforted and quieted and steadfastly prepared for everything— for God.

Sister, I call an eternal Hallelujah to you! You had courage in life, have it also in dying. If you remain, you remain for higher spiritual service to us and many others; yes, you especially remain for God and His aims.

Yours completely,

Hans - to his Liese and Franz!

He wrote his last letter to the F.F. Bargens, Carmen, Manitoba on January 29, 1933. He was unable to finish this letter. On February 5, 1933, he added a postscript with trembling hand, "I've become sick but don't worry. God be the Glory! Amen. Your Hans." Then an almost illegible script: "Periodic heart failures. Brother Paetkau will report everything!"

This letter was sent to F.F. Bargens after his death on February 21, 1933. Brother David Paetkau from Orenburg paid him the last honors.

Heinrich H. Voth
Teacher
Rueckenau, Molotschna

The widowed mother of Heinrich H. Voth lived in the village of Neukirch, Molotschna. Here, he received his first education. He then visited the nearby school of commerce in Alexanderkrone. He took his teacher's exam after completing the pedagogical classes in Halbstadt.

In the fall of 1918, he came to Rueckenau as a teacher in the two-room school. At that time, the head teacher was Jakob D. Harder from Lichtfelde, with whom I had worked for two years. In other words he filled my position. At that time, my family and I moved back to Friedensruh, the home village of my dear wife. I remained there for four years after spending ten years in Rueckenau.

It was already a time of unrest, and before long all religious instruction by teachers was forbidden. Meanwhile, in Rueckenau, the teacher Heinrich H. Voth had married the adopted daughter of the childless couple Heinrich Martens, Aganetha Toews, my former pupil. The Lord granted them six lovely children, of whom two died in infancy.

The Author

The further fate of the teacher H.H. Voth is related by his brother Johann H. Voth of Dalmeny, Saskatchewan, who in 1931 was the only member of his family to come to Canada.

My brother H.H. Voth taught school in Rueckenau for eleven years. The last years were very difficult for him. When the Soviet government banned religious instruction in schools he found it very difficult but stayed on, if only to prevent the feared communist teacher in his place. In 1928 he had to promise and sign that he personally would not attend any worship services during the school year. His pious mother counselled him to leave the school, but at that time he could not do so on account of the children. He clung to those children body and soul. He was also a generally beloved teacher in Rueckenau.

During Christmas 1928, he and his family went home to mother and kin in the village of Neukirch. During the last holiday, he went to the local church in the evening and attended the service. Someone who saw him complained to the local school authorities. At that time, there were already ample traitors in the Mennonite villages. The result: he had to pay a fifty ruble fine or leave the school. [He paid the amount and remained in school] though he was now on the government blacklist.

In the fall of 1929, I fled to Moscow with thousands of other refugees. I was the only member of my family to do so. I fortunately crossed the border to Germany and from there came to Canada in 1930. The following information comes from letters from the old homeland.

Before the school year commenced in the following year, the teacher Voth was handed a government questionnaire which he had to fill out. The first question read, "Do you believe in God?" He could only answer yes or no. One had to show one's true colors. He answered yes and that was the end of his teaching career in Rueckenau. The teacher Harder also left the school in Rueckenau, where he had been a teacher for thirteen years, for the same reason. What exactly happened to him cannot be established. Together with them all the teachers who did not want to deny their faith had to leave the schools. There were also those who denied their Lord in order to keep their teaching positions and to have bread and nourishment for their families. Hopefully, the Lord grants them repentance unto life, like Peter after his denial. Then all can be well again. Would we have remained steadfast? Who will condemn?

At that time, the government needed a reliable man to supervise a large account. H. Voth got the position and could remain in this work for three years. The godless know to whom they can entrust monies and those are the devout who trust God—is that not true? So God honors faithfulness, as in the case of Joseph in Egypt.

During these years, he and his wife buried two children. At this moment, it caused them great pain, though later they may have thanked God for it. But the Lord did not ease up, the valley became deeper. House searches were conducted by the GPU. He was arrested, taken to Melitopol and sentenced to a twenty-year exile. His wife remained in Melitopol with three children and later a fourth was born. Dear Neta, it seemed, was given over to the hand of fate. During the night she worked in a hospital in order to obtain bread for her and her children, and during the day she looked after her little children. They often starved. The reason for his exile related to a diary. He had also been in possession of letters from abroad. What invalid reasons, what mere pretenses for destroying a useful human life!

The Lord was, nevertheless, with him, even in exile. Because he had a good education, they only used him in the office to do written work. Because of good performance and model conduct, each day in exile was counted for two. Thus his punishment was cut in half, only ten years. But what does it mean to be cut off from wife and children for ten long years, and that in the solitude of the far north? Now and then I received letters from him in a roundabout way. He was treated reasonably well, received his daily rations. When he became ill, he was even cared for in a hospital which was not the case with many of the exiles.

His ten years were just up when Germany declared war on Russia. How he had looked forward to a reunion with his family. This is the last that we heard from him. His wife and children have also vanished without a trace. God alone knows where they are. I hope and wish they are with the Lord of Glory where there is no more suffering and sorrow.

My mother is still alive, and in June we hope to receive her here in Canada, provided God gives grace for the emigration from Germany. She is seventy-six years old and has experienced much tribulation and suffering. My sister, Anna, is with her and cares for her as best she can. We are also expecting my youngest brother, Jakob, at the same time. Since 1941 he has lost his wife and children. We have no news as to whether the other three siblings are alive. My sister Susi, Mrs. Isaak Walde from Neukirch, fled to Poland with two boys but

242

then disappeared. During the last years she had been with mother.

Heinrich P. Voth
Elder
Nikolaifeld, Sagradowka

Heinrich P. Voth was born on October 19, 1887 in Schoenau, Sagradowka. His father was Peter Voth and his mother was a Zacharias from Ohrloff, Sagradowka. His parents were farmers. After Heinrich had completed the village school at Schoenau, he attended high school in Neu-Schoensee and completed the pedagogical courses in Halbstadt, Molotschna, in 1906. He was baptized by elder Franz Martens in the same year.

He was a teacher in Tiege, Sagradowka where he also married Liese de Jager in 1912. As a teacher, he was strict and fair. His former students still speak of him with respect. Whatever he did he did thoroughly, and he demanded the same from his students. He took his profession seriously. To a young, up and coming teacher he wrote:

> I know from personal experience how rewarding the teaching profession can be. One can lead the child's soul into eternal truth and then with faithful care and cultivation produce something perpetual and lasting, which gives it the strength to keep faith amid the storms of life. After all, the soul is that element which, under the influence of the Spirit, unites itself with God and with eternity, and in this union finds peace and assurance.

From Tiege, he went to teach in his home village of Schoenau. In 1921 he was elected as minister and ordained by elder Jakob Rempel of Gruenfeld. It was a special celebration when he and four other brethren were ordained. The sermon of elder Rempel was deeply imprinted on the memory of the listeners present. "Five men dare to spring into the flood to rescue souls, five men want to work for the Lord with all of their strength."

In 1922 his dear wife died of typhus. The baby died soon thereafter and so left him with a son and three daughters.

In May 1923 he married for a second time to Susie Plantler from the Old Colony. He now gave up his teaching profession and took over his father's farm.

Soon after, the Nikolaifeld church elected him as their elder. He was ordained by J. Rempel, the elder of the Neu-Chortitza church on Ascension Day, 1925. The text: 1 Cor. 4:1-5. In his address he pointed to the duties and obligations, the sorrows and joys of serving a congregation, as well as the responsibilities of the congregational members. The church had just gone through a dark period of disruption. It was a tactful and firm presentation which brought the congregation together again and infused new life. The Bible studies inaugurated by his predecessor became popular. Well-known speakers from other churches were brought in and the large two-story church at Nikolaifeld was often overfilled.

Ministerial conferences were regularly held. Since ministers were in short supply, young men were appointed as evangelists at his instigation and later ordained as ministers. Thus he managed to gather a whole array of workers around him. He was especially concerned about the young evangelists. He encouraged them to take ministerial courses in the Molotschna and visited them there twice.

He developed his gifts for youth instruction in a special way. There was scarcely anyone who knew how to present the salvation truths of the Bible to young souls as well as he. Many came to a living faith and gave a joyous testimony before the congregation. The fruit of these efforts appeared later when, during the time of oppression, representatives of the young people came to him and requested that he lead a Bible study at least every second Sunday. He did this gladly, in spite of the dangers associated with such activity.

In 1929 he and many others fled to Moscow only to be sent back. Now a time of tribulation began for him. Soon, he had to leave his farm and move into the small janitor's house near the church. "There is room in the smallest hut for a loving couple," he wrote at the time.

Several months later he wrote,

> The instruction of youth is becoming difficult. If someone wants to go to church he has to walk and that is often a great distance. We are in a transitional period. There is a struggle

for the youth and the children. Circumstances are being constructed which will completely isolate the child from the family.
Our forefathers always left their homes when they threatened to
take their children and God always knew of other lands which
offered them refuge. In times of stress God knew how to save a
holy remnant which acquired the inheritance of the fathers and
allowed it to shine in new radiance. This holy remnant visibly
crystalized among us. All that is old, mouldy and antiquated in
our congregations does not hold up. It is collapsing. God is
showing us new directions. Our times are typified by the words
of our Savior: "Simon Jona, Satan has desired to have you, that
he may sift you like wheat."

A few months later he wrote,

Currently, things are very unsettled with us. Families are
being collected at night, taken to the station; destination unknown. You cannot imagine what kind of atmosphere we are
living in. We lay on our beds and are awakened by the noise of
the trucks. Startled, one sits up and thinks, "Will I and my
family be next?" Oh that the Lord have mercy on us! May He
give us the strength and grace to endure all the difficulties.

In the summer of 1931, he and his family were exiled to
the north for five years. Even there, his work was valued and
he won the confidence of his superiors. In recognition, his wife
received a position in the hospital which meant another ration
card. For eight children, they received eight kilos flour, 500
grams oat porridge and 250 grams sugar per month. Fortunately, several packages from America arrived at this time. It
would have been easier if they had been able to purchase something on the open market, but they were cut off from the larger
world. In summer, there was absolutely no access [to the
region].

One year later, he was dismissed from the office, and the
hospital where his wife worked was closed. There were illnesses. He, himself, came close to dying. He owed his life to
the steadfast care of his wife. During this period, a number of
his co-workers in Sagradowka died. There was blow upon blow
and yet on New Years 1934, he wrote:

The Lord has wonderfully led and preserved. Even in the
most difficult days when people were dying of starvation left and
right, our family was preserved.

A half a year later:

> We have experienced difficult times, times in which it seemed we would perish. Like the disciples we cried "Lord save us or we perish!" Our parents and the David Goerzens have helped us in a substantial way. There were also many berries and mushrooms in the forest which our children gathered and dried for the winter.

He was hurt that so few here in North America thought of him and that no one had words of encouragement and comfort for him.

On March 7, 1935 they were again relocated to Polowinka in Uraslskaja Oblast. Only one letter came from here. He wrote,

> We left the place where we experienced God's blessing and nearness for three years. We left Melkoje rich in inner experiences, affirmed through sorrow and suffering, strengthened in faith, rested for the future and journeyed to our new residence with a burning question in our hearts: "How will God appoint our situation here?" I am currently working in the forest. Perhaps the day of our salvation is not far off.

So far as we remember, there was one more letter in which he wrote that he and his eldest daughter had been sent even further. We assumed he arrived there.

P.S.

His son, Heinrich, and daughter, Liesbeth, returned from exile. In 1938 Heinrich was again sentenced to another ten years. Liesbeth came to Germany, then vanished without a trace. There is no further information.

Franz F. Wall
Administrator and Owner of the Muntau Hospital
near Halbstadt, Molotschna, South Russia

From the very beginning, the Muntau Hospital was a private work of faith. By government decree it was the property and risk of one family, their "risk of faith."

In 1889 the Mennonite minister Franz Wall of the Crimea, ostensibly a simple farmer, found himself deeply influenced by the work of the widely known man of faith, George Mueller of Bristol. Motivated by his love for Jesus and his fellowman, he felt irresistably compelled to dedicate his farm assets to God for the purpose of serving the sick. His wife endorsed the idea wholeheartedly, and so his work began. The project found widespread support. In the village of Muntau near Halbstadt, they built what at first was a modest hospital. It experienced a normal, healthy growth and expanded over time. People of all confessions and status, the poor who could not pay, and the rich who could, entrusted themselves to "Wall's House for the Sick," as it was officially designated by the bureaucrats in its founding charter.

From the very beginning, God granted the institution competent doctors who were respected by both the sick and the healthy. At first, it was the district doctor W.L. Pedkow, then his successor Dr. E. Tavonius, who headed the institution and dedicated his entire life's work to it, until he died of blood poisoning after the revolution. This doctor was a deeply religious man who enjoyed limitless trust among both the high and the low born. He attended the services of the believers, participated in Bible studies, prayer meetings, and the Lord's Supper. He pointed many a seriously ill patient, whose condition was hopeless, to the only One who could still help, Jesus. During the revolution, he saved many people from death. He fearlessly defended them before the Red officials, often at the peril of his own life. Like Dr. Hoffmann in the Old Colony, he possessed such authority that they did not dare touch him. Dr. Seiler, a graduate of the University of Dorpat, was his assistant for a considerable time.

The founder, Franz Wall, a deeply religious man, died in 1906 and left the institution to his widow and children. His son, Franz Wall, formerly an elementary school teacher, headed the institution as administrator. The oldest sister, Liese, was the head nurse and the other sister, Agathe, headed the maintenance department. Thus the good work was carried on in the spirit of its departed founder. After working at home for a lengthy period, the daughters sought to expand their knowledge abroad. The institution was steadily enlarged. A second story was added, which could accommodate many patients.

And what is the situation today in 1947? The owners and faithful workers have long since left under pressure from Red officials. What happened to the family Wall?

After some time, the dear old mother departed in peace. The daughter, Agathe, married "surveyor Janzen" of Memrik. The youngest son, Gerhard, perished tragically on the steppes during the winter. His body was only found and buried after a long search. This was a deep sorrow for the parents who were still living at the time.

The oldest son, Franz F. Wall, stayed at his post as long as he was tolerated. He was converted as a youth and lived a model Christian life. Among other things, he led the Christian youth program in Halbstadt. He married nurse Anna Ediger rather late in life. She was the daughter of Peter Ediger from Prangenau. They had no children of their own, but later adopted two.

For the following information the author is indebted to the Muntau Hospital nurse, Agaethe Loewen, who went to Friesland, Paraguay as a refugee and from there to Canada.

Franz Wall was able to continue his administrative service in the hospital until 1930. In 1929 all of us had to experience the so-called "purification," which the Reds undertook in all institutions. All undesirable elements were removed from such institutions as schools, offices, etc. Wall was subjected to a searching examination, but they found no reason for his dismissal. They tried to make all sorts of allegations but Wall was so faithful and exacting in his work and in his bookkeeping and accounts that no reason could be found to fire him.

Finally in 1930 under pressure from his opponents, he had to leave his post. He was disenfranchised and deprived of his civil rights. His possessions were simply taken from him and as an impoverished man, he had to seek accommodation and work. For a time, the family had its quarters in Halbstadt. Since they could find no employment, their existence was very marginal.

In 1932 Wall himself, and later his family, went to the Dneproges power station near Neu-Einlage. He received work in the chief controller's office thanks to his good education and long experience. Things were still difficult, since everything was very expensive. In addition to his wife and two adopted sons, he also had his two older sisters, Liese and Agathe, with him. The head nurse, Liese, had to leave after many years of work—they claimed she was too old for the job. The other faithful and proven sister had to leave her job as well.

Many of the respected members of our congregations were in Neu-Einlage and worked hard to earn their bread. There was also a vital spiritual life: services were held; communion was celebrated, etc. This was the situation until 1935. They were more or less left in peace. Sister Agathe Loewen visited there several times and met the minister Jakob Klassen, who had attended Bible school in the Crimea, as well as the minister and teacher Karl Friedrichsen, originally from the Crimea, then from Ufa. This was a sanctuary for those who had become refugees for the sake of their faith.

On April 6, 1936, Franz Wall was arrested and taken to a prison in Saporoshje. Sister Loewen visited him once and was able to bring him something, but they were not allowed to talk. In the fall he was sentenced to five years in exile. He was sent to Marinsk in the north as a political prisoner. His family remained where they were. They were able to send some things to him and carried on a correspondence. He experienced many difficulties in exile. He had to walk some twenty-six kilometers and the food was very poor. He never complained. The last word from him came in 1939: "We are sitting on our luggage awaiting further transport." At that time, his legs were completely swollen and his body had also begun to swell: he felt very tired and worn out. Mrs. Wall wrote a letter to him and sent him a parcel, but it was returned. One is now certain that he died as a result of his mistreatment. There was no further news from him, not even from others.

Johann J. Wedel
Pleschanowo, Neu-Samara

He was born in Rudnerweide in the Molotschna on May 15, 1877. In 1881 his parents and other Mennonite families moved onto an estate in the Dan region near the Sea of Azov. Here, he received his elementary school instruction.

In 1892 he came with his parents to the new settlement of Neu-Samara. He attended catechism instruction here and was accepted into the Mennonite church after baptism. Then he served in the forestry station of Anadol for four years.

Not long after the end of his service, he married Margaretha Warkentin from Dolinsk. For several years they farmed on Thiessen's estate in the vicinity of the settlement.

In 1909 they moved to the new settlement of Slawgorod in Siberia and lived in the village of Gnadenheim. There his dear wife died during a premature birth and left six children between the ages of two and twelve. Later, he married the widow, D. Braun, from Karatal who brought another six children into the marriage. After five years, another tragedy struck when his second wife died of a heart attack. Previously, two children from his first marriage died of typhus. The Lord gave grace, and he bore all this patiently.

He now married Mrs. Wall, a widow. She also brought children into the marriage. Through God's grace a happy marriage and family life was maintained. Several of the children had to work away from home and times were difficult. They joined the Mennonite Brethren church in Donskoy at this time. In 1926 they applied for their exit visas in order to emigrate to Canada. They were not successful. The visas were actually taken away from them. They tried again in 1927 but without results. They did not join the mass flight in 1929 and tried to ensure their livelihood in their old home. For a while, things went fairly smoothly, but then in 1930 the elimination of the kulaks and collectivization began and with this all hope for a quiet, peaceful life ended.

The Mennonite villages in Neu-Samara were small, yet in short order four to ten families were loaded on sleds in the cold winter and sent to far northern Siberia. Among them were the following families.

Dolinsk: Jakob Warkentin; Abram Warkentin; David Warkentin; M. Riesen

Donskoy: Peter Fast; Heinrich Willms

Pleschanowo: P.P. Dueck; Johann Willms; Daniel Neufeld, etc.

All these were sent together with their families.

The men had to work very hard in the swampy regions of the forest and received very meager and inadequate rations. The men all died in the first year. Daniel Neufeld, for example, sank into the swamp and was unable to rescue himself.

Neufeld's oldest daughter confirmed this when she returned from Siberia in 1935.

Collectivization was to be voluntary, but anyone who voted against it was put on the blacklist. Farming declined and people became so impoverished that they fed the cattle with the straw from the roofs of the houses. Then came the crop failures, the loss of cattle, etc.

Johann Wedel had to seek work elsewhere and found it on a dairy farm near Soroschinsk. Later, he had to return to the collective. Since he was older and weaker, he received work in the office as a bookkeeper and treasurer.

In June 1936, he was reading the local newspaper in the office. It described the difficult lot of workers abroad, especially in Germany, America and other capitalistic lands— how they were without work and hungry. J. Wedel questioned this in the presence of a fellow Mennonite, who reported this. Wedel was already arrested and sent away by the GPU the very next day. His home was searched but nothing compromising was found. They took his Bible and a few letters from Canada. He was accused of having contacts abroad.

Father, J.J. Wedel, was in prison in Soroschinsk and in Novo-Sergejewka for four months. He was allowed no visitors and could receive no packages. He was tried in October 1936. His wife and daughter, Anna, were present. Here they said goodbye to him forever.

The verdict was brief but severe. "Johann Wedel from such and such a place is sentenced to four years hard labor in a remote region for counterrevolutionary activity according to Section 58."

His difficult time began with a forced march to Siberia during the cold fall and winter. After a month's march they arrived at a concentration camp in the city of Barnaul. Soon after he became sick and had to be brought into a hospital. He could only write one letter a month which the relatives did not always receive. His wife wrote often but did not receive an answer. The family wrote many search letters to the camp administration, but they remained unanswered. Finally, they sent a letter directly to Kalnin in Moscow. After several months, a letter arrived in February 1938, containing father's death certificate. He had died on February 11, 1937.

The mother together with several of her daughters moved to her sister's in Konteniusfeld, Molotschna. She joined the great refugee trek first to Poland, then on to Marienburg in the vicinity of Berlin. They fell into Russian hands and were placed in a concentration camp. From here, the long and painful journey back to Russia began. According to reports, they spent some time in northern Russia, then were sent to the east.

One of the sons of his third wife, the stepson of the exiled J.J. Wedel, and Wedel's son by the exiled mother came to Canada as forestry workers after many escapades. We thank them and the brother of the exile Jakob J. Wedel, Abbotsford, British Columbia for this report.

Heinrich and Elisabeth Wiebe
Muensterberg, Sagradowka

Heinrich Wiebe was born in Nikolaidorf (this village was later abandoned and no longer exists), Sagradowka in 1877. He was the son of Heinrich and Susanna Wiebe, nee Wiens. In July 1902, he married Elisabeth Penner. Her parents, Abram and Katherine Penner, emigrated to Canada in 1903. H. Wiebe was a member of the Mennonite church in Nikolaidorf.

After their marriage, they lived in Nikolaidorf for a time and then moved to Muensterberg where they bought a farm. Here, they experienced the terror of the Makhno massacre in November 1919. Muensterberg was not far from the large Russian village of Tschestjerni. In this village, the Makhno bands massed together and prepared to overrun, rob, and massacre the Mennonite settlement of Sagradowka. The neighboring village of Muensterberg was a special target. The Russians had long wished to take the good land, beautiful gardens, and lovely homes from the hated Germans and to drive them out. Driven by mad violence, the robbers killed old people, men, women, and children in a bestial fashion. Hardly a person remained alive. The entire village was put to the torch and only ruins remained.

The H. Wiebe family had many good friends among the Russians and had always maintained good relations with them. One of the former servants named Titko was especially well-disposed towards them. He had warned the H. Wiebe family of the great danger and told them, "If you hear a shrill whistle quickly come to the river which passes your garden. I will have a boat ready to take you to us and hide you from the murderers."

That is what happened. In the evening before the terrible night, they took both of them and the children to the Russian village and hid them. They hid them singly in a large straw stack, in a large pile of chaff, etc. The bandits did not trust their own countrymen and even here searched in every nook and cranny for any hated Germans who were hidden. Again and again, they stuck bayonets and sabres into the chaff pile where a Russian woman had hidden H. Wiebe. When nothing stirred they left swearing. Later, when Wiebe emerged, he had several stab wounds and scrapes on his body, but he had not let out a sound or he would not have escaped with his life.

When the Machnovzi, frightened by an unusual light in the heavens, left, those who had been saved returned home. But what greeted them? The entire village was in ruins. The houses and their contents had been burned, the inhabitants massacred. They found accommodation in the village of Altonau and, with the help of their friends, built a small house at the end of the village. Even the Russians who were among their friends helped.

In 1925 the family Wiebe received an entry visa to America from their parents and family, but Wiebe could not make up his mind to emigrate. When the exiles in Russia began they were among the first to be sent to the Urals along with their three children. They were locked into a baggage car with many others, and after three weeks of hardships arrived at their destination. Here they had to work hard, but as long as they remained healthy they earned their daily rations. Both of them were not well, and this, combined with the poor food and hard work, weakened them so that they could no longer earn their daily bread. The children who had remained behind and friends in America all helped, but it did not seem to be enough. Even their Russian friends thought of them during this time of need. For a time, they set traps in the woods and captured little birds the size of sparrows. This proved most helpful. Often, they only had half a cup of coarse flour which they poured into a pail of water, boiled it, and that was their soup. Mrs. Wiebe often went into the woods to search for mushrooms but found nothing but lettuce leaves, since all the exiles searched for mushrooms. How often she called to God in the forest, but there was seemingly no answer. When Wiebe was very near death he said to her, "Take our last ruble and go to neighbor Hildebrandt and buy a little ground horse meat." It came from a horse that had died of starvation. Hildebrandt, in order not to starve himself, refused to give anything. [Wiebe's] wife passed her husband the dish of watersoup. He died while he was eating. He was buried deep in the virgin forest. It can be said of him as it is written in the Bible, "And no one knows the whereabouts of his grave until the present day."

So the mother and three children remained alone in exile. The place of exile was far away from other human settlement. In summer the sparse products were brought in by boat, in winter by sleigh. In spring and fall, there was a lengthy period where there was no contact with the outside world. Since the region was very swampy, walking or driving was dangerous. Thus, there were long periods of time without contact. The prisoners stood in long lines outside of the store where the foodstuffs were distributed. Often, they stood for hours in vain and had to return, empty-handed and tired and hungry to their barracks. Under these circumstances the Wiebe daughters had to leave at dawn and carry wood in the forests. They had no shoes, only rags on their feet. Sometimes, they were up to their hips in snow. The son was at another location where things were a bit easier.

In the middle of winter, the barracks were closed and the inhabitants sent elsewhere. Trucks came and loaded up the camp gear while the people, including the very sick and the weak, had to walk. The girls had been sent ahead. They did not want to leave mother alone, though they had been assured that she would be brought on the sleigh.

When the transport arrived somewhat later, mother was not along. The promise had not been kept. The mother had had to walk behind the sleigh and often collapsed in the snow from exhaustion. She picked herself up and dragged herself further. When they came to an empty barrack en route, she had decided to spend the night there.

When she did not arrive at her destination the next day, her daughters became concerned about her fate. Heinrich Voth, the elder of the Nikolaidorf Mennonite Church, who worked in the office, offered to go and find her. When he came to the aforementioned barrack, he found her lying dead on the doorstep. She lay face down, completely distorted, her hands frozen tightly to the ground. Voth laid her on the sleigh and brought her to the daughters. How great was the pain!

The daughters prepared the body for the funeral. The dear mother was brought to her last resting place. She and many others now awaited the great resurrection morning. The two daughters were finally freed and allowed to return home. The youngest, however, suffered so much as the result of all the deprivations and misery of exile that she died of consumption. These were all worthy to enter God's Kingdom through suffering.

Johann J. Wiebe
Teacher and Minister
Crimea, South Russia

Johann J. Wiebe was born on May 15, 1884. His parents were Johann J. Wiebe from Altonau, Molotschna and Anna Wiebe, nee Unruh, from the Crimea. His parents lived in the village of Schattenruh in the Crimea where Johann Wiebe also attended village school. After he had completed his exams, he went to Ohrloff, Molotschna where he attended high school for three years. There was no Mennonite high school in the Crimea.

At the time, his uncle Kornelius B. Unruh was a teacher in Ohrloff. The other teachers were J.J. Braeul and J.H Janzen. After he graduated from this school, he took his teacher training in Neu-Halbstadt and his teaching exam in the city of Melitopol. At first, he was a teacher in the village Busau and later in the village of Menlerdschik (both Tatar names) in the Crimea. Here, he married Justina Dueck from the same village. With the outbreak of WWI, he had to leave his teaching position and enter state service. He became a medic in the All-Russian Zemstvo Union. After three years of service, he returned home and was immediately elected as a minister by his home congregation and ordained not long afterwards.

Changing circumstances soon forced him to give up his teaching profession. He became a farmer. His combined activities as a minister of the Gospel, as a member of the Commission for Ecclesiastical Affairs, as a representative of the young recruits before the courts, and as an ecclesiastical negotiator frequently travelling to the capital of Simferopol— all this brought him to the attention of Soviet authorities. Before long, he was arrested and put in prison. He was imprisoned in 1928. He was freed once more but had to report regularly to the police.

When the mass flight of German colonists to Moscow took place in the fall of 1929 he, together with many others, was arrested because he was regarded as one of the originators of the movement, which naturally was not true.

Johann Wiebe was sentenced to death together with four other ministers. The other four were Johann Hiebert from Mare; A.J. Klassen from Spat, also a member of the commission; J. Dueck, Buslatschi; and pastor Hoerschelmann from the Lutheran German church near Yalta, Crimea. They spent twenty-seven days in single cells on death row awaiting execution of their sentence. When the verdict was changed to ten years exile to the Solowoki Islands in the White Sea in the high frigid arctic, brother Wiebe wrote among other things:

> After we were together in the cell for the first time we sang the song:
>
> Keiner wird zuschanden, welcher Gottes harrt
> Sollt ich sein der erste, der zuschanden ward?
> Nein das ist unmoeglich, du getreuer Hort
> Eher faellt der Himmel, eh mich tauescht dein Wort.

Doesn't this sound like Paul and Silas in the prison at Philippi (Acts 6:16)? Someone of higher authority had intervened on their behalf and had commuted the death sentence.

Following these events in the Crimea, all the prisoners were sent to the city of Archangelsk in the arctic. From here, they were to go further north. A Russian priest joined them. Brother Wiebe wrote, "Here all walls of separation collapse; we are all 'one in Christ Jesus.'"

Brother A.J. Klassen, Spat, died in Archangelsk. J. Weibe was able to visit him frequently, share his difficult hours, listen to his last wishes, and telegraph his family. Since it was a long, difficult journey Mrs. A. Klassen, unfortunately, came to Archangelsk too late. A mound of earth covered her loved one. They could only pray together at the graveside. What a sad return trip for the poor widow and her son.

From Archangelsk the path of suffering went to Solowoki, where in earlier years there had been an orthodox monastery. At that time the monks had tried to sustain their solitary lives through salt works.

The news from here was very occasional. In the winter, all communication between the island and the mainland was cut off for a lengthy period. After eight years had passed in August 1937, a final indirect communique indicated that brother J. Wiebe had left there and returned to the Ural region where, in the meantime, his family had been sent. He had been given two years time off for good behavior and faithful work.

Since then, there has been no more news.

Jakob G. Wiens
Elder
Tschunajewka near Omsk, Siberia

My brother, Jakob, was eighteen years older than I. Thanks to him, I received considerable recognition. Many who did not know me and heard me preach for the first time came and asked me if Jakob Wiens was my brother. When I asked them what gave them that idea, they said they had concluded it from my voice and mannerisms. I never realized I was so like my brother. Be that as it may, from a human standpoint I often wished I could be like him; otherwise, we want to be as Jesus Christ was.

Jakob Gerhard Wiens was born in the village of Rosenort in the Molotschna on February 15, 1857. His parents were Gerhard Friedrich and Susanna Wiens, nee Friesen. He was the third eldest son in a family of twelve children. His elementary school instructor was a certain Holzrichter who was a

257

teacher in the village for many years. Jakob possessed a studious disposition. If one of the older brothers had to stay home from school to help on the farm, he would gladly let the two older ones stay at home if only he could stay in school. He only obtained a simple village school education, but he read a great deal and broadened his knowledge through self-study. He remained in his father's wagon making business until he married.

At that time his parents were already living on the estate Woronzowka, also called Steintal, some sixty-five verst from the Molotschna Colony. It was located near the great coach road which led from the city of Orechov to Alexandrowsk and close to the river Konskaja.

His wife was a certain Anna Balzer from the city of Orechow, province of Taurida. When his father-in-law Franz Balzer built a steam mill, he worked in the mill. Later he moved to the Memrik settlement and lived in the village of Ebental.

During these years, he was converted to the Lord and was elected as a minister in the Memrik church. As a minister, he was very popular in his congregation and was subsequently elected as elder in the church. Instead of accepting the position, he declared that he had changed his views regarding certain church matters and joined the Mennonite Brethren church. This move was associated with many difficult experiences. In spite of misunderstanding and widespread contempt, he, nevertheless, calmly followed the path which he had chosen. This, after a diligent study of the Scripture, under the guidance of the Holy Spirit.

The Lord endowed him with a special speaking gift. Because he dedicated this to the service of the Lord he was much beloved as an itinerant minister.

From Ebental, he moved to a new settlement in the vicinity of Alexanderpol called Gnadental. There, he soon became the leader of the Alexanderpol Mennonite Brethren Church. The locality was not too far from the Ignatjewka Settlement where brother Hermann Neufeld was the leader of the Mennonite Brethren church. These two brothers consequently joined forces and often travelled together as evangelists. Many a soul accepted the Lord through their labors.

He lived on the Steintal estate for a time where his aged

mother, whose spiritual counsellor he became, also lived until her death in 1901. He and his family then moved to Siberia and settled in Tschunajewka, not far from the city of Omsk. Not long after, two large settlements, Barnaul and Pawlodar, were founded in Siberia. Thereupon, he moved to the Pawlodar settlement. Here, he became the elder of the Brethren congregations in the settlement until independent churches emerged. He then confirmed the new elders which these congregations elected. In addition to his work as elder, he also frequently participated in ministerial courses. He also remained active as an itinerant minister.

In his old age, he had some difficult experiences at the hands of the Soviet government. Since he was elder of the church, members who wished to emigrate came to him and requested their membership certificates, which then carried his signature. Red officials misinterpreted these and arrested him as an emigration agent which he was not.

Even before this happened, he had deep empathy for the brethren who suffered much on account of their faith. Yet he also understood the blessing of such suffering. When his wife expressed her pity for these brethren, he used to say, "You are grudging them the martyr's crown." He did not sense that he, too, would soon die as a martyr.

He was now arrested at age seventy-three and exiled to Novosibirsk in the north for three years. His family hoped to transport him there, themselves, and make his journey as comfortable as possible. He was in prison in Omsk at the time. When they received the permission, he had already been sent to Irkutsk with other prisoners. This later turned out to be the wise leading of God. Had he not been sent away from Omsk, his loved ones would have immediately taken him to Novosibirsk in the high north. Now he was in the group that would remain in Irkutsk until spring.

In Irkutsk the Russian believers learned about him and took him in. When he became ill in prison, they submitted a petition asking to take him and care for him. This permission was granted. When they arrived to get him, the Lord had already taken His dear old servant home. Before he was called home, the Lord gave him an opportunity to lead a soul to Him. One night in the prison in Omsk, he had the opportunity to sleep between two murderers. One of these murderers accepted salvation in Christ.

When a certain Russian brother named Popov learned that brother Wiens had died, he followed the example of Joseph of Arimathaea: he requested the body of the brother and it was given to him.

Because sister Wiens and the children lived far from Irkutsk, the burial was delayed two weeks because they felt someone might come for the funeral. During this time the family who lived near Omsk heard of the death of their father in prison and decided to hold a memorial service. When no further word from the family Wiens came to Irkutsk, they at last decided to bury the body of brother Wiens. Later,st it turned out that the memorial service in Omsk and the funeral in Irkutsk were held on one and the same day without one knowing of the other. What a wonderful leading of God!

We here in Canada had the good fortune of receiving a picture of the funeral in Irkutsk with the brother lying in the coffin. We treasure this picture very much as a remembrance of the blessed departed.

"Blessed are those that die in the Lord from now on. The memory of the righteous remains a blessing."

What a lovely testimony for the Russian believers in Irkutsk! "You have been participants in my sufferings." That applies to them as well.

J.G. Wiens
Winkler, Manitoba

GLOSSARY

Allianz   A new Mennonite church formed in Lichtfelde, Molotschna in 1905. It accepted all believers into its fellowship irrespective of the adult baptismal mode. It also practices open communion with believers from other groups. It was strongly influenced by the Blankenburg Alliance Conference in Germany, whose speakers frequently visited the South Russian Mennonites and whose writings enjoyed a wide-spread circulation.

Dessiatine   A land measure approximately equalling 2.7 acres.

GPU   Gosudarstennoe Politicheskoe Upravlenie (State Political Administration). The secret police, especially feared in the 1920s and 1930s.

Kulak   A wealthy farmer, literally "the tight-fisted one."

Makhno   A Russian anarchist leader who led his partisan band against the wealthier German settlements in the Ukraine during 1918 ad 1919. He eventually fled to the West and died in Paris in 1934.

MCC   Mennonite Central Committee. Founded in 1920 in order to facilitate relief work in war-torn Russia. The timely arrival of aid saved may Mennonites from death by starvation.

Politruk   A trusted communist appointed to observe and report. Such individuals might be present in schools, factories, prisons etc.

Pud   A measure of weight equalling 36 pounds.

Reaumur   A temperature scale established by the French naturalist Reaumur and used by Mennonites in Russia from 1830 to 1918.

Ruskapa   Russian Canadian American Passenger Agency which supervised the technical aspects of the Mennonite emigration from Russia in the 1920s.

Sovkoz   A state farm paying wages to its employees.

Torgsin   Stores established in towns and larger villages which only accepted payment in foreign currency or gold, silver and precious stones.

Some Notes

Mennonite **Umsiedler** presently living in Germany have supplied additional information for a few of the figures mentioned in the biographical sketches. More data might well emerge as the collective memories of this group are compiled.

John H. Fast

Fast survived exile and World War II and lived in Karaganda in the later 1950s. He was paralyzed by a stroke and carried on a counselling ministry from his bedside until his death in 1962.

Daniel Adolf Reimer

Reimer re-emerged in Kirighizia in the early 1960s and became one of the ministers of the large Russo-German Baptist Church in Frunse. He died in the late 1960s or early 1970s.

Heinrich H. Voth

Voth was active as an accountant in the Karaganda in the 1950s. He retired to Kant in Kirighizia in 1960 and participated in the local Russo-German Baptist Church both as treasurer and minister until his retirement at the age of eighty-five.

Heinrich P. Voth

Voth survived his incarceration and eventually moved to Tokmak in Kirighizia. For a time he served the Mennonite Church in Tokmak and died there in the early 1970s.